ROUTLEDGE LIBRARY EDITIONS: EDUCATION AND MULTICULTURALISM

Volume 5

EDUCATING ALL

EDUCATING ALL

Multicultural Perspectives in the Primary School

ELIZABETH GRUGEON
AND PETER WOODS

LONDON AND NEW YORK

First published in 1990 by Routledge

This edition first published in 2017
by Routledge
2 Park Square, Milton Park, Abingdon, Oxon OX14 4RN

and by Routledge
711 Third Avenue, New York, NY 10017

Routledge is an imprint of the Taylor & Francis Group, an informa business

British Library Cataloguing in Publication Data
A catalogue record for this book is available from the British Library

ISBN: 978-1-138-06461-4 (Set)
ISBN: 978-1-315-16030-6 (Set) (ebk)
ISBN: 978-1-138-06826-1 (Volume 5) (hbk)
ISBN: 978-1-138-08041-6 (Volume 5) (pbk)
ISBN: 978-1-315-15812-9 (Volume 5) (ebk)

Publisher's Note
The publisher has gone to great lengths to ensure the quality of this reprint but points out that some imperfections in the original copies may be apparent.

Disclaimer
The publisher has made every effort to trace copyright holders and would welcome correspondence from those they have been unable to trace.

Educating All

Multicultural Perspectives in the Primary School

Elizabeth Grugeon and Peter Woods

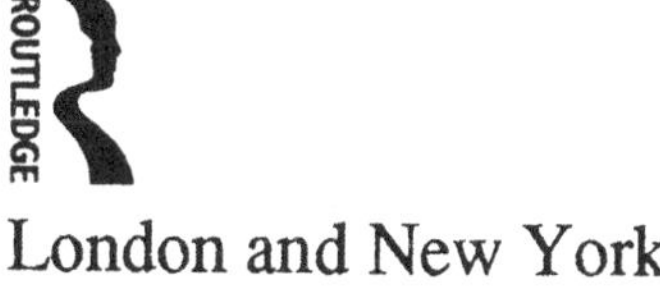

London and New York

First published 1990
by Routledge
11 New Fetter Lane, London EC4P 4EE

Simultaneously published in the USA and Canada by Routledge
a division of Routledge, Chapman and Hall, Inc.
29 West 35th Street, New York, NY 10001

Typeset by LaserScript Limited, Mitcham, Surrey
Printed and bound in Great Britain by Mackays of Chatham PLC, Kent

British Library Cataloguing in Publication Data

Grugeon, Elizabeth
Educating all: Multicultural perspectives in the primary school.
1. Great Britain. Primary Schools. Multicultural education
I. Title II. Woods, Peter, *1934–*
372'.011'5

ISBN 0-415-03642-9
ISBN 0-415-03643-7(pbk)

Library of Congress Cataloging in Publication Data

Grugeon, Elizabeth.
Educating all: multicultural perspectives in the primary school / Elizabeth Grugeon and Peter Woods.
p. cm.
Includes bibliographical references.
ISBN 0–415–03642–9. — ISBN 0–415–03643–7 (pbk.)
1. Intercultural education – Great Britain. 2. Education, Elementary—Great Britain—Aims and objectives. 3. Children of minorities—Education (Elementary)—Great Britain. 4. Race relations in school management—Great Britain—Case studies. 5. School integration—Great Britain—Case studies. I. Woods, Peter. II. Title.
LC1099.5.G7G78 1990
370.19'6—dc20 89–71068
CIP

Contents

Authors' acknowledgements

We are grateful to a number of people who have commented on parts of previous drafts of the text. These include Andrew Pollard, Will Swann, David Grugeon, and members of the Conference on Ethnography and Inequality held at St Hilda's College, Oxford, in September 1987. Special thanks go to Sheila Gilks for expert and unfailing secretarial assistance. Finally, the book would be nothing without the teachers and pupils who feature within it, and who helped to produce it. We would like to dedicate the book to them.

The research on which this book is based would not have been possible without a research grant from the Open University.

Chapter 4 ('Becoming a junior') first appeared in A. Pollard (ed.) (1987) *Children and their Primary Schools*, Lewes, Falmer Press; and parts of chapter 6 ('Learning through friendship') appeared in H. Burgess (ed.) (1989) *Teaching in the Primary School: careers, management and curricula*, London, Croom Helm. Our thanks go to the editors and publishers for permission to reproduce them here.

Preface

The issue we address in this book is that of 'race' and education; more specifically how, in that respect, schools might provide a fair and just education for all their pupils, how they might counter racism, and how they might promote multicultural perspectives. The urgency of the issue is underlined by the increasing incidence of racial unrest and disorder, increasing evidence of the permeation of racism in society, and of the part played by education in promoting inequalities and divisions.

Schools can do more than just modify this effect, however. Some may argue that the basic problem is in the structure of society; in, for example, the distribution of jobs among different groups, the low representation of blacks in key professions, and their comparatively weak political position. However, it might be argued that, if there is to be any structural change, it has to be preceded by new forms and levels of understanding and awareness of the experiences of ethnic minorities in multi-ethnic societies, and the inculcation of democratic values that show a concern for equality and social justice. Schools clearly have a major part to play here.

The problem was highlighted by the Swann Report (1985). This noted that

> racism. . . damages not only the groups seen and treated as in some way inferior or manipulable, but also the more powerful groups in that it feeds them with a wholly false sense of superiority and thus distorts their understanding of themselves and the world around them. All members of a racist society suffer from feelings of fear and insecurity, and, as we have seen, it takes little to fan the flames of suspicion and mistrust into open hatred and violence.
>
> (Swann Report 1985: 36)

At the heart of the report, therefore, were the recommendations of 'education for all' and how it was to be achieved, since all members of society were affected – not just ethnic minorities, and not just the inner cities.

The report was forced to note elsewhere, however, that multicultural education had been little-researched in terms of actual practice at school level and individual teacher attitudes. This is particularly true of primary schools, and yet it is known that attitudes on matters such as 'race' are formed very early. There seemed to us to be quite a lot of activity in primary schools that went under the general heading of 'multicultural education', but there was little thorough evaluation of it, little consideration of how it was conceived and put into effect, or of the impact that it had upon pupils. This, then, was the origin of the 'Pupils, Race and Education in Primary Schools' (PREPS) research project we undertook, which is reported here.

PREPS' aim was not just to document and assess examples of activity in the area, but to help promote the general cause. As will be seen, collaboration and democratic procedures were at the heart of much of the successful teaching activity, and we applied this to our own research methods. We worked to a model of teacher development that has the teacher and the teacher's own practice as its motive/force, rather than, say, a body of knowledge or skills conveyed to the teacher by external 'experts'. It involves collaboration between teachers and researchers, democratic procedures in research, the encouragement of 'reflectivity', and the principle of 'learning by doing'. It recognizes that no practice is perfect, and that in the 'doing' the ends will often fall short of the aims. This is true of almost any activity, let alone teaching where so many factors obstruct and complicate the best intentions. But it also admits of the possibility that at times aims are realized. In the teacher's quest for the conjuncture of circumstances that bring about varying degrees of success, external researchers can be a useful resource. We saw ourselves as facilitators, therefore, joining with teachers in a common aim.

Initial discussions with teachers interested in joining us in this research led to a number of case studies addressing different aspects of the issue depending on their definitions of their own problems and interests in the area. A number of these form the core of the book in chapters 2 to 9. Some readers may choose to go straight to these, and to select amongst them according to their own interests and concerns. Alternatively, of course, the book may be read as a whole. There are certain integral themes common to all the case studies, themes to do with research method, teaching method, theoretical perspective, and the issue under examination. These are introduced more fully in chapter 1, and reviewed in chapter 10 in the light both of the case studies of this research and of other, related work.

The audience we address includes teachers, teacher-trainers, advisers, inservice workers, youth and career guidance officers, all those who work in race and ethnic relations, other professionals interested in the model of professional development, and social scientists interested in the research method. Primarily the book is seen as a contribution to the debate initiated by the Swann Report, which we turn to in chapter 1 in a little more detail, together with more extended discussion of the origins of the research.

1 Researching education for all

'EDUCATION FOR ALL'

In 1979 a committee was appointed to inquire into the 'education of children from ethnic minority groups'. Its final report, known as the Swann Report after its chairman, was submitted in 1985 under the title *Education for All.* It had a mixed reception. The right-wing Hillgate Group maintained that it represented a current of opinion which 'threatens to destroy altogether the basis of our national culture'. Others criticized it for being an exercise in containment rather than reform; for concentrating on 'black underachievement' (a dubious concept; see Troyna 1984, Rattansi 1988) rather than racism within schools; for a certain blandness in its recommendations for 'education for all' in the face of growing demands for 'mother tongue' teaching and separate schools; for inadequate attention to structural factors, structural divisions, and conflicts of interest; and for viewing racism primarily as individual prejudice (Naguib 1985, National Antiracist Movement in Education 1985, Brandt 1986, Troyna 1987a, Gurnah 1987).

We are less concerned here with those debates than with the principles set out in chapter 6 of the report, which would inform an approach of 'education for all'. At heart this recognizes that issues such as the academic achievement of ethnic minority pupils and the need for education to reflect the multiracial nature of British society are of more general concern than had been recognized. The former was often perceived as a 'problem' caused by ethnic minority pupils, while the latter was invariably seen as an agenda only for multiracial schools. Both of these are misconceived. The Swann Committee stated that they

> look ahead to educating all children, from whatever ethnic group, to an understanding of the shared values of our society as a whole as well as to an appreciation of the diversity of lifestyles and cultural, religious and linguistic backgrounds which make up this society and

> the wider world. In so doing, all pupils should be given the knowledge and skills needed not only to contribute positively to shaping the future nature of British society but also to determine their own individual identities, free from preconceived or imposed stereotypes of their 'place' in that society. We believe that schools also however have a responsibility, within the tradition of a flexible and child-oriented education system, to meet the individual educational needs of all pupils in a positive and supportive manner, and this would include catering for any particular educational needs which an ethnic minority pupil may have, rising for example from his or her linguistic or cultural background.
>
> (Swann Report 1985: 316–17)

Such an education 'must reflect the diversity of British society and indeed of the contemporary world'. It must aim 'to help pupils understand the world in which they live, and the interdependence of individuals, groups and nations' (318). 'The richness of cultural variety in Britain, let alone over the world, should be appreciated and utilised in education curricula at all levels' and in all schools, whether they contain ethnic minority pupils or not. 'Education for all' is thus 'essentially synonymous with a good and relevant education for life in the modern world.' Failure to broaden perspectives in this way is consequently 'mis-education' in that it does not help to equip children to function effectively as citizens of the society and wider world community of which they are a part.

Education also has a 'major role to play in countering the racism which still persists in Britain today .. by ensuring that the degree of ignorance which still persists about ethnic minority groups is not allowed to remain uncorrected' (Swann Report 1985: 319-20). A crucial element is 'to seek to identify and to remove those practices and procedures which work, directly or indirectly, and intentionally or unintentionally, against pupils from any ethnic group, and to promote, through the curriculum, an appreciation and commitment to the principles of equality and justice, on the part of all pupils' (320). We must help our students 'to understand the social and economic origins of prejudice ... [and to acquire] the power of critical reflection, the ability to explore ideas and attitudes with understanding and detachment, and the ability to challenge information. They should acquire the confidence to question established authorities and to think independently, and should learn to justify opinions in a rational manner' (320).

Such an approach is 'even more necessary in "all white" areas and schools'. Their task and indeed that of others, is not 'cultural preservation' so much as 'cultural development', in terms of 'helping [pupils] to gain confidence in their own cultural identities while learning to respect the identities of other groups as equally valid in their own right' (325). This is not something that can simply be 'added on' to the existing curriculum. 'It must permeate *all* aspects of the educational experience' (325).

While the Swann Committee believes such an approach will be a benefit to all children, it recognizes that some will still have special needs, which will have to be catered for to offer 'true equality of opportunity'. There are language needs, since 'a full command of standard English is and will remain a key factor in success both in academic terms and in adult life' (325). There are pastoral needs, where 'a pupil's parents are not familiar with the British education system and may not be fully fluent in English'. This calls for 'particular sensitivity and appreciation of the situation in the school's arrangements for home/school liaison in order to enable the parents to play their full part in supporting their child's education'. Such special needs are basically no different from the educational needs any child might have, and which schools have a responsibility to meet. They must be met in a spirit which offers not just 'acceptance' or 'tolerance' but rather 'true equality of opportunity and treatment within a framework which regards cultural diversity as a valuable resource to enrich the lives of all and in which all children are able to benefit both from their own cultural heritage and also that of others' (326).

Among those welcoming the Report, Rex, while critical of some other aspects, agrees with the above principles, noting that it

> emphasizes the notion of equality of opportunity; it does not base its concept of multiculturalism on a paternalistic and caricatured concept of minority cultures; and it targets racism both indirectly through a syllabus for all which treats minority culture with respect and directly through anti-racist teaching . . . It is up to us to see that its principles are fully implemented.
>
> (Rex 1987:15; see also Patterson 1985)

The Swann Committee (Swann Report 1985: 327), however, was unable to offer any examples of 'good practice' based on the principles it enunciated. As J. P. Cornford notes in an annex to one of the chapters:

> Many of the recommendations of this report are as it were acts of faith, based upon experience and commonsense. If, as we hope, they are implemented, they will become hypotheses to be tested to see whether or not they have the good results we expect.
>
> (Swann Report 1985: 182)

How, then, was 'education for all' to be advanced? It was anticipated that the Schools Curriculum Development Committee (as it was then) would produce subject-specific guidelines and examples. One might also expect there to be specifically funded school-based projects, local authority initiatives, courses in awareness raising, and so on. Some feel that it is the formulation of whole-school policies within the school, and the thoroughgoing evaluation of their implementation, that is considered important (Lynch 1987). We also are of this view. Further, as well as policies specifically designed to meet the Swann Report's principles, we strongly suspected, despite the Committee's failure to locate it, that some teacher-initiated school-based work of that kind already existed (Antonouris 1985), though it might be hard to find in some 'white hinterlands' (Verma 1989).

Our initial plans, therefore, involved identifying and documenting such practice. The quest might also reveal attempts that fell somewhat short of the mark, or missed it completely, but which nonetheless might prove instructive in the analysis. As these were teacher-based initiatives, they involved a focus on the teacher, but we had a related interest – the pupil. To meet the principles of 'education for all', and to plan, process and evaluate curriculum initiatives, we need to understand pupil identities and cultures. The complexities of these and their importance for educational outcomes have been well demonstrated in respect of social class and gender. Willis (1977), for example, was concerned with 'how working-class lads chose working-class jobs'; and a large literature now attests to the influence of gender on the development of pupils, both in respect of how boys and girls choose their identities, and of how they are pressurized to conform to certain patterns of behaviour and attitudes (see, for example, Weiner 1985, Mahony 1985). As for race, the Swann Report (3) argues that

> membership of a particular ethnic group is one of the most important aspects of an individual's identity – in how he or she perceives him or herself and in how he or she is perceived by others. A particular ethnic group may be characterized by . . . certain shared cultural attributes, which may be open to change or choice but which can also serve as powerful forces in maintaining that group's distinctiveness.
> (Swann Report 1985: 3)

The dynamics involved here between identity and culture we have hardly as yet begun to examine, though there have been some studies touching on this at secondary school level (Furlong 1984, Mac an Ghaill 1988, Gillborn 1988). This follows the former imbalance of studies of pupil cultures typical of the 1960s and 1970s. It could however be argued that pupil beliefs, attitudes and values have already been shaped, to a large extent, in the formative years of primary school. They will certainly have made adaptations to school, and developed learning and coping strategies that will serve them throughout their school career. If we are to exert an influence upon these in the interest, for example, of combating sexism and racism, we need to find out more about their origins.

The research reported in this book had two broad aims, therefore: first, to identify and evaluate school-based projects which were either specifically designed in response to the Swann Report, or which emerged in school activity in line with Swann's recommendations; and second, to monitor certain aspects of the influence of 'race' on pupil development in primary schools.

COLLABORATIVE RESEARCH

A third aim was to develop collaborative research with teachers. There is a developing tradition in this kind of enterprise stemming especially from work at the Centre of Applied Research in Education (CARE) and at the Cambridge Institute of Education. Sociologists are steadily becoming more prominent in this kind of activity as they seek to address theoretical gains to policy and practice (see, for example, Connell *et al.* 1982, Burgess 1985, Whyte *et al.* 1985, Hustler *et al.* 1986, Woods and Pollard 1988, Woods 1989). Teachers have a sound basis for theorizing about their work (Elbaz 1983, Tripp 1987), considerable reflective capacity though working in considerably constrained circumstances (Pollard and Tann 1987), and not a little research experience of their own (Woods 1986). There is also the growing realization that if educational change is the end product of the research, then teachers have to be involved in its formulation and execution. Certainly, reform of the nature envisaged by Swann can only be achieved with the whole-hearted co-operation of teachers. We were not interested, therefore, in researching teachers, but rather in exploring with them their pupils' development, ways in which they themselves adapted to the demands being made on them, and their own continuing professional development, and in helping them to gauge the success of their endeavours. If teachers are required to change, they must do so from the strength and conviction of a knowledge base which is theirs (McLaughlin and Marsh 1978). Further, it must be characterized by an openness to new insights and powers of critical scrutiny which can be applied to their own practice. They have little time themselves for research in the ordinary course of events (Taylor 1987). However, external demands for radical change in areas that challenge fundamental belief and attitudes can promote an entrenched defensiveness rather than critical openness. Nixon, for one, is 'aware that [his] uncompromisingly critical stance may have the effect of alienating teachers whose work [he has], by implication, called to account' (Nixon 1985: 34).

Teachers thus have to come to terms with the implications for themselves and for their teaching of revelations of racism in schools and society, and they have to do it whilst subject to many other pressures that limit their freedom to contemplate and initiate change. Hargreaves (1988a), for example, has outlined a number of factors that constrain teachers to acting in routine ways and adhering to didactic, 'traditional' teaching methods which, according to general agreement, seem to be inimical to multicultural anti-racist teaching, and indeed to any kind of curriculum change. These include the problems of having to deal with large cohorts, the pressure of examinations, situational constraints, the isolation of individual teachers, the emphasis on subject-related pedagogies, and status and career factors. We might add to these the fact that cohorts are not only large but differentiated. Eggleston *et al.* (1981) speak of

> the experiences of many of the teachers we have interviewed faced with the day to day and minute by minute problems of working in classrooms with children whose cultural, community, intellectual and linguistic situations are diverse and which they only incompletely understand.
>
> (quoted in Arora 1986: 57–8)

There are, for example, 170 spoken languages in inner London (Craft 1989). It is no wonder, then, that the teachers featured in the Eggleston (1981: 91) report, *Inservice Teachers Education in a Multicultural Society*, used short courses to acquire 'survival skills' rather than to obtain more ambitious equipment. There are also a host of reformist pressures brought about by the Education Reform Act of 1988 and events preceding it, including demands for greater accountability, appraisal of teachers, and a weakening of their control over the curriculum, examinations, and school processes in general. Thus they have even less power to influence the kinds of constraints discussed.

It may be that some of these factors bear less heavily on teachers in primary than in secondary schools. They are certainly similarly concerned with cohort control, a range of situational constraints, and status and career factors but, arguably, less bothered by examination pressures, teacher isolation, and subject-related pedagogies, though the latter are becoming increasingly important, and the total effect of the 1988 Act remains to be seen. It is also generally acknowledged that children's motivation is less problematic in primary schools. The smaller size and integrated curriculum of primary schools also means a better chance of a whole-school policy developing among the staff, as with the teachers involved in the mathematics project of chapter 8. Large comprehensive schools are more likely to show more ideological divisions and subject-centredness, which work against such integration, though this is not necessarily the case, especially where the school has a distinctive ideology of its own (see, for example, Hewton 1988, Gates 1989). In this respect, some primary schools might be hampered by what Alexander (1984) has described as the 'primary ideology'. Among the chief features of this are (1) 'sequential developmentalism', an attachment to Piaget's notions of child development which hold that the average child is incapable of abstract thought until the stage of 'formal operations' which, in turn, lies beyond primary school; and (2) an idealist conception of childhood which views children of this age as innocent and therefore to be protected from the more troublesome and disputational issues of the world (see Carrington and Short 1987). However, it would seem that inroads are being made upon this position (Hartley 1985, Carrington *et al.* 1986, Pollard 1987), and on the whole there would appear to be the possibility for more flexibility in teaching in primary schools.

There certainly appears to be a need to be flexible. We know that racial prejudice is acquired early (Horowitz 1936, Jeffcoate 1979, Davey 1983, Milner 1983, Thomas 1984). Also, there is growing evidence that children of primary school age can 'cope conceptually with both individual racism and with structurally determined forms of racial inequality' (Short and Carrington 1987: 232; see also Lee and Lee 1987). Such evidence is challenging 'sequential developmentalism'. Furthermore, the teacher's role is a key one. It is to provide assistance to the pupil through the 'zone of proximal development', defined by Vygotsky as 'the distance between the actual developmental level as determined by independent problem solving and the level of potential development as determined through problem solving under adult guidance or in collaboration with more capable peers' (Vygotsky 1978: 86). Bruner talks of 'scaffolding' the learning task, whereby the teacher aids the pupil as a 'vicarious form of consciousness until such a time as the learner is able to master his (sic) own action through his own consciousness and control' (Bruner 1985: 24–5). The scaffolding at any particular age is constructed 'in terms of the child's way of viewing things' (Bruner 1960: 33). It is not therefore the age of the child that is crucial in these matters, but the skills of the teacher.

Problems in collaborative research

There are obviously dangers of 'going native' and other problems, such as giving teachers too much control of the research to the detriment of objectivity (Jenkins 1980). Teachers work in separate institutions from researchers, with their own occupational cultures. These institutions have intricate social structures, with their own hierarchies, sectional interests, power struggles, and career routes. Unsurprisingly, their outlooks are not infrequently touched by such considerations. They would have good reason to resist certain critical interpretations of their work. The nature of the teacher's work also demands a certain conviction, a decisiveness, and a sureness of execution. Almost by definition, it is change-resistant (Waller 1932); and this is not helped by the social conditions in which it takes place, as discussed earlier. On the other hand, teachers might argue that in some attempts at joint work, researchers have indulged the traditional model, retaining too much control, defining the area of research, nominating the problems, initiating and supervising execution, analysis and writing in ways that make it difficult for teachers to access. Impenetrable 'researcher speak' often characterizes such work. While it may advance sociological, or other disciplinary, knowledge, it does little for educational practice (Otty 1972, May and Rudduck 1983, Degenhardt 1984).

We certainly experienced some problems. Collaboration represents quite a shift in research model from that with which we had worked previously. There were new psychologies involved as we tried to move from academic-directed research to participative research, to which academics and teachers contribute on an equal basis. There were new roles, with the teacher as co-research worker, inputing practical knowledge, the academic contributing specialist knowledge of theory and method and a more generalized overview, acting as 'critical friend', liaison person, and co-analyst and -writer. For their part, most of the teachers took some time to adapt to the point of the study. They, too, were entrenched in an 'academic' research model, and at first were concerned to know 'if we were getting what we wanted', 'if what they were doing was of interest to us', 'was such-and-such of any use'? We, the 'academics', were tempted at times to be more directive, but in truth this was easily resisted as there was so much happening that was of interest that we felt compelled simply to record. The feeding-back of this documentation advanced the collaboration a stage. As teachers gradually got used to us, and we them, so we came to operate more as a team, or rather as teams. Here, the same 'participatory democratic' rules applied as between other parties within the school, with, we trust, similar benefits. We were able, for example, to share our knowledge and experiences of multicultural anti-racism with each other. We lent them what evaluatory skills we possessed; they shared with us their pedagogical knowledge and skills, and demonstrated and articulated theory-in-use. Like most ethnographic-type approaches, it took time to negotiate access and develop the trust and rapport essential to the enterprise. But when it gathered pace in the various separate areas, the potential began to take shape. With what results it is for the reader to judge, but we feel that it is another approach among a range that might be brought to bear on the issue. Governed by the same principles that apply to other relationships and decision-making processes in the schools concerned, it is one, we believe, that has much to offer to the advancement of causes in equal opportunities.

Initiating the research

Such an approach has implications for the selection of schools and teachers that take part. Not all teachers wish to engage in such activity. Some who do may be at cross purposes in the aims of the exercise, in some scenarios, perhaps, even seeking to advance their own brand of racism. We had to find schools and teachers who were not just prepared to allow us into their schools and classrooms, but who were as enthusiastic about the project as we were, were well disposed toward teacher research, and were genuinely sympathetic to the aims of the Swann Report. Though we might work with particular teachers, we also wanted to do so within whole-school policies, and where all welcomed thoroughgoing evaluation of their implementation (Lynch 1987, Chivers 1987).

We took advice from advisers, other educational institutions, and private sources, as to which schools appeared to meet these criteria. Then we wrote to them asking if they were interested in discussing the project, enclosing a summary of what we were proposing. The proposal, for a 'teacher–researcher' project, stated the basic aims of: (1) identifying the characteristics of policies and processes that advance 'education for all' and that might be taken as instances of 'good practice' judged by those principles; (2) studying aspects of pupil development within primary schools with particular reference to multiculturalism; and (3) developing methods that involve teachers and researchers in close collaboration over the research. The precise objectives were to be worked out with the teachers concerned, but examples of possibilities were given. These included the monitoring and evaluation of teaching and curriculum initiatives, the study of a particular child or group of children, perhaps ones with special needs, and pupil adaptations to school and to majority cultures. It stated the resources available, the methods that were on offer, and summarized the pilot work that had already taken place.

It will be noted that we used the term 'multiculturalism'. This was partly because it is a much less threatening term to teachers than some others we might have chosen and partly because, at the level of practice, we have found it difficult to distinguish between some forms of multiculturalism and anti-racism (see also Antonouris 1985). Certain forms of multicultural teaching which entail including projects from a variety of cultures, or adjusting one's curriculum to a variety of cultures, but leaving racism untouched, have been somewhat discredited (see, for example, Troyna 1987b, Finn 1987). However, some forms of multiculturalism might be seen as a stage on the way to anti-racism. Arguably some attempts under this banner, notably from the Schools Curriculum Development Committee (SCDC) and the Commission for Racial Equality (CRE) have done something in raising awareness of racism (Taylor 1987, see also Arora and Duncan 1986). Some, like Cohen, have found the anti-racist versus multicultural debate 'sterile and self-destructive', and prefer to try to 'find ways of combining the positive elements in both approaches while avoiding their negative features' (Cohen 1987: 4). There is, in fact, some indication that moves to include anti-racist strategies within a multicultural education context are having an influence on teacher perspectives (Antonouris and Richards 1985). It is possible that the anti-racist critique has had its effect on multiculturalism, exposing its more tokenist forms, and imbuing it with more positive lines of action to combat racism. Similarly, multiculturalism might have modified the more extreme forms of anti-racism. According to Foster:

> Despite the proliferation of prescriptive literature in this area, anti-racists especially have failed to map out how they see their particular educational ideology being practically applied in schools. They have preferred to adopt a critical stance towards LEAs and schools, pointing out faults in existing practice and provision, sometimes correctly so, but at other times with little understanding of school processes, teachers, and the constraints under which teachers operate. Teachers are often viewed as, at best, cultural dopes naïvely reproducing the social structure, at worst, as racist monsters ensuring the failure of every black student they teach.
>
> (Foster 1989: 505–6)

The debate now, we would argue, should move to the field of action, the school, and the classroom. As Cohen notes, 'it is at the level of teaching methods that both anti-racist and multicultural education are at their weakest; there is, for example, no detailed ethnographic study of the *process* of such work' (Cohen 1987: 4). Demaine and Kadodwala agree that 'it is much more constructive for teachers and their pupils to examine specific forms of practice within the institutions in which they live, work and play' (Demaine and Kadodwala 1988: 199).

With such aims it was essential that teachers and researchers felt comfortable with each other. This was extremely important for both parties. If there were to be meaningful collaborative work in such a sensitive area, there had to be a large degree of trust from the outset, such that teachers felt able to continue with their work in the usual way and to say what they thought, without fear of it being misappropriated or misrepresented. This raises the question of criticism. Is not such a method a recipe for blandness, and in the difficulties that might be caused by raising points of criticism likely merely to reinforce the status quo? Might this not also be the product of assessing achievements within given frameworks? If this were to happen, it would mean the selection process had gone awry.

There are signs that in some schools teachers are becoming more self-critical and more reflective, and are inculcating an openness in their teaching that invites it being screened by others (Pollard and Tann 1987, Hewton 1988, Gates 1989). This is a far cry from the jealously guarded autonomy of the closed classroom which is held by some to be almost an essential feature of schools, and by others as one of the biggest impediments to change (Waller 1932, Denscombe 1985, Hargreaves 1988a). Our teachers were willing to countenance criticism of their own practice, but, in the spirit of the collaboration, the criticism was better coming from them rather than from some 'authoritative' external source. In the event, there was no problem over this. They needed no prompting. Our custom was, after the initial research, to draft a paper giving our descriptive view of the issue or project. Thus an individual teacher, looking at one paper in the cold light of day, two weeks afterwards, picked out one section of a lesson as being particularly anti-educational (it had not initially appeared so to the observer). At another school, the staff responded to our evaluation of a whole-school project by nominating one of their number to sharpen the criticism in the paper and to begin to formulate a response. Elsewhere, a head teacher's first reaction to our discussion document presented to him and his staff was that 'it was very hard-hitting'. In this case, the objective documentation of their project by an independent observer revealed things they had not suspected, or had glossed over. We made no judgement – the criticism was in their own perceptions.

We have also found that teachers are not unwilling to countenance criticism when it is constructive, relevant, and likely to enhance their own professionalism. This was the message behind our reference to 'good practice'. It is often assumed that everybody who has ever had anything to do with teaching knows what 'good practice' is, without making the criteria explicit or considering who specifies them. We would have to do this, of course, but for the moment it was intended to convey our purposes – to locate examples of interesting and effective teaching in the area, and to disseminate news of it. Not only, then, was this offering a means by which teachers might be helped to evaluate their own practice, but it was also hoped that it would be able to inform them of what others were doing. It left the actual objectives open, merely giving a range of examples of what might be proposed.

RESEARCHER AND TEACHER ROLES

The form of the collaboration also facilitated constructive critical discussion. To meet the central principle, to encourage rapport, to appreciate more acutely the teaching experience, to contribute towards the schools' main functions, and to help release teachers for other (perhaps 'research') activities, it was proposed that the researchers be participant observers. This has largely gone out of vogue in British educational research, but, apart from the cognitive benefits, this now has a great deal to offer teacher–researcher collaboration. Most importantly, it offers to the class teacher opportunities of release from teaching responsibilities for sufficiently lengthy periods to observe the class herself from a different perspective, to cultivate reflectivity (Pollard 1988), to plan, and to write; in short to take a full, active part in the research. In this scenario the 'teacher–researcher' takes on new meaning, for it recognizes the problems associated with combining two roles and workloads within one person, and instead shares out the two roles as equally as possible between two people.

It should also be noted that, while the primary aim of the project was research along the lines indicated, a notable contribution might also be made to the teaching of the particular classes studied, for the field worker is an extra resource to the teacher in the classroom. They may devise new schemes together, team-teach on occasions, do group work without penalty to other groups, attempt other tasks that singly they would shy away from, feed off each other's ideas and experiences. Thus the activity of 'teaching' is not one separate from that of 'research'. Indeed, in this particular conception of collaborative research the researcher doing teaching is the logical corollary of the teacher doing research. The two functions become combined, to their mutual benefit, within the two people concerned.

This, then, was our conception of collaboration. The extent to which practice met the principles involved varied from school to school and from teacher to teacher. On the whole researcher-teaching tended to be auxiliary rather than relief, and perhaps only bold planning and timetabling at the outset can secure the model's full operationalization. But we feel we moved a considerable way towards it. An extended example of the method in operation is given in Grugeon (1989).

RESEARCH METHODS

'Experiencing' education for all draws attention to our attempts to join with teachers and pupils in sharing their experiences, empathizing with their feelings, seeing things from their point of view. Research methods, therefore, were ethnographic, and aimed to build up a detailed, true-to-life picture of the groups under study in their schools, and the factors that bear on them in their various interrelationships. The main techniques used included observation, naturalistic interviews, conversations, diaries, and study of documents (Burgess 1984, Woods 1986). Pupils and teachers were seen and conversed with in many contexts and on many occasions. We sat in classrooms with them, acting the roles variously of observer, pupil, and associate teacher. We observed and chatted with pupils in the playground and joined in discussions with teachers in the staffroom. We accompanied them on trips. Field notes were taken, a research diary kept, and tape recordings, where agreed, were made of interviews and lessons. On occasions we used a radio microphone for tuning in, again with the participants' agreement, to pupils' conversations and work in groups.

This method would seem the most appropriate for the study of cultures which should be 'empathetically described in their own terms' (Swann Report 1985: 329); and for the study of the 'detailed texture of school life', of 'what teachers actually do' and for the 'detailed classroom observation' demanded by Marland (1987: 119–21). It would seem suitable, too, for investigating 'the roots of racism in the child, the relationship between attitudes and unconsciously held theories, and pedagogic strategies to intervene' (ibid.: 127). This use of ethnography in the evaluation of a specific policy is a development of the method in the service of (a) practical reform, as argued in Woods and Pollard (1988), and (b) collaborative research with teachers, as discussed in Woods (1986).

THE SCHOOLS AND AREAS INVOLVED IN THE STUDY

We eventually chose a number of schools (and they chose us), because they seemed to meet our criteria of selection and to represent a reasonable comparative base. We shall describe them later in the appropriate places. They were divided between two neighbouring LEAs, each of which had made recent statements of intent in the area. In one, for example, a curriculum document noted that:

> While the framework applies to all children and students, there are recent social changes which have led to greater cultural diversity in communities. This means that at this stage in the development of educational thought, special attention needs to be given to ways in which all young people can be helped to appreciate and enjoy the similarities and differences amongst people that are evident in a multicultural, multi-racial and multi-faith society .... Every conscious effort must be made to increase the esteem and understanding of all children and students and their teachers for one

> another in order to dispel racial prejudice and discrimination. Racism has no place in our schools. The curriculum should be designed at every stage to promote racial harmony between those of different races, cultures and creeds.

While in the (largely rural) county as a whole there is a much lower proportion of ethnic minorities than in the large urban conurbations, as the document from which the above quote is taken makes clear, the authority is very alive to educational needs in a multicultural society. They had circulated an aide memoire to all their schools as a follow-up to the Swann Report, and invited responses, as a first stage toward action.

The second area was also largely a rural county, though the large town where we worked had a high ethnic mix. They had produced a recent report of their own, wherein they stated:

> A multicultural society will function most effectively and harmoniously on the basis of a pluralist approach which enables, expects and encourages members of all ethnic groups, both minority and majority, to participate fully in shaping the society as a whole within a framework of commonly accepted values, practices and procedures, at the same time allowing and, where practicable, assisting all groups to maintain their distinct ethnic identities within a common framework. Education should prepare people for life in the wider community and help them to develop attitudes and ways of behaving which are appropriate to living in a society which wishes to eradicate racial prejudice and the social scars it produces. All pupils and students (whether belonging to majority or minority groups) need to have their awareness heightened of the multicultural society within which they live.

Clearly both authorities seem very much in sympathy with the principles expounded in the Swann Report.

CONTENT AND ORGANIZATION OF THE BOOK

This book consists of a selection of the issues and projects that we examined with the teachers concerned. The first part focuses on pupil development and, particularly, points of transition. Chapter 2 is about 'becoming a pupil'. Not much is known about this (though see Barrett 1986, Ghaye and Pascal 1988, Woodhead 1989), even less about the pupil's experience of it, and still less about that of the minority ethnic child. Abbas was a five-year-old Asian boy who could speak very little English and who had had no pre-school formal educational experience. Teachers at his school had noticed that such children often adopted strategies for survival in the early weeks which later hindered their development as autonomous self-motivated pupils. This chapter describes how, from his own perspective, Abbas 'learned to learn', how he became a 'pupil', how he encountered and overcame difficulties, became progressively more able to participate in school routines and take part in his peer group culture. Such a case study, we argue, highlights problems common to many children at this stage – though 'writ large' in this case – and we suggest ways of tackling them.

Abbas made a successful adaptation in that he found ways of coping with the demands made on him. This does not necessarily mean an end to all the difficulties he would experience, but it did ensure his absorption into mainstream education. This was not the case with Balbinder, the son of Kenyan Asians. An unduly high proportion of minority ethnic children find themselves in the lower streams or sets, or otherwise marginalized (see, for example, Wright 1986). A device at primary level for pupils who are thought to have special needs beyond the resources of the school is 'statementing', and in some areas this can mean transfer to a special school. Ostensibly done in the interests of the child, it remains questionable whether this is the case. From some points of view it would appear that Balbinder was being given more opportunity; from others that he was being 'ruled out'. We simply raise that point here. What we are mainly concerned with is charting the process of statementing from initial conception to execution, particularly from the pupil's and his mother's point of view. Chapter 2 illustrates how these decisions involve and affect the whole family, particularly the mother, whose career as 'mother of normal pupil' is disrupted, and the difficulties of comprehension experienced by the family in grappling with the legalities concerned with statementing.

Chapters 3 and 4 discuss transitions at age 7 and 9. As Bennett *et al.* have noted, 'Although there have been a number of research studies on transfer at the age of 11, none has investigated this at the age of 7. Thus we have no knowledge of the impact of this change on children, or their learning experiences at this age' (Bennett *et al.* 1984: 129). The same might be said of transition at nine. We consider both of these in a multi-ethnic context. Chapter 4 looks at the whole class of 7-year-olds in a multi-ethnic school, and considers how transfer has affected their development as pupils. The implications for their learning, the formulation of identities, and interrelationships with others are all examined. Some of the problems of minority ethnic children experiencing different cultural forms are illustrated, as are their various ways of coping with them. Gender identities and cultures are becoming more strongly established, and represent a much firmer division than 'race'. In fact the class appeared fairly well integrated in this respect, apart from one or two exceptions. At this age in this particular class, 'race' seems to figure as an attraction in inter-pupil relationships, though not in every case.

Chapter 5 looks at the experiences of a group of black girls following transfer from a lower to a middle school at age 9. Studies of transfer at age 11 and 12 have emphasized the importance of curriculum continuity if the pupil's learning impetus is to be maintained. It is argued by some (for example, Measor and Woods 1984) that at that particular age, some *social* discontinuity is not amiss as it might aid the transition from childhood to adolescence. There is no such advantage at age 9. The dispersing of pupils to different middle schools, or *within* different middle schools with the influx of pupils from a number of lower schools can be a considerable problem especially if the transfer school does not have the same kind of multicultural policy as the feeder school. Thus pupils from a lower school that has taken the matter seriously may experience worries and difficulties if transferred to a school that has hardly begun to consider the matter. Again, while the education of all will suffer as a result of this omission, black pupils in particular will be affected, and we monitor some of their experiences here. The need, clearly, is for consistency in multicultural policy throughout school systems, built into the social framework of schools as well as their curricula.

The second part of this book presents evaluations of a number of projects which seemed to us to be of special interest within the schools concerned, and to be instructive to others. Chapters 6 and 7 consider two inter-school projects. The first involves an exchange between two classes of pupils, one from an urban, multi-ethnic school, the other a rural, all-white school. During our eighteen-month association with the multi-ethnic school, this certainly seemed to be one of the high moments, the activity being a catalyst for the whole of the curriculum for the whole of one term, though the exchange itself lasted only two days. It was of particular significance in the area of personal and social development, and we were particularly interested in the interrelationships among the pupils concerned. Thus both pupil development and cohesiveness were enhanced in a particularly striking way, with the multi-ethnic factor being especially prominent. The success of the venture, in our opinion, also had much to do with the learning theory that underpinned it, and the way it was implemented; and with the rather special kind of inspiration infused into the project by the teachers concerned, which was in turn captured and taken up by the pupils.

The exchange also afforded an introduction to comparative religion. However, what pupils make of other religions, let alone their own, is not something we know a great deal about. One of the LEAs put great store by a 'multi-faith evening', to which many schools in the authority would contribute with plays, songs, and dance. It was hoped that the event itself, and the preparations for it, would broaden pupils' perspectives on religion by offering some essential features of a number of religions in a dramatic, appealing and memorable way. It might be anticipated that this would certainly be true of those children of one religion, who were involved in the presentation of another. But was this the case? Preparations were thorough and time-consuming. The event, attended by the participating children, parents, teachers, and advisers, appeared to be a great success. But what sense did the children involved make of these proceedings? What meanings did they attribute to the various presentations, and were they those intended or hoped for by teachers? How was the event followed up in the schools? In what ways, if any, had pupils' understanding of other faiths and cultures been enhanced? How did different preparations, presentations, and follow-ups differ in this respect? Chapter 7 will offer a view on these questions.

The next two chapters, 8 and 9, present descriptions and analyses of two contrasting whole-school projects, one emergent, one planned. While planning is essential in teaching, the best results sometimes seem to occur by accident. This of course is not always the case, and we shall be at pains in chapter 8 to identify the conjuncture of circumstances that gave rise in one of our schools to a mathematics project that was particularly well attuned to the multi-ethnic composition of its intake. It developed from small beginnings involving the youngest class later to embrace the whole school and other areas of the curriculum. As with the 'exchange' project, it was informed by a learning theory that emphasized the value of relevance, participation and practice, and that encouraged the fostering of growth points which then led on to further developments. It was symptomatic of that particular form of creativity – of both teachers and pupils – that is often claimed to be the distinctive hallmark of British primary schools.

By contrast, the project discussed in chapter 9 was planned most meticulously in an all-white, Church of England school. This was a term-long project on 'Living and growing', occupying a third of the curriculum and infused with a 'multicultural perspective' in response to the LEA's aide-memoire which in turn was a follow-up to the Swann Report. The staff were keen to respond, but were in need of advice and resources, with no tradition or experience in the area. The chapter therefore illustrates the problems such schools face even when well-disposed toward rising to the challenge. We monitored their efforts. To what extent, and in what ways, did pupils 'appropriate' the multicultural aspects of this project? What opportunities were realized by the teachers, and what ignored or rejected? What are the conditions for effective multicultural implementation in this kind of environment? We shall consider to what extent such a programme is a 'superficial irrelevance' (Mullard 1984), and how far it might be seen as a necessary prerequisite for a broader anti-racist strategy in the long term.

In the final chapter, we reflect on some possible lines of development that might help promote multicultural anti-racist education in our schools. It seemed, from our several case studies, that the more successful efforts were informed by a model of teaching for which there appears to be growing general support. Chapter 10, therefore, presents the framework of this model within the context of other studies in the area.

2 Becoming a pupil

The first term at school

> Some ethnic minority children, especially Asian children, face problems at the moment of entry. These problems are of three kinds. There is the problem for the non-English speaking child of approaching his school work with the linguistic capacity he or she actually commands; there is the problem of maintaining his or her skill in the mother tongue; and there is the problem of acquiring sufficient English to be able to work with English as the medium of instruction.
>
> (Rex 1986)

The purpose of this study was to see whether regular observation of one child by a researcher and a class teacher would provide information about the way children for whom English is a second language cope with transition from home to school at age 5, and to suggest ways in which teachers might be able to help these children. The school in question was 'Avenue Lower', a nineteenth-century town centre school with over 200 children on the roll, with a small minority of pupils from the New Commonwealth and Pakistan. There were also other children of different nationalities, whose parents, from Europe, the Middle and Far East, were studying locally. There was also a number from local Italian and Chinese families. The school had a strong sense of its multicultural nature and was proud of having a 'United Nations' identity. At the time of our research, Section XI provision was not strong, but awareness of individual children's needs was high on the agenda. The catchment area of the school had been fairly mixed, socially and racially, but had recently become a popular area of the town centre for upwardly mobile families. The school has also reflected this shift and has become a flourishing and popular local school.

It had been noticed by teachers at the school that children with little English and no pre-school experience often adopted strategies for survival in the early weeks, which later hindered their development as autonomous, self-motivated pupils. The teacher of a reception class agreed to join in a collaborative study of one particular boy in her class. He was observed in the classroom by the researcher for one day a week for a period of one term. At the same time the class teacher kept a diary of significant developments, initially every day and gradually as a weekly summary. Towards the end of term, a radio microphone was used to record the child's language.

The class teacher's first encounter with Abbas was on the first day of term in April. His parents had not come to the meeting for new parents which had been held in March, nor had they brought him to either of the two afternoon sessions for new children. He was one of three ethnic minority children in a reception class of eighteen. All three had school-age siblings. Two of the three had been accounted for before the term started. The researcher and class teacher had visited one at home, the other had attended both afternoon sessions. One spoke Chinese at home, and the other Punjabi, but both were fluent English speakers; they seemed confident, sociable 5-year-olds. One had been at nursery school, the other at playgroup in the previous year. Only the third child seemed likely to have problems in starting school. A local playgroup leader, in conversation with the class teacher, had described this child's brief appearance at the group, screaming and clinging to his mother. He had not stayed for long and had never returned.

THE FIRST WEEK

On the first day, Abbas arrived with his father, who stayed with him for a while. It was when his father left that the class teacher realized that Abbas was going to need a lot of help. He was, as she put it, 'awful'. He had dived for the door and had to be physically restrained. 'He is a big boy and very strong.' She coaxed him on to a chair and gave him a jigsaw but 'he just sat and stared'. He held her hand and she stayed with him at playtime. 'He did want love.' The only word he said during the morning was 'coat', indicating that he wanted to take his jacket off. At lunch-time his father collected him and afterwards brought him back, taking him to the toilet. For the rest of the day Abbas was not happy. 'He was so pathetic, he didn't shed a tear but kept holding his nose.' The other children who were all, as the class teacher said, 'on a very thin line themselves', accepted her explanation that he was unhappy, but by the end of what she felt had been a fairly traumatic day, they were all a bit tearful.

After school she had seen a much more hopeful side of Abbas. He had brought his parents into the classroom on their way to 'Mosque school' and given them a guided tour. 'When he brought his mum, he had the most beautiful smile' and, interestingly, 'he showed his mum all the things as if he had done them.' So it would seem that, while he had been sitting near to tears, he had been watching the other children, taking everything in.

Although he wasn't ready to take part yet, he could imagine himself being able to. When he talked to his mother in their own language, it was as if he had done all these things, played with the sand and water, used the bricks and lego and been into the play house. It would, in fact, be a long time before he felt confident enough to undertake any of these things on his own initiative.

The second day was more promising. Abbas had seemed much better. He had smiled a lot, taken part in creative work, and made a butterfly. But an unexpected problem emerged, one which would persist for some time. At the end of the morning when everyone sat on the carpet, he insisted on having a chair; his large size appeared to be a problem to him.

The researcher's first visit took place on Abbas's third day. First impressions of Abbas were that he was a large child. He was tall, overweight, with a self-consciousness that seemed related to his bulkiness. He tended to stand slightly apart from the other children, with his hands in his pockets. He waited at the end of the line when the class went into the hall for singing. In the front row the new children all seemed slightly lost; they couldn't join in most of the songs yet. Abbas appeared to be in a dream.

Playtime was another problem in these early days. The new children were not sure about the timetable. Several did not want to go out. Abbas went reluctantly. He sat on a low wall apart from the boisterous mêlée, watching another child, Jeetinder, who was surrounded by an animated group of older boys. One of them seemed excited, pointing at Abbas, seeming to encourage the group to approach him. Gradually they moved nearer and stood in a semi-circle around him. Abbas folded his arms and smiled. The boys began to run and jump about as if they were putting on a show for him. They circled round, running closer as they passed, waving their arms at him. Abbas eventually responded with great deliberation. He unfolded his arms and aimed a mock punch at no one in particular. This received instant acclaim. The running and jumping became more excited and hilarity increased. Abbas became the focal point of a more structured game. The aim was to provoke and dodge his swinging punch. Abbas stood up, adding effect and weight to the movement. Several other boys, attracted by the excitement, were drawn in and began to respond to Abbas's punching gestures. The game was quickly developing momentum and rules. Abbas stood with his back to the wall punching rhythmically, as the others ran past him aiming near misses. It all seemed good-natured to an onlooker, but may have seemed threatening to Abbas himself.

Learning school routines occupied much of the first week. Lining up in the playground was still a new idea. Jeetinder was quite certain, standing in first place while the rest of the class gradually formed up behind him, with Abbas at the back. He was last to go into school and immediately vanished into the toilets, rejoining the class later. By the time he arrived they were already sitting on the floor. He struggled on to the carpet behind Jeetinder where he proceeded to fidget, taking no part in the action songs and clapping rhythms. Instead, he quietly and unobtrusively provoked Jeetinder, pulling his hair, and putting his hands round his neck. The class teacher ignored the way he was disturbing the children nearest him but praised him when he joined in: 'Good boy Abbas! You joined in the clapping.' From the beginning the class teacher used positive encouragement, always noticing and praising appropriate responses. She was alert to Abbas's movement, utterances and moods, helping him to understand what he was doing, reinforcing the behaviour that she wanted, often turning a blind eye to less desirable aspects of behaviour at this stage.

Abbas's size was a real problem. He had to struggle to get up from the floor. He would look round for a chair or table to hold on to, and with difficulty haul himself to his feet. And getting on and off the floor was not the only problem. He was chosen to do some painting but did not go over to the table where the paper and paints had been laid out. He eyed it mistrustfully and when spoken to, shook his head vehemently, looking unhappy. Light dawned on the teacher – none of the painting overalls was large enough. He was gently persuaded to paint without one and seemed to enjoy trying out a number of different colours. A larger overall was acquired during the lunch hour. When he had finished painting he washed his hands at the sink and showed the researcher the bin for wet paper towels.

After lunch, the class had indoor play. When the researcher returned the class teacher was sitting with her arm around Abbas. She said he did not want to do anything and seemed miserable, and she wondered whether people had been unkind to him. At this stage communication was difficult, involving a lot of guesswork. Abbas relied heavily on gesture to express his intentions and found it impossible to explain what was troubling him. It was hard to ascertain how much English he was able to use. His comprehension seemed good, he rarely seemed confused by instructions, quickly learning to watch other children to see what the teacher intended. When the whole class listened to a story or sat together he was bewildered and simply switched off, but in a one-to-one situation he made an effort to listen and respond.

The class teacher and the researcher both felt that he understood quite well at a functional level but that when he wanted to initiate communication he was using two languages. For example, when he wanted to sit down he repeated a word which obviously meant 'chair', seeming to be unaware of the fact that he was using his home language. He was to continue to operate in two languages for several weeks.

The researcher played with the lego alongside Abbas, hoping to discover more about his language competence. They built a wall, Abbas persisting in trying to force square shapes together despite being shown that he had to check whether they had holes or ridges on the bottom. He did not speak at all but communicated by emphatic gestures, often physically pushing or obstructing the researcher. He proceeded in a haphazard way, picking up pieces to fit together randomly and then discarding them. He seemed to have no idea what could be done with lego and expressed a restless frustration. At first, when the researcher pointed out colours, he repeated their name and looked for more of the same colour in the box. As he became more relaxed he began to speak to her in Urdu. He opened and shut the door of a box saying what she took to be 'open' and 'closed'. When she said this in English he repeated his own version, making no attempt to say it in English. While they were clearing up, he threw the lego into the box and she sensed a feeling of aggression and frustration in not being able to communicate.

Many of the children were reluctant to go out to play. Abbas in particular hung back. What had seemed harmless ritualistic play in the morning had become open baiting by the afternoon. Abbas was in a corner now, four boys were running up to him leaping, laughing, and waving their arms. His previous ponderous punching had become a short run out of the corner, head down, punching the air. The provocateurs ran screaming into the centre of the playground, Abbas retreated, and they did it again. It seemed inevitable that in the excitement the mock punches would become real ones. Back in the classroom for the last half hour, Abbas squirmed and wriggled, prodding and poking the other children throughout the story.

On Thursday Abbas's father came to school to complain about Abbas being bullied, so clearly the child had found the activities of the previous day distressing. His father explained, 'He is a fatty.' Abbas's teacher mentioned the problem to staff doing playground supervision and noticed that at the end of play Abbas lined up with the second year boys who had been bothering him and seemed altogether happier. She also noticed that he was teasing and distracting other children during quiet times.

Another problem was going to the toilet. Abbas's father took him in on his way back after lunch but on this Thursday afternoon he vanished for a long time and refused to come back to the classroom when two boys were sent to fetch him. He could not explain what was bothering him. This was repeated on Friday; his class teacher wrote in her diary,

> Abbas got himself very upset about the toilets. I sent the children off together and Abbas became very agitated and wouldn't go but it was obvious he needed to. He spoke only in Urdu so I took him to Mrs

> Chand. She spoke kindly to him and asked him the matter – he refused to speak to her but as soon as we left he spoke to me in Urdu. As we came past the toilets they appeared empty and Abbas dived in.
>
> At lunchtime I spoke to his father and asked him to find out the problem. It seems Abbas is very shy and will only go to the toilet when alone.

However, it seemed unlikely that this problem would last very long since his father was aware of the difficulty and would be able to talk to him about it.

So far, Abbas was finding some aspects of school life alarming or incomprehensible. His teacher recorded, 'He always appears last when we go into assembly. He always goes last and then hangs about the door while I settle the class. I go back for him and settle him by himself.' However, by the end of the week he had been given the task of closing the door and, perhaps more importantly, had given himself a job: 'If another child wants my attention and I haven't noticed, Abbas makes it his business to make sure I do.' He is aware of the importance of being able to communicate with a teacher although he finds this very difficult himself.

A summary of Abbas's first week

At the end of his first week his class teacher wrote, 'He is very kind and helpful. He understands a lot of what I say and is anxious to communicate his needs.' Already Abbas had made great strides. The child who sat holding back tears on Monday was taking positive initiatives on Friday. Among other things he seemed to have learned

- the pattern of the school day: when to come, when to go and where to meet his parents;
- to line up on the playground at the end of breaks;
- to sit on the floor with his class for different activities such as assembly, singing, listening to stories;
- to identify with a group of children that he had never met before and to know most of them by name;
- to attract his teacher's attention in a number of different ways;
- to experiment with painting, drawing and cutting out – 'He did a lovely drawing of himself walking to school in profile';
- to be wary of other boys on the playground.

He achieved the above with a very limited command of English. Since communication was difficult he had to rely on gesture, facial expression and a very emphatic use of a few words. The frustration this caused sometimes showed itself in a seemingly stubborn rejection of other people's attempts to communicate, an undue loudness of voice, or aggressive physical contact.

Some problems also emerged. These ranged from short-term ones which would probably disappear when he became more secure in school, to longer term ones. The short-term included:

- his worries about going to the toilet;
- staying for school lunch;
- his relationship with older boys on the playground;
- embarrassment at answering the register.

Longer-term problems which might have benefited from outside intervention seemed to be:

- his very poor command of English;
- his weight.

THE SECOND WEEK

Abbas's mother came in on Tuesday of the second week. She seemed to be less attentive than his father, but noticed that Abbas was sitting on a chair. When it was suggested that he found it difficult to sit on the floor, she remarked, 'He is very heavy.'

In a discussion of the names of different tools involved in a sorting game, Abbas knew screwdriver and hammer. However, he continued to speak a mixture of English and Urdu. On Wednesday, when the researcher played picture lotto with him and three others, he joined in enthusiastically, naming many of the items in Urdu. He did this in a very confident and teacherly way, seeming to want everybody to know his words as well. He immediately recognized a butterfly card and, although he couldn't remember the word, drew everyone's attention to the one he had made last week. He seemed to be actively making links and matching. He was particularly concerned to pick out cards with a green background, repeating the word 'green' each time. Sitting on the rug, he seemed much less self-conscious and made a good attempt at joining in the action of 'Five little ducks went out one day'. However, things had not improved in the playground.

Abbas came out on to the playground last, and reluctantly. The same group of boys were waiting for him and approached him in a good-natured, boisterous way. There was some pushing and a few threatening, punching gestures. Abbas didn't seem alarmed but as they gathered round, he was driven against the wall and started kicking out, probably in fear rather than aggression. At this point an adult intervened. After break Abbas and others helped to plant seeds in pots. He filled several pots with compost, using a trowel quite competently, then handed it over and went to play with a jigsaw. He was good at jigsaws and was now sufficiently confident to move from one task to another without being directed.

Another of his achievements this week had been answering the register. He kept his hand over his mouth and was barely audible but he was making the appropriate response. 'He's done it again,' one of the class remarked approvingly. After registration they all wanted to talk about the playground, who had hugged whom, who was kissed, who was someone's friend. Ann said, 'While we were playing Hokey Kokey, some of Mrs Lowe's class came and broke our game and one of them kicked us.' Abbas was evidently not the only child to find the playground threatening. Sadly, he could not join in and share his experience.

In the afternoon the children could choose what they wanted to do until afternoon break. The researcher observed Abbas from 1.50 to 2.30 p.m. and was able to document the way he was becoming able to choose and carry out an activity on his own:

1.50 He was sitting alone arranging a set of dominoes in a square, fitting them together carefully.

1.55 He moved to sit on the edge of the carpet. Four children, three boys and a girl, were playing with the Brio train set. He watched them.

2.00 He picked up a piece of the track, put it down and got up. He had to turn himself round and push up to a kneeling position before he could stand. He went to the class teacher, pointed to the railway. She told him that there were rather a lot of children on the carpet. He indicated that he would be careful. She hugged him. He returned to sit on the edge of the carpet and watch the other children.

2.05 He spoke to Jeetinder, asking a question, and then claimed a spare truck. He waited a while before taking two pieces of track that no one was using. He put these together and pushed his truck up and down. When Jeetinder left the carpet, he took another truck, joined two together and continued to play on the very edge of the carpet, keeping well out of the other children's way.

2.08 A drama took place as one of the children wrecked the extensive layout and long train that someone else was playing with. Abbas, sitting on the edge, took the opportunity to enlarge his collection, gathering a few more items while the other children were distracted.

2.15 The wrecker was removed, his friend tried to repair the damage. Abbas now had a complete train and access to more track. He put it together and played with it.

He continued to play for fifteen minutes, becoming visibly more confident. He seemed physically more at ease as he moved about on the carpet pushing his train and adjusting the tracks. He played alone despite the fact that there were two other children on the carpet.

2.30 He stood up, looked on the teacher's desk, briefly played with the percussion chimes and went back to the dominoes, laying them all out again. When the teacher called everyone to sit on the carpet he packed them away tidily in their box.

Comment

During this forty minute period there were many interesting clues to Abbas's growing understanding of his role in the classroom:

- He chose the dominoes and seemed to have set himself a task. When he had completed this to his satisfaction, he looked about for something else to do. This was progress, as he had been inclined to wait until someone made a specific suggestion and showed him what to do next.
- He spent some time watching what other people were doing before he decided that he would like to do it too.
- He seemed to have understood the rule of not more than four people at any one activity and went to ask permission. This was impressive. It showed considerable maturity and the ability to defer pleasure until the correct procedures had been gone through.
- He seemed to be exercising considerable patience and self-control in gradually collecting trucks and pieces of track, always making sure that they were not being used by anyone else.
- He spoke only twice during this period but on both occasions he used language to negotiate and to obtain permission. He was anticipating quite complex syntactic and semantic structures, asking whether it would be all right for him to act in particular ways. Linguistically, he could not do this yet, but he achieved the same end by a very skilful use of gesture and single words.

At break the researcher observed how he came out of school, looked around, walked to the centre of the playground, approached two boys, Ravi and Tony, when they came out and when the same punching routines began, retreated to the steps in the shelter of the doorway. He stayed there until he had to line up with his class to come indoors. In the afternoon he joined in the actions of the song. Going home at the end of the day he gave his jersey to his smiling father, who was waiting on the edge of a crowd of parents, and strode along beside him as they left the playground.

By Thursday of the second week, his teacher felt that he was 'coming out of himself'. She was worried by the fact that he still tended to put his hand over his mouth when he spoke but was pleased that he answered the register and seemed to be speaking a little more. He was allowed to choose whether he wanted to sit on a chair or on the floor. She felt that he was beginning to know what he wanted to do but still did not join in the more social games, like playing with sand and water. The other children did not seem bothered by his communication problem and often joined him in whatever he was doing. He seemed quite bossy. PE and games remained a problem. He would throw and catch balls and beanbags with a partner but refused to join in running and skipping. His weight seemed to limit what he could do.

A major hurdle *was* overcome, however. Abbas wanted to join in a painting session but refused outright to put on an apron. His teacher ignored him and let him watch. The next day he wouldn't do PE. The alternative was to help to paste a car the class was making. In order to do this he had to have an apron on. The class teacher describes how he was finally persuaded to do this:

> He was very near tears but I came out straight with, 'Get the blue apron, it is a big one.' He went to get it but didn't know which one was the blue apron. We looked at the blue bear, etc. but he couldn't match it. Somebody helped. Hopefully he now knows the apron is comfortable .... He kept the apron on and after the story he wandered over to the water. I left him playing while I saw the children out and sent his dad to get him. It had never struck me that he didn't play in the water because he had no apron but this is now obvious – poor Abbas.

The blue bear was one of a number of different coloured bears which had been strung across the room to help Abbas with colours. At this point, he knew green but was unsure about the rest.

A summary of Abbas's second week

During the second week Abbas had consolidated some of the achievements of the first week and continued to take more responsibility for his actions. He:

- was talking more;
- was beginning to relate positively to the other children in the class;
- answered the register without prompting;
- had overcome his dislike of wearing an apron and discovered the new possibilities which this permitted;
- was going into the play house;
- and although he still found the playground threatening, he was learning to avoid confrontation.

THE THIRD WEEK

During the third week the whole school was working on a project called 'safety', with a particular emphasis on the development of primary craft, design and technology (CDT). The topic for the summer reception class was road safety, and they had also started to learn about electrical circuits. They were working on a prototype for wiring bells, buzzers, and, eventually, traffic lights. They had to fill in a diagram to show the way the wiring worked – a hard task for 5-year-olds. Abbas surprised everyone on Monday. The teacher noted that 'Abbas's big success today was his work with the circuits. He very quickly understood the principles and did a beautiful diagram – superb observation and pencil control.'

On Tuesday, his growing self-confidence was beginning to show in the way he often interrupted the end of afternoon story with single words. He seemed to realize that he could make a contribution, although he was not sure when it was appropriate to do so. The class were going out to put road safety into practice on Wednesday afternoon; to compare a busy road with a quiet street, to use the crossing island and the pelican crossing, and to try out the Green Cross Code. Parents had received a booklet explaining the purpose of this walk, indicating the vocabulary involved and suggesting discussion points; several were coming to join in.

The morning activities were preparation for the afternoon outing. Abbas played traffic pelmanism with three others. This was useful for matching and recognizing different vehicles. Abbas collected tractors zealously. They were probably the easiest to recognize. He did not seem interested in the others. Later on, everyone coloured in a writing worksheet, tracing arches to make a bridge and colouring in the different vehicles going under it – buses, cars, lorries, boats, and a train. Abbas fetched his name card and copied it neatly on to the worksheet, and talked to the researcher as he coloured in the different items. When she said, 'That's a van', he said emphatically, '*No*, truck.' He mentioned 'dad's car', but for most of the time he responded to the researcher's 'What's that?' in Urdu. He often talked quite volubly, seeming unaware of the fact that he could not be understood. During story time at the end of the morning he watched intently and joined in some of the actions, accompanying a rhyme about frogs, and while the story of *The Three Little Pigs* was being read he loudly and repeatedly said 'Pig!'

On the walk Abbas pointed to lorries and lamp posts, saying 'green'. On the main road he repeated 'lorry', 'truck', 'car', 'bike', and 'ambulance', as these were pointed out to him. Gradually he began to make observations himself: 'car', 'lorry'. At each crossing, the class practised the Green Cross Code. Abbas went through the motions. Whether he understood what he was doing was difficult to tell.

At break, the playground was less fraught for Abbas, as the big boys seemed to have lost interest in him. He sat on a bench looking around. He saw Alan and got up, putting his arm round him. They walked along together looking like Laurel and Hardy – tiny Alan, large Abbas. Occasionally they held hands and ran together. The running developed into a game of tag. They ran and touched other children, wanting them to join in, Alan calling 'I'm going to get you!' At the end of play they joined the line together, bringing up the rear. In the classroom Abbas sat on his chair and tried to pull Alan on to his knee. They hugged each other lovingly and then sat at the back of the carpet fidgeting and playing about while the story was being read.

By the end of the week it seemed that the toilet had ceased to be a problem. Abbas went before school, after lunch, and at other times went on his own, simply saying 'toilet'. A pattern of absence from school for no apparent reason was developing, however. When he was away one morning his father said he had a cough. Abbas's version was, 'Boys hit me.' When this was mentioned to his father he did not seem to think that it was a problem, feeling that boys had to expect fights at school.

During the week, Abbas began to show a real interest in the technology side of the project. He seemed particularly fascinated by the electricity box and experimenting with the motor. He proved to be good at sawing and hammering. His teacher observed, 'Coupled with his careful nature it makes him very useful.' Trying to tell the teacher about his bicycle and finding that he hadn't got the words to describe it, he produced a meticulous drawing which showed excellent observation. Now when she asked, 'What colour is?' he could reply, '*That* colour', and show her what he meant. He had found a strategy for coping with his language problem.

Comment on the third week

At the end of this week Abbas seemed to be making very encouraging progress. He:

- had found a particular friend;
- had developed a real interest in something he could do more competently than many of the other children;
- was listening and responding to stories;
- was beginning to participate in group activities, such as songs and action rhymes;
- rarely wanted to sit on a chair when the others were sitting on the floor;
- used the toilet confidently;
- and although he had to rely on gesture and one- or two-words utterances, he did feel confident enough to contribute – his one-word observations may have been interruptions but they were definitely progress at this stage.

On the negative side, he:

- still refused to do PE and did not appear to have any PE kit.

THE FOURTH WEEK

This was the last week before half-term and Abbas had come a long way. At the beginning of the week his teacher observed that he was now able to say what he wanted to do. Moreover, he was not easily deterred once he had made up his mind. His teacher observed:

> Sometimes when he isn't chosen, he goes on and on but I have become usually firm that he finished the first task. He always maintains his high standard even if he wants to move on. In turn, I always let him then go on to that task.

This suggests a considerable maturity on Abbas's part. Again there was evidence that he was able to defer a pleasure until the appropriate moment.

On Wednesday, groups were drawing, painting, and cutting out pictures of fast and slow things. Abbas picked up an Argos catalogue, and quickly found the page he wanted. 'Toys', he said, sounding pleased. He then selected a very small catalogue of model trucks, lorries, and diggers, and proceeded to cut out a small lorry. He was very dexterous, cutting with good control. He removed a neat oblong and thoughtfully pushed two fingers through it before stirring and mixing the pot of glue, lifting the spatula to let it trickle in circles. After he had played with the glue for a while he stuck the lorry on a piece of paper and proceeded (very carefully) to cut out a picture of a boy on a tricycle. Later, when the class were sitting on the carpet, the class teacher introduced them to some of the characters from the reading scheme. There was a set of models standing on a table, and children went to fetch different people. Abbas was asked to bring Mr Red Hat. He looked carefully and chose one of the 'Red Hat' family. His ability to recognize colour, and to relate the colour to only one attribute of a small model, seemed again to indicate considerable growth in his understanding: another step forward.

At the end of a long day, their teacher read the story of *The Tinder Box*. Abbas was now much more alert. He sat watching intently, really paying attention. He was using much longer utterances, sometimes complete sentences, 'that is a . . .' or, 'this is a . . .'. As she read he pointed to the pictures, saying loudly 'dog', 'cakes', and later, his longest utterance, 'that a dog is'. Sometimes he repeated words he did not know, trying them out. No one knew what 'trail' meant and, as the teacher explained, Abbas repeated the word several times, appearing to be trying it out for himself. There was another small social milestone – at the end of the afternoon he turned to the researcher with a charming smile and said, 'Right, bye!' before leaving the classroom.

Comment on the fourth week

After half a term his teacher wrote in her diary:

> The everyday pattern of school life is becoming much more familiar to Abbas. Things like lining up, assembly, play times seem to hold no fears for him. He has cultivated a very cheeky grin and you have to be quite firm with him as he thinks he can win you with it.

As far as his social development was concerned he was beginning to relate well to teachers and other children in his class: 'The other children often tell me they have seen Abbas in the park and he nods and grins.' His language development was accelerating. As he became more confident about the routines of school, his urge to communicate seemed to increase. He used his limited resources impressively, making his immediate needs understood by a combination of gesture, intonation and repetition:

> He has only cried real tears once when he was hit in the mouth . . . . He obviously has a bad tooth. We went to the dentist this week and

> Abbas indicated in his own inimitable way (little language, lots of gesture) that I should tell the lady about his tooth. She was very understanding.

He was, however, often very difficult to understand, and listening sometimes required considerable time and patience. The effort to communicate must often have seemed very frustrating.

THE FIFTH AND SIXTH WEEKS

Abbas was unaccountably absent several times in the fifth week. Coincidentally, it was the end of Ramadan and there was much to celebrate in the Muslim community. In the sixth week, swimming had started and Abbas's newly won confidence received a blow. He most emphatically did not want to go. He was absent again this week. His teacher recorded, 'He becomes quite nervous when swimming times come.' There was no explanation for his absence from school but towards the end of the week when he realized that no one would force him to go he became more relaxed and watched the other children getting changed with great interest.

On Wednesday the technology side of the project was much in evidence. Abbas was instructed to show the researcher the traffic lights which had been added to the model street they had been constructing. Abbas showed her how to make the lights change from red to amber to green. He did not answer questions about what the different colours meant but said, 'That's green' with enthusiasm. He had done a very careful and recognizable pencil drawing of a saw. The work experience helper had said Abbas was the best in the class at using the saw and that when Abbas had been helping him he had not had to do anything. Abbas had beamed proudly at this praise.

Later in the morning, the class went on with the road safety story they were writing together. This involved making suggestions which the teacher wrote on large sheets of paper and the children then 'read' back to her. The adventures of Peter and Melissa were coming on. Today they were going to the park. There was much talk about who went to the park and who lived near it. Someone said, 'You live near the park, Abbas', but he looked nonplussed. When class discussion took place, he sometimes seemed to get lost trying to follow the other children's rapid exchanges.

On the playground, he seemed much more confident, tugging at the researcher's sleeve rather aggressively as she helped him into his coat. He then ran lumberingly on to the playground where he chased any children who were prepared to play with him. He stopped to have an animated conversation with Ravi who seemed to invite Abbas to chase him; others joined a 'running away from Abbas' game. As they were all much more fleet of foot, there was no danger of anyone being caught. Abbas looked happy but when the researcher left the playground before the end of play, he followed her, saying something about boys fighting him. He was with Alan by now and they went off together. Playtime was still slightly threatening, it seemed.

There was considerable evidence of language development during the fifth week. Abbas's class had been practising a road safety song and were ready to sing it to an audience. Abbas joined in all the actions and some of the words. After a singing session in the hall, he did some number work with the researcher. They went outside to count the steps, the seats, bikes and daisies before settling down to play with pegs and rods. He could count from one to six quite well.

Abbas was very chatty, asking 'What's this?' and seeming ready for conversation. 'Have you got a brother?' his teacher asked. He nodded. 'Is your brother at school?' He replied 'Yes', and then told her, 'My brother is Kafief', and 'I fight my brother'. He indicated the size of his brother with a raised arm. She asked, 'How many people live in your house?' He looked puzzled, so she prompted him, 'Mummy, Daddy, Kafief and . . .?' 'I' he said confidently. He could sustain quite a long conversational exchange, reply to questions and give information. He arranged the plastic rods in a neat pattern and said 'This, heater.' When the bell went, he said loudly 'Bell!'

However, both the class teacher and researcher agreed that for most of the time it was very hard work sorting out what he was trying to say. It was hard to see where he needed help. Certainly he would have benefited from a chance to use his mother tongue in the classroom, more opportunity for extended talk in English with an adult, perhaps some structured language teaching and an immersion in books and stories. There seemed to be a shortage of suitable books in the classroom. Access to picture books would have provided a wider range of language experience than he was probably getting at the time.

In the afternoon the researcher put this idea into practice, reading *Mr Gumpy's Outing* with Abbas. He snorted at the pig but could not follow the story, and when it was finished wandered away. Books with very little text but plenty of pictures to talk about, or books like the Spot series which involve reader participation, much anticipation and prediction would have been useful. If Abbas was going to make sense of learning to read he would need experience in handling, looking at, and familiarizing himself with a lot of books before, or alongside, embarking on this process. There were no dual textbooks available in the school, at the time.

Comment on the fifth and sixth weeks

During the fifth and sixth weeks:

- Abbas's fear of swimming dominated these weeks; when the class was swimming he had to join another class and take part in alternative activities, yet he seemed reluctant to do this;
- he again showed a very positive interest in the technology project, becoming successfully involved in a number of different activities;
- he was much more relaxed on the playground, initiating and joining in games – yet there was still some slight trepidation;
- his language was noticeably more confident – he used complete sentences and two- and three-word utterances more frequently.

THE SEVENTH WEEK

This week, the class teacher's diary recorded only one event, which is worth quoting in full:

> *Monday June 15th*
> Abbas decides to stay for school lunches. His father is (not surprisingly) finding it tiring coming home for lunch. He works in town and uses his lunch break to pick up Abbas. He has asked the Headteacher if he can come in with Abbas for the first day or so. I must say I admire him as I would feel very conspicuous. He sits with Abbas at a table which rather cuts him off from other children.
>
> I have sat near and watched. His father stands in the queue with him and suggests food. He is very 'picky' and eats very little. He is obviously very uncomfortable. It's a very sad, tense scene. They go into the playground and sit on a bench together; other children gather round and talk to Abbas's dad. This has lasted for a week and it has been decided that Abbas should go home and try again in September. I can't help thinking that if he was left to fend for himself he might fare better.

When the researcher arrived on Wednesday the class were anxious to tell her the good news, 'Abbas comes to dinner with us.' Everyone wanted to talk about it. 'He likes beans, he likes them.' They all seemed to share the feeling that this was a big step for Abbas. They had been talking about different kinds of food in class to help Abbas recognize what he was eating. Abbas sat silently, looking embarrassed by the attention he was receiving.

Sadly, this was not going to be the achievement everyone had hoped it might be.

Abbas's ability to communicate, however, was continuing to make strides. On Tuesday, Simon had accidently cut Ann's finger while they were working together. Abbas told the researcher about it, indicating Ann's injury. 'Hurt! Cut, it was Simon,' he told her. He used his limited resources impressively and seemed much more confident about initiating conversation and making a contribution.

He was helped enormously by the sensitive way the class teacher enabled him to do this. He could easily be swamped by more competent, voluble English speakers but she often noticed his quietest murmur or gesture in response to a question, picked it up, developed it and gave him credit for it. She asked the class why using pins to hold some pieces of material together would not be a good idea. She noticed Abbas's attempt to indicate a sharp point and shaped an answer from his gesture, giving him credit for the suggestion that pins would be dangerous. She showed the class a strip of embroidered tape. 'Oh yeah, it teddy bear,' Abbas said. She immediately asked him whether he had a teddy bear. He nodded vigorously.

After play, they were continuing with activities related to the road safety project. The class teacher suggested different activities and children put up their hands for the group they wanted to be in. Abbas did not put up his hand. She asked, 'Abbas, would you like to make a person for the road? Go and sit over there.' Abbas listened very carefully and pointed to the chair she had indicated, obviously wanting to be reassured. He seemed uncertain. He went over to the table where six children were already sitting and came back again. He said 'Mrs Smith', very quietly, and then went back to the table. He knelt on a chair and leaned on the table in a non-committal way. He did not follow instructions to get some pencils and sat down only briefly before getting up to watch the teacher cutting up card. The other children fetched the felt-tip pens and settled down to draw small figures on pieces of card. Abbas spent a long time choosing a red pen, carefully removed the lid and fitted it on the end and then drew a neat circle on his piece of card. At this point, he leaned forward to see what everyone else was doing, before settling down to draw himself. He then drew several people, seeming engrossed in what he was doing and was very keen to cut them out when he had finished.

He did not always immediately understand what was required, but he had developed a strategy for coping which involved certain delaying tactics, like not fetching the tools for the job immediately, taking his time going to his place, and waiting until he could see what other people were doing before embarking on the task himself. His slowness was not a lack of enthusiasm nor a lack of understanding. It seemed rather to suggest caution, since once involved in a task he was generally keen to do it carefully and to complete it.

Comment on the seventh week

During the seventh week:

- Abbas experienced failure – he was unable to stay for lunch, something that everyone, especially his father, had hoped he would be able to do. It is difficult to know whether he was distressed by this;
- there was much evidence of his ability to undertake and complete a task – he was less likely to want to move on when he thought he had not finished, and could say, 'Not finished';
- he appeared to work very deliberately and carefully;
- he could discuss an event in the past tense ('It was Simon') another important step forward.

THE EIGHTH WEEK

The class were printing snail and rocket patterns on white cloth. Later in the morning, Abbas chose a book about a snail and took it to the researcher. In this, he was making connections between different activities and different media. He printed a snail pattern, taking great care to get the right amount of paint on the foam-rubber shape, then spent a long time painting a large cardboard car which he had helped to make on Tuesday. He did a lot of painting this week. His class teacher described the way he painted the model traffic lights, 'He had done it very carefully and got none of the paint on him, which is no mean feat.' She also commented on the way he completed worksheets, 'He is very absorbed when he works.'

She felt that he had considerable staying power when he was doing something he wanted to do and that he was a very determined child. However, this had a negative side, for if he did not want to do something it was very hard to persuade him otherwise. She wrote in her diary: 'When Abbas can't go swimming he has to go to another class. He goes very reluctantly. I have to physically push him in the direction of the classroom. Poor Abbas, he doesn't want to go swimming or to another room.' Most of the class were ready to start on the reading scheme and were taking home the first books in the series. Abbas was not ready to start on the scheme. Instead he was taking home 'books he has enjoyed when we have read them and number, a b c, and colour books.' His father had agreed to help him with these.

He was much more obviously becoming a pupil now and conforming to the behaviour of the group. He sat on the carpet more often than a chair; he found his own place at a table rather than waiting to be told; he started work without having to be given individual directions. A glance from the teacher was enough to make him stop what he was doing when he realized that it was undesirable. Thus a reproving look stopped him from playing with another child's jersey when the teacher was waiting to start reading a story to the whole class. Earlier in the term he would not have been able to interpret that sort of non-verbal signal.

THE NINTH WEEK

Abbas was becoming increasingly chatty. He had acquired grammatical structures which helped him to introduce a topic. He relied less on gesture and intonation, and more on language itself. Walking across the playground with the researcher he said, 'There's a tractor.' This was a great improvement on the pointing and naming he was using a few weeks earlier.

As his linguistic competence and confidence increased, his teacher became aware of a different kind of problem:

> Abbas is becoming quite a 'nuisance' in story time. How much do I let him interrupt? It is lovely to hear him communicate but nobody else is allowed to interrupt. Sometimes I have to put him down in the gentlest way possible, I am really aware that I could destroy his confidence. Mind you he always comes bouncing back. His favourite bit of news is that he is going to London with Daddy to watch the cricket and then buy a car this big (he shows this with his hands, it gets bigger every time he tells me).

He was definitely understanding and talking more. The other children talked to him a lot and he responded. How far they understood each other and how far Abbas's language development depended on his relationship with other children is more difficult to assess. Persuading Abbas to wear a radio microphone for a short time while he was playing with Jeetinder in the sand box gave access to a wider range of language than had been possible hitherto. Using this during the eighth and ninth weeks the researcher was able to test Romaine's hypothesis that 'Linguistic input from peers is important in shaping emergent communicative competence' (Romaine 1984: 25), and to describe some of the different things Abbas was able to do with language.

Comment on the ninth week

At the end of the ninth week it was possible to use the tape transcripts to see how far Abbas was participating in his own learning and how far interaction with his peer group contributed to his language acquisition. A short extract recorded as he was playing with sand illustrates one of the ways he was learning new vocabulary and practising his existing knowledge:

1	ABBAS	There we are Tinder - da Tinder. [*Da sound which could be 'there'*.]
2	JEETINDER	Write your name
3	ABBAS	Let go in. (*Inaudible.*)
4	MRS SMITH	Pardon Abbas. What was that?
5	ABBAS	(*Makes funny noise.*) This one.
6	MRS SMITH	What's this? (*She points to the sand.*)
7	ABBAS	(*Sounds like. . .*) Berba.
8	MRS SMITH	Sand, sand.
9	ABBAS	Sand? (*Very surprised and questioning tone.*)
10	MRS SMITH	This is sand. (*She goes away again.*)
11	ABBAS	What this Tinder? What this Tinder? Tinder.
12	JEETINDER	A spoon.
13	ABBAS	There we are Tinder. Sand, Tinder. (*Long pause when only sound is scraping in sand.*) One, two, three, number – not in here.
14	JEETINDER	We're making a sandcastle, come and look what we made here. We're making a sandcastle.
15	ABBAS	I don't know sand. (*Another long pause.*)

In this extract the process by which he learned a new word is quite evident.

7 He used a word of his own to answer the teacher's question.
8 She gave him the English word.
9 He repeated this.
10 She elaborated, putting it into a sentence.
11 Abbas asked Jeetinder a similar question, practising a method for finding out for himself.
13 He used *sand* for the first time, telling Jeetinder about it.
14 Jeetinder introduced *sandcastle*.
15 Abbas used *sand* in a complete sentence. He had told himself about it and made it his property.

It is interesting to compare the way Abbas talked to Jeetinder in the sand box with the way he talked to adults. When he talked to Jeetinder his utterances were longer, more frequent, and he often took the lead. When he said, 'I don't know sand', he seemed to be taking control of his own knowledge in a quite sophisticated way, thinking about the new piece of information he had just received.

THE TENTH WEEK

This week the school was looking wonderful. The safety project had ended and in Abbas's classroom the display of work illustrated everything that the children had done this term. Abbas would be able to show his parents what he had been doing; there was his drawing of an electrical circuit, a chart showing that he had helped with wiring, sawing and painting to make the traffic lights. There was even a photograph of him painting them. He could show them paintings of the street at night, the snail he had printed, the bicycle and fire engine he had drawn. He would be able to help them to listen to the tape of songs and rhymes that the class had taken several weeks to learn and record. And he could show them how to switch the traffic lights on and off on the model street they had been adding to throughout the term. He could show them the big cardboard car and the model of a small boy and tell them about the consequences of a collision. They would be able to see the book of cautionary tales that the class had enjoyed making up, and look into the play house which had become a café, with the car, which Abbas had spent so long painting, parked outside. He had taken an active part in so many of the things that were on display that he would certainly have a lot to talk about. In the event, his parents did not come to the school. His teacher recorded, 'Sadly, Abbas's parents did not come to the Open Evening. I was sad because he could have told them so much and would perhaps have got that sense of belonging that these evenings foster.' His father came in on Tuesday because he was worried that Abbas might be forced to go swimming. This was still a problem. He did not like going to another classroom either, and had been rude to the teacher who had to have him. However, he seemed happier in the playground this week. A boy who was related to him had returned to school after a long absence, providing someone he could talk to if he wished.

On Wednesday he was persuaded to wear the radio microphone for most of the day. This made observation of what he was doing much easier to record. He had an important piece of news which he wanted to talk about. He told the researcher 'I go . . . I not come . . . I not come . . . I go in London, I not come.' She did not hear at first so he laboriously told her again, but could not answer her question '*When* are you going to London?'

He told the class teacher and again he was not heard at first. The rest of the class were leaving the room to go swimming. Somebody asked, 'Abbas's going to London?'

MRS SMITH	Abbas – going to London?
ABBAS	I no com aschool.
MRS SMITH	You're not coming swimming? Why not?
ABBAS	No, I no com aschool.
MRS SMITH	You're not coming to school. When?
ABBAS	I a go London.
MRS SMITH	You're going to London. What are you going to see?
ABBAS	Toys.
MRS SMITH	Some toys in London. What sort of toys?

(*Abbas made a huge gesture indicative of something very large.*)

He still could not answer *when* but had an appropriate answer for 'What are you going to see?' He had more trouble when he talked about a 'scooter bike'; this was heard as 'goodbye'. Being able to talk about his everyday life, something the rest of his class found easy, was enormously difficult for him. Despite the fact that he was often misheard and misunderstood he struggled on impressively, trying to make himself clear.

SIMON	He's going to see big toys.
TEACHER	He's going to see big toys in London.
ABBAS	Es gooderbye, goodbye. (*This is what it sounds like but clearly is* not *when replayed on the tape*!)
TEACHER	Goodbye?
ABBAS	No, a scooter. A *scooter bike*. (*He enunciates this carefully.*)
TEACHER	A scooter bike.
ABBAS	I, a scooter bike, I have one.
TEACHER	You've got one.
ABBAS	No.
TEACHER	You're going to get one?
ABBAS	I go in London, das too big.
TEACHER	I see yes. You're going with your dad?
ABBAS	Mm.
TEACHER	And your mum?
ABBAS	Kafief. (*His intonation indicates* and *Kafief.*)
TEACHER	Kafief.

The problem of getting through to an adult with a piece of personal information is one all 5-year olds can experience; perhaps for Abbas, it was particularly difficult. He walked away at this point and seeing a towel and swimming trunks on the floor, immediately drew attention to them; 'Who are dis? Who dis?' He spoke with some urgency, evidently aware that one of the swimmers who had just left the room might have left them behind. When he had sorted this out, he picked up some lego and said, 'I'm playing this.' This was progress, he not only chose an activity but was able to express his intentions for the immediate future.

From 10.05 to 10.15 a.m. he played on his own in silence, then went across the room and picked up a book. The researcher brought several more over to the table where the other children were playing. Soon, someone asked her to read a story. At this point it is interesting to compare three different extracts from the transcript of the recording. In the first one, shortly before he settled down to play with the lego, he had a brief exchange with the researcher, looking at some of the items on display in the classroom. He had attracted her attention by calling her name and showing her the model traffic lights.

RESEARCHER	Yes. What's that Abbas?
ABBAS	Plate . . . orange.
RESEARCHER	Very good. Did you make that?
ABBAS	No . . . green.
RESEARCHER	What colour's that one?
ABBAS	Orange.
RESEARCHER	And this one?
ABBAS	Red.
RESEARCHER	What does the red light tell you?
ABBAS	I dunno.
RESEARCHER	What does the green light tell you?
ABBAS	Green . . . I dunno.
RESEARCHER	Can you see the green light? What does it say?
ABBAS	Dunno.

In a one-to-one question and answer exchange Abbas will still often respond minimally, and will retreat from questions he cannot answer, with his newly acquired 'dunno'. In another situation he may seem far more confident and linguistically capable. In the second extract, recorded not long after the first, he and Matthew are listening to a story, *Tariq learns to swim.*

1	RESEARCHER	Shall I read this to you?
2	ABBAS	Das a photo. (*Points to the cover of the book.*)

3 RESEARCHER I don't know. I think it's about a boy called Tariq.
4 ABBAS I know – Tariq. (*He remembers reading this story before.*)
5 RESEARCHER What does he do Abbas?
6 ABBAS Swimming.
7 MATTHEW He learns swimming, he learns to swim.
8 ABBAS Das go dat. (*Abbas mimics holding his nose and jumping into water.*)
9 RESEARCHER He's got arm bands. What are they for?
10 MATTHEW Keep them upright.
11 RESEARCHER Is that right? Do you have armbands?
12 ABBAS Not swimming.
13 RESEARCHER Let's read the story shall we?
14 ABBAS (*Slowly.*) I'm in a scooter bike. (*He is talking half to himself – this comment refers to an earlier conversation. He is obviously thinking about it.*)
15 MATTHEW What does that say?
16 ABBAS (*Looking at the picture.*) Football. I'm going park football play. I know T-shirt and that's a T-shirt. (*Points to his own shirt.*)
17 RESEARCHER Yes, that's your new shirt.
18 ABBAS Mm.

Out of eighteen utterances in this stretch of the tape, Abbas made eight contributions. Many of these show that he could take the initiative and introduce his own observations. These are not simply responses to the researcher's questions but a direct response to the book, 'Das a photo', 'I know Tariq', 'Das go dat', 'I'm going park.' At (16) he made the longest utterance and seemed to be trying to relate the story to his own experience. There were also things he could not do yet. Matthew, the native English speaker, answered with more sophisticated syntax, and could use alternative versions, 'He learns swimming. He learns to swim.'

In the third extract Abbas has taken over. He picked up a book, starting at the back and turned over the pages.

RESEARCHER Do you want to read that?
ABBAS No, not yet, I looking there.
RESEARCHER Right, you read it to me. (*Necklace of Raindrops.*)
ABBAS Look at that. (*He turns the pages.*)
MATTHEW He can't read that.
RESEARCHER He can tell me about it.

And this is what he proceeded to do, turning the pages rapidly, making incomprehensible comments, 'That's boff', 'That's dayout', hurrying over pages without pictures, remarking 'nothing here', or 'More ting ere'. 'Ting' was obviously 'writing' and he wanted to find the pictures.

He changed books to find one he wanted.

0	RESEARCHER	What's that?
1	ABBAS	Teddy bear. Teddy bear
2	RESEARCHER	A teddy bear is it?
3	ABBAS	Not teddy bear . . . Ah, that's what that . . . pah, *dass* one. (*He points to the picture and then to a large construction on the table near him.*)
4	RESEARCHER	Oh *yes* – that pattern, is just like the lego isn't it? Do you think that's lego? (*The picture is of a patchwork cover.*)
5	ABBAS	Mm.
6	RESEARCHER	Yes, very good.
7	ABBAS	Pah! That's ting.
8	RESEARCHER	That's writing.
9	ABBAS	Not wri-ting.
10	RESEARCHER	Writing.
11	ABBAS	Das ting, das ting. (*He turns the pages where there are no pictures.*)
12	RESEARCHER	Lots of writing.
13	ABBAS	That's number, look!
14	RESEARCHER	Yes.
15	ABBAS	Look, one, two, look, look one, two, three, . . . hold it there, hold it there.
16	RESEARCHER	You want me to hold it there. (*He goes on turning the pages of the book.*)
17	ABBAS	Nothing (*Pronounced nutt-ing.*) dair. (*There is a long pause as he looks at the picture.*) Green.
18	RESEARCHER	Oh that's nice.
19	ABBAS	Dats bus.
20	RESEARCHER	That's a bus.
21	ABBAS	There's cat.
22	RESEARCHER	There's a cat. What's this? (*Looking at a picture.*)
23	ABBAS	Ers doing. I dunno.
24	RESEARCHER	What's she doing?
25	ABBAS	I dunno.

In this extract Abbas really took over, showing what he had learnt during the term about the way books can be looked at and talked about. He pointed out the similarity between the patchwork in the picture and the lego nearby (4). He commented on the amount of writing involved and showed that he can understand the difference between words and numbers (13, 15). He knew what he was looking for. 'Nothing there' (17), he said, as he turned pages, pausing to enjoy and talk about a picture ('Dats bus', 'There's cat', (19, 21). 'Hold it there', he said, reversing roles with the researcher, 'That's number.' Finally, he found an economical way to tell her that he did not understand something. 'Ers doing, I dunno.' This is typical of the versatile and creative way that he often used his limited resources.

At break, Abbas ran about rather aimlessly with one of the non-swimmers before starting to play with Jeetinder. He raised his arm and Jeetinder ran under it, Abbas trying to stop him by bringing his arm down. It was very orderly. After play Abbas's table were given a worksheet. He was still wearing the radio microphone, so it was possible to listen in to the way they tackled this task and to the kind of conversation it generated. Listening to the recording gives some idea of the extent to which Abbas's language learning was dependent on his interaction with his peer group.

Abbas's group was given a worksheet to do.

MRS SMITH	Right, you four – this is a new letter sheet. Does anybody know the sound this letter makes? Tom?
TOM	Hat.
MRS SMITH	Good, there's hat here. So what's the sound?
TOM	A.
MRS SMITH	Not an *a* – *h* – at.
TOM	H.
ABBAS	Har. (*But he isn't heard*)
MRS SMITH	Good, a 'h' – this is h, h for?
TOM	Hat.
MRS SMITH	Can you think of anything else which would be h for?
ABBAS	Dog. (*He makes this suggestion rather quietly.*)
TOM	Top Hat.
MRS SMITH	There is a top hat there. H for hat. What else Abbas? H for happy. Can you look happy? Happy with a hat on your head. That's nice, what a lovely smile. What else? H for?
TOM	Head.
MRS SMITH	Good boy and put the hat on your . . .?
TOM	Head.
MRS SMITH	Right – that's right.

MRS SMITH	(*Demonstrates how to trace the letter h.*) Down, up, up half way, down. I'd like you to do the letters *first.*
OLIVER	Mrs Smith I've done it.
ABBAS	Not yet. (*Sounds aggrieved.*)

Abbas does not speak, but occasionally hums. The conversation around him is about pencils and rubbers, 'Can I have the rubber?' 'Why are we waiting?'

ABBAS	Done it!
MRS SMITH	Do you want to stop now?
ABBAS	Yes.
	(*After some time.*)
MRS SMITH	That's *beautiful* Abbas, well done!

By 11.30 a.m. Abbas had traced his letters and sat back to wait to be told what to do next. He played with two pencils, making them stand up. 'Look Miss!' he said to the researcher who was sitting near him, helping another group to complete a difficult diagram. Abbas had done this diagram yesterday, and when he saw that neither she nor the person she was helping had got it right, he leaned over and pointed out, '*No*, not there, mm, *there*', showing them exactly where the wires connected.

At 11.34 a.m. the whole table were using pencils as chopsticks. Abbas took two green pencils from the box and experimented. Simon showed them how to hold them properly and pick up a rubber. Eventually the teacher suggested he should get on with his work:

MRS SMITH	Can you get on with your hat now please.
ABBAS	Hat!
MRS SMITH	Hats, yes. Good boy, now your hats.
ABBAS	Colour!
MRS SMITH	Yes please.

Everyone coloured hats. Abbas did not speak; he was concentrating on very careful colouring in.

By 11.40 a.m. Abbas had meticulously coloured less than half the brim of a sombrero in green and orange. Others on his table were singing 'The farmer wants a den'. It is interesting to listen to the group talking as they colour their hats. Abbas interrupts the singing:

ABBAS	More red! (*He wants a coloured pencil.*)
OLIVER	More red?

ABBAS	More red.
OLIVER	More red. (*This has become a game.*)
ABBAS	Two reds . . . man.
OLIVER	And what about more greens?
ABBAS	No!
OLIVER	You don't like greens.
ABBAS	No (*Said very playfully.*) I'm see you park.
OLIVER	Pardon? You come to my park?
ABBAS	No! You my park, I'm see you doggy.
OLIVER	(*Giggles.*) I don't have a doggy.
ABBAS	I'm see you.
SIMON	Have you got a dog?
TOM	No. I've got nothink, not animal.
ABBAS	Yes, ave dog, dog, is ave dog, is avin dog, is, is avin dog.
SIMON	I've got a cat, the dog chased the cat.
TOM	No.

This example shows that Abbas had the confidence to become involved in a playful use of language with his peer group. 'You don't like greens' could be interpreted as a teasing reference to Abbas's school lunch failure since it was common knowledge that Abbas liked the colour green. It was one of his first words and is often referred to by the children. In this extract Abbas was not only confident about his relationship with the group but took on a teasing role himself. The repetition of 'more red' leading to 'two reds' showed that he had grasped the formation of the plural. He was starting to use the possessives 'my' and 'your'. He had not quite perfected the latter, but had nearly done so 'my park, you(r) doggy'. Despite his confusion with verbs 'I'm seeing you', 'is ave dog', the other children knew what he meant and it is likely that it is in this sort of exchange, which relies on imitation and repetition, that he would begin to pick up correct forms without more structured teaching.

After lunch the researcher noticed that Abbas still covered his mouth with his hand when he answered the register. The rest of the class answered quickly and clearly. As usual Abbas could not contribute to the very lively exchange of news and stories that took place at this time every day. At 2.30 p.m. he completed the work he had started in the morning. He had coloured in three hats, traced the letters and carefully written his name at the top. He wandered over to the brick box and joined three other boys pushing cars along the floor. As he played he talked quietly to himself. He seemed to be playing with language as younger children do in their mother tongue, practising sounds and meanings. At playtime he took off the microphone and went out. He seemed very relaxed and ran about with Sajid. For the last part of the afternoon the whole school had singing. Abbas was beginning to join in songs in the security of his own classroom, but seemed to opt out in larger groups. At the end of the afternoon his parents were waiting on the playground, standing slightly apart from the other parents. As Abbas approached, his mother bent down as if to hug him. He neatly avoided her, gave a letter about the open evening to his father, and set off walking beside him. His mother dropped behind and followed them to the car parked round the corner. Abbas got into the front seat, his mother sat in the back.

Comment on the tenth week

During the tenth week:

- on Wednesday Abbas put up his hand and volunteered to match a word with the same word on a chart relating to the road safety topic. This was the first time he had joined in this kind of activity and his teacher felt very pleased. She had chosen the word well – *green*!
- the transcripts made during this and the ninth week reveal more precisely than anything else to date what Abbas could do with language, and give some idea of the problems he was encountering everyday in the classroom (a separate list of these achievements follows below);
- he had given further evidence of his ability to understand complex relationships in his explanation of the wiring diagram to another child;
- he still refused to join in PE lessons or swimming.

What Abbas could do with language at the end of his first term at school

Ask questions to find out.

What land is? (*Intonation made it clear that this meant 'What's that thing?'*)
Ah! What's on there? (*Pointing to a photograph.*)
What's this? (*As he picks up an object.*)
What it called?
Who is this . . . what doing?

Who are dis? Who dis? (*On finding someone's swimming kit.*)
What ter matter? (*Said while playing on his own.*)

Tell or give information

That's you! That's you! (*Pointing to a photograph.*)
I don likey dat. (*When he wants to remove the microphone.*)
I'm playing dis. (*Meaning he is going to play with something.*)
I'm not yet finished.
Das gone, no das gone, there.
Not finished yet.
Das a photo.
I know Tariq.
I football like.
I know that one.
I want that one.
This is red.
I'm see you park.
I'm see you doggy.
Is avin dog. I'm not come 'ere.

Show or demonstrate

Look at that.
That's bus.
Das go dat.
There's a cat.
Look Miss!
Nothing there.
That's number look.
This one that way.

Describe

That's broke.
That's good.
That's a T-shirt.

Ask

Gimme rubber.
I on a rubber.

Instruct

Hold it there.
Wait a minute.

Use negatives

I not com.
No, a *scooter*. (*Correcting a mishearing*.)
No this one, not anymore.
Not same.
Nothing here.

Plan and comment

That's gone there . . . I need there . . . that's gone there.
I going park football play.

Compare and contrast

That's same, that's different. (*He shows how the stripes on his shirt match his shoes*.)

Giving instruction to another child

ABBAS	You hold them. You go there, go, go. (*They are opening out a concertina book*.)
MICHELLE	I seen it before.
ABBAS	No, go there.
MICHELLE	Oh Abbas there.
ABBAS	Not you.

Responding to questions

TOM	What are you doing, Abbas?
ABBAS	Paint.
TEACHER	Painting. Good boy. What are you painting? What are these?
ABBAS	Traffic lights.

Coping with school routines

OLIVER	Mrs Smith, I've done it.
ABBAS	Not yet . . . Done it!
MRS SMITH	Do you want to stop now?

ABBAS	Yes.
MRS SMITH	That's *beautiful* Abbas, well done!

Negotiating with his peer group

CHILD	Can I have a dark blue.
ABBAS	Not dat from that's my red.
CHILD	You're not having my pencil.
ABBAS	Hey! Gimme dat.
CHILD	He's got one.
ABBAS	No! (*Continues to colour his picture and keeps the crayons he is using.*)

Give a reason

He did not often answer questions which asked him *why* or *how*. He could give a reason using a causal connective ('because'), but this seemed to be a recent acquisition as there was only one example in the recording:

CHILD	I'm Superman 'cos I can fly.
ABBAS	I'm say Superman, that's cos colour Superman.

At first he seems here to be imitating the previous child, but his sentence has a different and more complex structure both syntactically and semantically: 'I am say(ing) Superman that (is) because (I) coloured Superman.' This is confirmed by the other child's response: 'Yeah, he coloured Superman.'

Imitating other children

At this stage imitation is crucial and Abbas often repeated single words that he had heard several times. Sometimes he repeated part or all of phrases he had heard:

CHILD	Cor! That was hard work.
ABBAS	Cor! I going out. (*He uses exactly the same intonation.*)

Playing with language

There are many examples of Abbas experimenting with both sound and meaning when he was playing on his own. This involved practising and repeating words and phrases: 'That's good . . . other girl, this girl, that girl.' It allowed him to try out structures: 'You having that, Simon, you having that.' When he played alone he often played with nonsense sounds and meaning: 'What's it called? No! Look at it, gis in da, ooh! Who is this? They co, this is her. What doing? There, I see–ee up, up, up.' He often made strings of expressive noises which were impossible to transcribe, combined with syllables and real words, 'Mm, yah, playtime, bye-bye, sting firs, oo-ee?'

With other children he was also able to respond to jokes and even initiate and sustain a joking sequence:

ABBAS Simon, Simon.
CHILD I'm not Simon.
ABBAS Yes, you me, I'm Simon.
CHILD No I'm . . . (*Sounds like Superman.*)
ABBAS I'm Superman.
CHILD No I'm Superman.

Experimenting with limited resources

One impressive feature of Abbas's language development at this stage was his determination to communicate and the way he struggled to make himself understood. In one afternoon he produced many different ways of saying the same thing. He started hesitantly 'I go . . . I not come . . . I go in London, I not come,' and then at intervals tried out the following,

I not com aschool.
I go in aLondon.
I no com aschool.
I a go London.

All these convey a sense of the future, although he could not yet use this tense.

THE ELEVENTH WEEK

The last two weeks of term had been busy. The open evening in the tenth week had drawn crowds of parents to look at an impressive display of work on all aspects of safety. Tuesday morning of the eleventh week was sports day; Abbas and his parents had not turned up for either. He had come back to school on Tuesday afternoon and drawn a picture in his 'Busy Book' with the caption, 'I like sports day.'

On Wednesday morning, when the researcher arrived, the class was sitting busily drawing pictures, and the teacher was beginning the end of term sorting out and tidying up. Abbas wanted to know a word that seemed to be connected with running. After several demonstrations, everyone agreed that the word he wanted to know was 'skid'. He showed the researcher three pictures he had drawn in his book. One picture said, underneath 'This is my dad.' The researcher asked who it was and Abbas replied, 'That's my dad' – a well-structured, correct response; a long way from the single-word answers of ten weeks ago. Looking at the next picture, captioned 'A pretty picture,' Abbas said, 'That goes round and round', another thoroughly competent utterance which any native speaker might be expected to produce. The third picture, 'I like sports day', he seemed less sure about, speaking indistinctly. He seemed to say 'Kafief jumping.' There appeared to be a correlation between his commitment to the drawing and the correct linguistic response.

It had been a wet playtime and when the teacher and researcher came back to the classroom Abbas was practising his new word. 'Hey Miss! Look at me!' he called out, running a few steps and skidding dramatically. He watched as the researcher wrote in her notebook. 'Write my name,' he said imperiously. When she did not, he tried again, 'Give me my name.' She continued to write and he said, 'That's not my name. Give me my name. Give me my name.' His command of the imperative was well developed! When she finally wrote 'Abbas', he took the pen and added his surname.

Back in his seat, he drew a picture and asked, 'Where go Simon?' as children left the room. Later he went to join them in the hall where they were trying out jigsaw puzzles made by older children. Abbas was good at jigsaws (his teacher thought he may be doing them at home), and he confidently fitted shapes together on the hall floor. 'Let me here,' he said to the researcher, indicating that she was to sit on the floor beside him. 'Put hand here,' he said, touching his knee and saying 'Ow!' in pretend pain, evidently suggesting a bruise. 'Come sit down,' he added insistently. He was finding ways of using language to organize other people as well as his own life.

Back in the classroom, he drew with a red felt-tip pen, experimentally holding it still to watch a darker spot grow on the paper. Inspecting both sides at intervals, he made an interesting pattern and was obviously testing out an idea. Later on, when he sharpened a pencil on to the floor, he seemed surprised to be asked to clear it up, picking up pieces in his fingers in a most ineffectual way until one of the girls produced the dustpan and swept up for him. He was becoming rather good at using 'I dunno' when he did not want to do something! A clue to some of the inexplicable aspects of Abbas's early responses to school was unexpectedly provided during this week. It had been decided that it would be best for Abbas to join the Autumn reception class next term instead of moving on with his present group. His father had come to talk to the new class teacher and told her that

Abbas had spent his early years in India and had only returned to England shortly before starting school. This could explain, among other things, Abbas's reaction to playgroup, his very poor command of English, his father's over-protective behaviour, his seeming rejection of his mother and his fears about taking off his clothes, doing PE, and going swimming. It also made the way he had adjusted to school even more remarkable. In many ways, he was now a fully-fledged member of the school community. His teacher's final comment reads, 'On the last day Abbas was told off by the Head in Assembly; he tried one of his melting grins – needless to say it didn't work. But Abbas really wasn't upset!'

CONCLUSION

Some points for discussion

By the end of term Abbas had clearly made considerable progress. He had become progressively more able to participate in school routines and to take part in his peer group culture. In retrospect, it would have been helpful to have known more about Abbas, his family, and their recent history.

More detailed background and biographical information might have made it possible to help him in practical ways. Coping in a foreign language for long periods every day was undoubtedly very stressful. If it had been possible to arrange for someone who spoke his own language to spend some time with him, even an older child, the evident trauma of his first weeks might have been alleviated. His teacher would have welcomed help of this kind, and some of the frustration that both she and Abbas had experienced might have been averted.

In starting at a school where he is very much in a minority, he will have had to make cultural adjustments. As a Muslim from the Indian subcontinent, it is probable that he found little to relate to in the school environment. Although there were familiar faces among the children, there were few cultural representations in the form of pictures, stories, or artefacts. Obviously, he does share a common cultural experience with the other children in his class since they live locally, shop and play together, and must have many domestic routines in common. The transcripts of his talk also suggest that television is a common cultural experience, and the local park a shared playground. However, Abbas tended to seek out other Asian children on the playground and seemed more relaxed in their company.

It would have been helpful to have had stronger links with Abbas's home. Attempts to visit informally had failed and contact with his mother had been minimal. Father was extremely attentive but had failed to communicate important information at times when it would have thrown light on Abbas's problems. More effective communication might have enabled the parents to discuss Abbas's weight. This had contributed to his distress in the early weeks, and continued to make him a target for teasing, preventing him from joining in many of the normal physical activities of his peer group. Also, his poor attendance during the first term was never accounted for by his parents. Perhaps the school could have taken the initiative in enabling these parents to communicate their anxieties more effectively and in return learn about matters which were of concern to the school.

Abbas might have benefited from access to a wider range of picture books, to familarize himself with the relationship between image and text, and to give him a sense of the pleasure of looking at and handling books. Some of his class will have had this kind of pre-reading activity at playgroup or nursery. Such experience would have been useful to him before he embarked on the more structured work of the reading scheme.

Summary of Abbas's achievements

Abbas had made real headway in the two crucial areas facing 5-year-olds on entry to school; he was learning to be a pupil and learning to learn. School routines, how and when certain kinds of behaviour were appropriate, no longer troubled him and he had become a member of a group of children of his own age with whom he could hold his own.

At first, his teacher was afraid he might become a class pet, as another child had the previous year, becoming almost unable to operate independently. She had tried to avoid this and although he seemed to be much loved by the other children, he did not seem unduly dependent. Listening to their talk shows the extent to which he could communicate with other children on his own terms. At the same time, it shows how the children, taking their model from the teacher, were sensitive to Abbas's limited repertoire and often included him in conversation by making reference to things they particularly associated with him. For example, the conversation which Abbas opens with, 'I'm see you park' is not random but part of a pattern. Another child had opened up the possibility of an exchange by saying directly to Abbas, 'You like green'. 'Green' was one of Abbas's earliest words and one they all associate with him. The park is also a point of reference. At news time, when sharing experiences takes place, the children often referred to seeing Abbas in the park. Now they enabled Abbas to reciprocate and probably for the first time, he claimed to have seen one of them in the park. The children often seemed to enable Abbas to extend his linguistic competence by elaboration, repetition and imitation. Observing Abbas during this first term at school revealed many different ways in which he had been an active participant in his own learning and the extent to which this had been made possible in a classroom where all the children were encouraged to take responsibility for their learning within a secure and structured framework.

The development of Abbas's communicative and social competence

The detailed description of Abbas's progress in his first term at school may have seemed unnecessarily laborious. After all, four weeks into the second term he seemed to have settled into his new class. He did not seem any different from the other children. Language was not the handicap that it had seemed five months before. Some of the new children were less confident than Abbas and there was one boy whose language was no better. Mahmum had just returned from Pakistan, having started school earlier in the year. It was interesting to see them together, Abbas, self-propelling, wanting to communicate and find out, Mahmum painfully quiet and shy. Both of them had had to cope with disruptive experiences which would almost certainly affect their progress in school.

Most children will probably experience a certain amount of trauma when they start school. The transition from home to school is a move from primary to secondary socialization, from the security and familiarity of home routines to the uncertainty and diversity of school experience. For children like Abbas and Mahmum, whose lives have already been interrupted by other kinds of transition, it is hard to say when and where their experience of secondary socialization might have begun. During the first five years of his life Abbas lived in two different continents, and recently he had had to relate to a new family. Without more detailed information about his early years in India, it is impossible to imagine the kinds of adaptation he had had to make, both linguistically and culturally. The lack of continuity between his previous experience and that of school is likely to have been more pronounced than for children who have lived locally for most, or all, of their lives.

Certain assumptions can be made about children entering full-time schooling whose mother tongue is English. They can be assumed to have developed an adequate mastery of the basic structures of their native language (Wells 1981). Presumably, the same assumptions can be made about Abbas. His linguistic repertoire in English may be limited but since he appears to be a fluent speaker in his mother tongue, he must possess many or all of the grammatical structures, knowledge about language, which we would expect English-speaking children to have brought to school. This may explain his versatility in using stress, intonation and gesture to make himself understood. He seemed to be able to transfer skills from one language to another; he understood the turn-taking rules of conversation and the basic uses of language for exchanging information, asking, telling, and listening.

Looking at the transcripts of his talk, many features are still very undeveloped. He rarely used definite or indefinite articles to present information: 'That's bus', 'There's car', and he was not yet at ease in forming interrogatives: 'What's this?', 'What doing?' He quickly learned to use request forms, however: 'I *want* rubber', '*Give* me rubber', 'I *need* tyre.' Interestingly, these directives are among the earliest and most frequent forms used by first language learners. There has been much discussion in the past as to whether errors are caused by interference from the speaker's first language or by developmental factors. However, there seems to be much evidence to suggest that most errors made by bilingual children of Abbas's age will be developmental (Saunders 1982). These developmental features are not errors. Many of the examples from the transcript may seem to be straightforward mistakes which could be corrected. However, they have been identified as 'transitional constructions' (Dulay *et al.* 1982), interim structures which show that the second language learner is engaged in an active process of deciphering and producing a new system. Formal instruction or correction at this stage seems unlikely to be particularly effective. The errors Abbas was making are similar to those found in the speech of first language learners (Brown and Bellugi 1964). Research evidence suggests that the successful acquisition of communicative skills in a new language depends on the way the learner subconsciously filters and organizes the new system. The new learner, like any first language learner, has to build up the rule system in order to generate sentences. Children seem to filter the incoming language, attending only to parts, in order to acquire phrases and sentences which are essential for social participation. In order to achieve this, children choose their models, preferring their peers to teachers or parents, and members of their own ethnic group to non-members (Dulay *et al.* 1982).

As we have seen with Abbas, one of the major steps in the first term is learning to participate in the discourse of the classroom (Romaine 1984). The development of his communicative competence is essential before he can begin to add the skills of reading and writing, and it will have to take priority. It has been demonstrated that other children make a very important contribution to the development of second language learners, providing a powerful context for learning (Wiles 1979, Dulay *et al.* 1982).

We can see how Abbas's linguistic development is an active and creative process and by listening carefully we have some idea about his linguistic repertoire at the end of his first term. What we have almost no idea about is his repertoire of cultural knowledge (Houlton 1986). He spends much of his time in a cultural context which the school knows little about, in his Muslim home which will involve him in different language, different cultural rules, and different social roles. Most of what he experiences in school will relate to a very different set of norms and practices.

It has been suggested that cultural differences can affect language development (Rex 1986). Some of the problems facing children like Abbas in the development of conversational ability, or what has come to be known as 'oracy' (Wilkinson 1982), have been shown to stem from culturally based differences relating to communicative expectations (McTear 1985). There are often differences in ways of structuring information and of speaking. They may involve, among other things, the way a speaker uses intonation or para-linguistic cues. Failure to recognize cultural differences in these cues may lead to inter-ethnic miscommunication. The use of an inappropriate tone of voice may be construed as rudeness or aggression by a member of a different cultural group. Abbas's loud, peremptory tone, which sometimes seemed rude and even aggressive, could be attributed to this kind of difference.

The taped material illustrated specific ways in which Abbas was learning to participate in the classroom discourse, both in the structured learning conversations which took place in larger groups, and in small group interaction with his peers. In both contexts he seemed to be gaining invaluable practice at skills which he would need if he was going to add the linguistic skills of reading and writing to his repertoire. As far as these are concerned, he was still at a considerable disadvantage compared with many children of his age. What kind of extra assistance, therefore, might enable Abbas to achieve the competence which can be taken for granted as a starting point for most native English speakers on entry to school? And what else has to be taken into account if school is going to enable him to fulfil his potential?

The study of Abbas's progress has shown him to be an active participant in his own learning. It has also shown that peer group talk has been an effective means of learning. However, recent literature also warns that it may not be enough to leave second language learners to 'pick up' incidental language from their peers (Saunders 1982, Edwards 1984). Collaborative small group talk may also be beneficial if it is structured and encouraged by the teachers. The promotion of talk in the classroom is particularly important for second language learners. They need access to the widest possible range of opportunities to communicate, so that they can try out the rules that they are developing.

Perhaps Abbas should have the last word. Waiting in line to leave his classroom in the fourth week of his second term at school, he enquired, 'Where we going? What we doing?' Everyone concerned with the progress of ethnic minority children who start school with little English could well be asking similar questions!

3 Ruled out or rescued?

The process of statementing

> Their own expectation that hard work brings results, causes them to urge their children to 'work hard' in school, and they ask for evidence of such hard work in practices familiar to them: spelling words, 'learnin' lessons', and doing homework. Yet on those rare occasions when their children confront them with what they must do at school, they cannot grasp the ultimate purpose of the activities called for . . .
>
> (Heath 1983: 46)

> The successful education of children with special educational needs is dependent on the full involvement of their parents: indeed, unless the parents are seen as equal partners in the educational process the purpose of our report will be frustrated.
>
> (Department of Education and Science 1978: 50)

A recent report on a national conference entitled *Asian Children and Special Education* (ACE Bulletin 1989) highlights how little is known about the assessment of learning difficulties in children from bilingual and minority cultures. In Britain at present, we know very little about the nature and extent of actual or potential educational difficulties faced by Asian children. These questions have been more seriously debated in Europe and the USA than in Britain, but the publication of *Bilingualism and Special Education* (Cummings 1984) has led to debate on assessment, language, and bilingualism, and has made some educational psychologists critical of what has been described as 'the educational disabling of minority pupils'. There has been a move to discuss working with schools, teachers, parents and community over the assessment of bilingual and bicultural children.

However, relations between Asian parents and professionals can be problematic where referral, assessment, and statementing for special education has taken place. Questions about the most appropriate curriculum for Asian children who are placed in special schools, including the question of a non-racist curriculum, have scarcely been raised and the problems of parent–professional contact are still to be tackled. Many ethnic minority parents face language barriers and cultural differences. At best this may lead to misunderstanding; at worst, to inappropriate referral.

A long-standing friendship with an Asian family who were neighbours of Elizabeth led to her being involved in the process of statementing their youngest child, Balbinder Singh. He was six years old and had been at the school for three terms when the headteacher, knowing that Elizabeth was a neighbour and friend of Balbinder's mother, invited her to go with Mrs Singh to a meeting with the educational psychologist. The headteacher explained that he and the class teacher felt that Balbinder was making little progress, and they were worried about his lack of concentration and poor language. They were considering the possibility of a place in a special school for children with moderate learning difficulties which could offer smaller classes and more individual attention. His transfer would involve a lengthy and complicated assessment procedure, and they wanted Elizabeth to help to explain this to Balbinder's parents and to reassure them. If the process were to be set in motion immediately it was possible that he would be able to transfer in September. Balbinder's parents would almost certainly find this hard to comprehend. This chapter is an account of how the process happened, seen largely from the family's perspective. Below, Elizabeth tells the story as it unfolded.

EVENTS LEADING UP TO STATEMENTING

I had known the family for some years as I had been Mrs Singh's English tutor on a local authority adult literacy programme. Balbinder was 3 years old when I first started visiting the house, a very sociable child who eagerly awaited my arrival and the chance to play with the bag of toys I always brought with me. Over the years in my role as a home tutor I had had a privileged relationship with Balbinder and his family. By the time he started school I had already been an intermediary between the family and the town hall, the DHSS, the local social services, the medical profession, and the school. Mr and Mrs Singh kept most of their official correspondence between the pages of their telephone directory, and on my weekly visits we sorted out the milk tokens, rates demands, post office giros, all of which made linguistic demands which were beyond the level of their competence. Mr Singh, a Kenyan Asian, confessed to me, after I had been a friend of the family for several years, that he was neither fluent in Swahili, the language of his education up to 13 years old, nor in Punjabi, his mother tongue. He was certainly not fluent in English. However, the family spoke Punjabi exclusively at home and had very strong views on the need to do this. They were concerned that the boys should not lose touch with their language and culture.

The two older boys, aged 5 and 7, were competent in both languages. Balbinder seemed slower to talk and his mother was worried about his reluctance to speak English. As both parents spoke to him in Punjabi for most of the time this did not seem surprising. I reassured Mrs Singh that once he started playgroup there would be an improvement. In fact the health visitor diagnosed a problem at his screening at age 3, and he began attending the local health clinic for speech therapy. Mrs Singh mentioned this once or twice but did not seem to have much confidence in it. She continued to express concern at what she felt to be his backwardness at speaking English. I wondered how many people he had the opportunity to speak to outside his family.

Both the playgroup and the school he was to attend had a small number of ethnic minority children, so it seemed likely that his English would improve. Neither of his parents seemed to feel that Punjabi was causing any problems but this may never have been discussed in relation to his slow development in English. Certainly, when the educational psychologist produced evidence to suggest that he was suitable for transfer to a special school, no mention was made of his competence in his mother tongue – only of his deficiencies in spoken English. The school's educational psychologist had made contact with the family before, when he had been involved in the assessment of Balbinder's older brother Jeetinder, now in the fourth year at the school. There had been concern about his progress at much the same time as there now was for Balbinder's. Mrs Singh had been visited at home and the headteacher had arranged for me to be present so that I could explain and reinforce any suggestions. In the event, I had found it difficult to help Mrs Singh to implement these suggestions, as they seemed inappropriate. The psychologist had suggested, among other things, that Mrs Singh could help to improve Jeetinder's spoken and written language by reading to him at bedtime, and could help to improve his numeracy by encouraging him to spend and account for his pocket money. Both ideas were culturally alien to Mrs Singh. There were no English children's books in the house, and the boys did not shop on their own nor have regular pocket money. Neither parent was fully literate in English *or* their mother tongue. Mrs Singh had seemed mystified by the advice, as she believed the school should be responsible for progress in English and mathematics, and shrugged helplessly when I suggested that parents also had an important role to play. As Sikhs they felt that they were educating their boys in particular ways, and by speaking Punjabi in their home they believed that they were preserving their cultural heritage. In my

English lessons with her, I had often stressed the need to play with and talk to pre-school children. But at the end of every lesson, Mrs Singh would collect up the toys and books I had brought with me and offered to leave behind until my next visit, insisting that I should take them away. Balbinder always played quietly and absorbedly with my lego, puzzles, cars, paper and crayons, while I helped his mother to read and write.

The playgroup run by local parents had not been the success for Balbinder that we had hoped. There were complaints about his behaviour. He did not seem to know how to play, would not settle down, ran about too much, and fought with the other children. At home, whenever I visited, he always seemed the same docile, attractive child sitting silently watching television in the impeccably tidy and attractively furnished living room of the very small terrace house. In the house, the lives of the three young boys seemed quiet, calm and disciplined. But the large hall at playgroup, the number of activities, different experiences, and other children seemed to produce excitable and often aggressive behaviour in Balbinder. The staff were also worried about his speech, not seeming to take into account the fact that this was the first time he had come out of a Punjabi-speaking environment and was having to cope with new experiences in a foreign language. His mother's flowing though inaccurate English and confident manner may have led them to expect more of him.

Mrs Singh worried about Balbinder a great deal, and was often very angry at his apparent lack of progress. She wanted him to learn to count, begin to write, and above all to speak in English. She and the children visited my house regularly at this period, so that I could hear the oldest boy Ravi read. He had already overtaken his mother and she did not know how to cope with the graded readers he brought home from school, or with his teacher's request that she should hear him read. Whenever they visited me I listened to him reading. He was quite fluent but seemed to read without comprehension. I felt that the texts he was reading did not speak of familiar experiences, nor use vocabulary he was familiar with. I remember him struggling with a story where understanding of the narrative depended on the reader knowing about canals. He could read the words – 'canal', 'lock', 'barge' – but the illustrations of an urban canal with tall industrial buildings and long, painted boats portrayed an unfamiliar landscape. At 8 he was rapidly becoming a non-reader. The idea that reading might be for pleasure had not occurred to him. Balbinder was always pleased to come along for these sessions, to play with my children's toys and run in the garden. Mrs Singh brought her letters and forms for me to elucidate. For a year or so she was quite ill, suffering from high blood pressure and a serious gynæcological problem. Often she was clearly too tired to cope with her English lesson, and often she was depressed. Her husband remained unemployed, his social life caused her great concern, and, as she saw it, the boys were not making good progress at school.

I had had the task of explaining school reports to her for long enough to be aware of the way the two older boys were, in the estimation of their teachers, falling behind. While I knew that her aspirations for the children were unrealistic it did not seem unreasonable that she should want her children to fulfil their potential more effectively than they seemed to be doing. But how could she intervene or express her feelings when the processes of the education system were so mystifying, so partially understood, and seemed so effectively to exclude her? I was constantly surprised at the extent to which she needed explanations for even the most taken-for-granted aspects of junior school life. The list of clothing for a school trip included 'night dress' and 'sponge bag'. The Singh children slept in their underpants, and she wondered whether I could lend her a 'night dress' for Ravi, and also a sponge. Almost all documents sent home from school were incomprehensible. Letters inviting parents to 'join the parent–teacher association', visit the 'Spring Fayre', to volunteer for 'parent–governor elections', or attend a 'Maths Workshop', were put in the bin after my attempts to explain them. Schools unwittingly erect a language barrier which must exclude great numbers of parents. End of term reports contained phrases like 'his development of spatial awareness . . . ' or 'his confidence on the apparatus . . . '. However, phrases like ' . . .is working hard', '. . . always tries his best', '. . .is beginning to show some improvement' did not fool her. She interpreted them quite accurately to mean that her children were under-achieving and the message she took from them was almost always a negative one.

On one occasion Mrs Singh had asked me to go with her to visit one of the boy's teachers. The teacher was brusque and busy. She brushed aside Mrs Singh's assertions that her son was not making progress by telling her repeatedly that it was unreasonable to expect anything more; she used phrases like, 'He is well below average', 'He is slow', 'He is in the bottom set, you must accept that. You can't put it there if it's not there.' She showed Mrs Singh his English books full of neatly written exercises. The mistakes he was making suggested lack of understanding. In his story book he had written briefly about Odysseus and had been asked to copy out a short piece related to the class topic. This was displayed on the wall. Mathematics consisted of answers in a printed book and Mrs Singh was told he was making progress. Mrs Singh was not satisfied. She wanted to know why he never brought anything home, why he had no reading book. His teacher explained that homework for 8-year-olds was not school policy, and Jeetinder was called in to show his mother that he could read. He produced his reading book, one of the Pirate series by Sheila McCullagh, and read quite fluently. The teacher suggested that Mrs Singh could help by reading with him, Mrs Singh to read one line, Jeetinder the next; she was evidently unaware of the possibility that Jeetinder's reading could be more competent than his mother's.

Looking at a piece of work on the board, Mrs Singh said she wanted her son to write like that. The teacher, by now worn down by Mrs Singh's refusal to accept Jeetinder's limitations, told her that it had been written by 'a highly intelligent girl'. She continued to try to convince Mrs Singh that although Jeetinder was in the bottom set he was doing well and was not 'the bottom of the bottom set'. None of this convinced Mrs Singh, who left the classroom saying in an unusually dictatorial tone to the class teacher, 'I want you to sort him out and bring homework home.' Later, I tried to mollify her by pointing out that the teacher had said what a nice boy he was. Looking me straight in the eye she replied, 'Nice is in every child.' She wanted her children to be able to cope with life more effectively than she and her husband seemed to be doing. She knew that education was the key.

Shortly after Balbinder had started school, Mrs Singh had to have major surgery followed by two weeks' convalescence in a hospital twelve miles from home. This cannot have been an easy time for Balbinder. His father took him to school and members of the family rallied round. But for many weeks family life was disrupted. After the operation, Mrs Singh's health improved, and with it her energy and enthusiasm. She took up part-time work as a seamstress. Her English lessons with me became infrequent, but invitations to visit her and sort out forms, letters from school, and to listen to her worries, increased. On the morning the headteacher had asked us both to meet the educational psychologist, she had approached me in the school foyer, handed me a bag full of letters, and burst into tears. I realized that I hadn't visited her for some weeks and agreed to go to her house after school.

The headteacher had explained to me earlier that Mrs Singh had been coming to school regularly to express concern about Balbinder's lack of progress. The class teacher and the headteacher were also worried; they felt that, 'after four terms at school, he is the slowest in the class.' Their concern was that in September, when he should be moving into the second year with his age cohort, he would be left behind. The headteacher had asked the educational psychologist to come and assess him. Standardized tests had shown that whereas his two older brothers had scored better on verbal ability than on visual motor ability, Balbinder had performed equally poorly on both. As a result, the educational psychologist had been investigating the possibility of a place at a local special school for Balbinder. They now wanted to explain all this to Mrs Singh and hoped that

I would be able to explain the implications of what they were going to say in a more informal situation later on. My knowledge of the family made me feel some misgivings about the way they might respond to a suggestion that Balbinder should transfer to a school they had never heard of, which was also several miles away from their home.

PREPARING A STATEMENT OF SPECIAL NEEDS

At the time I knew little about the assessment and statementing procedures in which the Singh family were to be involved. Balbinder would be assessed under Section 5 of the Education Act 1981, in order that the local authority could determine special educational provision for him and issue a written statement as to the nature of this provision in due course. The 1981 Education Act defines a child with special needs as one who has 'significantly greater difficulty in learning than the majority of children of his age'. Since the Act, children are no longer allocated to one of a number of categories for which separate types of provision are made, but are assessed in order to discover their individual special educational needs. Assessment should be seen as 'a means of arriving at a better understanding of a child's learning difficulties for the practical purpose of providing a guide to his education' (Department of Education and Science 1983, para. 4). Following the recommendations of the Warnock Committee (Department of Education and Science 1978), the Act also gave parents new rights to be involved in the process of assessing and preparing a statement on their child. In theory, this meant that parents were to have more information and be more involved in the decisions.

For many parents, however, the rhetoric of the act falls far short of the reality that they encounter. More often than not, it seems that the placement of a child in special provision has been decided *before* formal assessment takes place, and the system of provision is unable to respond to or to satisfy even seemingly reasonable parental wishes (Swann 1987: 193). In the case of Mr and Mrs Singh, the notion of parental participation in decision making would depend on their understanding the issues involved. My conversations with them revealed that they were often struggling to make sense of a system which continually mystified them and which seemed unable to provide the results they hoped for. Both of them had spent less than three years in British secondary schools in the late 1960s. The primary school that their children attended seemed very different from their own early years in Kenya and the Punjab. Understanding the intricacies of special educational needs and provision would be hard for them. They simply wanted reassurance that whatever was going to happen would be best for Balbinder.

As an outside observer drawn into this process by the professionals involved, I had a neutral but not disinterested role. I kept a diary of events and attempted to chart the process by which 6-year-old Balbinder was removed from mainstream education.

The process of statementing

March

Meeting with the headteacher, the school's educational psychologist, Mrs Singh and myself at school.

The headteacher explained to Mrs Singh that Balbinder was not making much progress and that, because of class sizes he would be unlikely to receive the kind of attention he needed. He explained that at Cedars (the local authority's provision for children with learning difficulties), where classes are small and the teachers are specialists at coping with Balbinder's sort of problems, he might do better. He stressed that it was essential for Balbinder to start at Cedars as soon as possible, if he was going to catch up. At this point he seemed to be suggesting that once Balbinder had been at Cedars for a while, he might be capable of re-entering mainstream education at middle school transfer. Certainly, in conversations afterwards I realized that Mrs Singh had understood it this way. It was an idea she was to hold on to throughout the process.

Both the headteacher and the educational psychologist stressed the positive value of Cedars and the likely problems for Balbinder if he stayed on at his present school, which they told her did not have the expertise to cope with his needs. By suggesting this, they began quite unwittingly to undermine her confidence in the school and in herself. She became very upset and confused, clearly feeling that Balbinder's failure was her fault. She cried a lot, repeatedly saying, 'he always wants to play . . . he just wants toys'. When she was calmer, she also made it clear that she felt that a stricter approach that forced Balbinder to concentrate and work harder was all that was needed. She felt that he was not doing well because he was not trying hard enough, and that his teachers were not making him try hard enough. She listened intently as they explained the statementing procedure. They stressed that the decision to send Balbinder to Cedars would be made by Mrs Singh and her husband. The initial stage would be to visit the school and then to return to discuss the matter again. A date was arranged for the following week for both events, and I agreed to go with them.

What I did not realize at the time, but discovered later, was that Mrs Singh had no idea that transfer next September had been suggested – she expected that it would happen straight away.

> After she had left, the headteacher and educational psychologist explained the statementing procedure to me in more detail. In the past, they had waited until after the 7-plus screening, but they now felt that this was leaving it too late. In Balbinder's case it was not simply that he was a slow learner. There were what the head called 'social concerns' behind his transfer. He was developing 'social control', but found it harder on the playground where it seemed that he was easily influenced by other children to behave badly. As he put it, 'He reverts when he is with naughty children.' They had not given these reasons for transfer to his parents; yet they were clearly important considerations as far as the school was concerned. At times, Balbinder was seen to be a disciplinary problem.
>
> It was not a foregone conclusion that there would be a place available at Cedars, since there is a lot of pressure on special education in the county. As the headteacher of Cedars was making his entry list for September already, and would have to submit it by the end of the week, the educational psychologist was going to request a place for Balbinder before statementing him. Thus it was essential to get Mr and Mrs Singh's agreement as soon as possible. Later on the same day, I visited Mr and Mrs Singh at home. Over tea and food we talked about the school's suggestion. Mrs Singh was upset; she felt rejected by the school her children had been attending for five years. She was depressed and angry with Balbinder. She had been crying and said that she had been 'feeling awful' all day. She clearly found it hard to sort out the implications of what was being suggested. However, we agreed to visit Cedars together in a few days time.
>
> The difficulty she was having in making sense of the boys' education was illustrated by the packet of letters she had brought to school in the morning. One from the LEA was about her 8-year-old son's transfer to middle school, an event generating a great deal of paper including a list of the available schools; another letter from the LEA explained parents' rights of choice and appeal, and also dates of open evenings; yet another letter from the school he had been allocated to required the parents to sign the tear-off slip and return it to their present school. I noticed, fortunately, that he had been given a place at a different school from his older brother and that it

was actually a matter of filling in the appeals form requesting a place at that school. I suggested that they should also accept the invitation to take him to visit his new school's open evening. Mrs Singh said she would go if I came too, but not otherwise. Another letter from the middle school was about a visiting theatre group and asked for money as well as containing a tear-off slip. We discussed with her 10-year-old son whether he wanted to see the play and we put the money for a ticket in an envelope. To his chagrin we threw away the letter about a skiing holiday. At nearly £400 for a week in Austria, his parents were not interested.

In the evening I consulted a friend who is also a local headteacher. Her school has a high proportion of ethnic minority children where I felt Balbinder might not have seemed such a problem. In her opinion, it was unlikely that he would get a place at Cedars at such a late stage in the year. She also felt that age 6 was too early to make what she saw as a drastic decision – once out of mainstream education she felt he would be unlikely to get back in.

At this stage in the proceedings, my own feelings were mixed. If the school felt it could not cope with Balbinder then maybe he would be better in a more sympathetic environment. On the other hand, Mrs Singh would lose all her social contacts in the local community once she did not have to take him to school every day. The school gave her a point of reference and contact with other mothers. The middle school which both her older boys were to attend was a long walk from her home and made little or no attempt to involve parents; positive home/school links were nonexistent. If Balbinder was bused to Cedars every day she would effectively be cut off from any real involvement in her children's schooling, and from an important part of her own role within the community as the mother of a young child at the local school.

On the other hand, I knew that her confidence in Balbinder's school had been profoundly shaken by the interview with the headteacher and educational psychologist. If Balbinder didn't get a place at Cedars this year she would become even more anxious about his progress.

March 9: visiting Cedars school

The headteacher at the school made us very welcome. He began by talking to Mr and Mrs Singh about the school. He stressed the normality of the children who attend it. He explained that children came to Cedars when their own school could not give them the individual help with basic skills which they needed. He explained that when a child becomes anxious he or she may stop learning.

Cedars, he told them, was a special school because it had special teachers with special skills and training. All of the sixteen teachers in the school were experienced in teaching children with learning difficulties. Another special feature was the size of the groups; ten in the first year, twelve in the second, and fifteen thereafter. Balbinder would be in a group with ten children.

Mrs Singh seemed to be listening intently, but I guessed that a lot of what was being said went over her head. I am not sure that she even knows the word 'special', and phrases like 'learning difficulties', 'becomes anxious', 'experienced', are not necessarily familiar. After a while she asked, 'These children, do they learn it at the end?' The headteacher replied that the school offered ideal circumstances and that most children responded positively. There is an annual review in which a report is made on the child's progress. All parents, he told them, have the right to say, 'I want my child to leave,' and he said, 'Our job is to help the child go back.' They review this possibility annually, and he explained that when they have identified children who will go back they let them go into mainstream school for at first a morning and then one day a week. At the moment six children would be going back into middle school in September. At this point Mrs Singh said comfortably, 'They have learned, that's nice.'

The headteacher went on to explain that the school's job was to understand each child's problem. He told them that many children learned more slowly. He illustrated different ways in which reading, for example, could be taught, and how some children may not be 'mature' enough to cope with a 'look and say' approach, or may not develop that way. He explained how 'look and say' uses eyes, while phonics uses ears. Mr and Mrs Singh listened politely but were possibly confused by all this specialist terminology.

He went on to tell them about the school. The children started at age 5 and could stay until the age of 16. They could also leave at any time. Each part of the school – lower/middle/upper – resembled mainstream school, the difference lying in the size of the teaching group. At 16 plus they go on to college for up to two years and follow courses which will lead to work. Several of the 15-year-olds were on work experience at that moment.

He then took us round the school, showing Mr and Mrs Singh everything. The lower school had its own grassed and paved play area with plentiful equipment. The rooms were small, purpose-built, had carpeted floors, and each teacher had a non-teaching assistant, or para-professional. It was an intimate, small-scale, non-threatening environment. I was particularly impressed by the art room. The workshop and home economics area were also impressive, and the school had three computers. Outside it was very pleasant also, with views over open fields and a local park. Part of the senior side had been landscaped to make an attractive outdoor work area containing wooden tables and benches made in the workshop. There was a swimming pool and a distant view of the donkey field. There seemed to be few ethnic minority children, one in each class perhaps, certainly none in the youngest group.

After the visit, the headteacher talked about the importance of parental involvement. He explained that regular contact and discussion of ways in which parents can help at home was vital: 'Together, we can achieve more.' The school had an open door policy. He then put it to Mr and Mrs Singh that they would have to think about whether they would like Balbinder to come to the school. He explained that there were a limited number of places, with sixteen to seventeen taken up for September already (I wondered whether this meant Balbinder might be unlucky, but did not like to ask).

He explained the procedure by which Balbinder would be given a place. The educational psychologist would prepare notes on Balbinder. He himself would visit Balbinder at his present school. He stressed, 'We only want him to come if it's right. Nothing happens until you say yes.' Then Mr and Mrs Singh would come again with Balbinder, and finally they would receive a letter from County Hall. Again, he stressed that the final decision lay with them: 'He will not come until you sign it in the end you decide.' Mr Singh asked his first question: 'Would it be next September?' The headteacher said that that would be the case and that Balbinder would stay for as long as he needed their help. However, they could make the decision to take him away 'at any time'.

Mrs Singh asked, 'Do you have the same holiday?' and then spoke for the first time about Balbinder. She seemed distressed; 'I mean, Balbinder, he used to just sit by the telly, even now he still . . . he want toys . . . he doesn't want to do the things, he want to do all the time what he wants to do . . . ' The headteacher nodded reassuringly, seeming to listen, but he did not encourage her to talk about Balbinder any more. Instead he went on to tell them them that the shortest time they kept pupils for was two years, but that usually they tried to move people back into mainstream education at the time of transfer to middle/upper school.

He told them that the educational psychologist was very good, and really knew the children. Mrs Singh, still pursuing her own thoughts, said, 'I wish he was just like other children, like my other children.' The headteacher said it was important to think about 'whatever is best' for Balbinder, and went back to what the school catered for – 'People think it's a school for the mentally handicapped'. 'It doesn't look like one', said Mrs Singh very positively. The headteacher told them that there were many different special schools in the county, and explained where and what each one was for, reassuring them that Cedars is 'a school for children who have difficulty getting started with basic skills'. Its job is to help children 'who are struggling'. He gave Mr and Mrs Singh a school booklet and saw us out. We rang for a taxi, and while we waited looked at books of photographs of school plays, trips, art work, and sports days. Both Mr and Mrs Singh seemed surprised and relieved by the normality of the school. Mr Singh told me that one of his brothers-in-law had told him it was a school for mentally handicapped. This had clearly been worrying them both.

When we got home they both expressed their surprise and relief that everything at the school had seemed so normal. They seemed quite clear in their minds that Balbinder's transfer would be their decision and that they would choose 'whatever was best for Balbinder'. They both seemed almost convinced already, and I could see that they were ready to agree to the move. It was also evident that they had not weighed up the consequences. It all seemed easy – they sign on the dotted line and Balbinder would be virtually taken out of their hands. Despite the school's stated intention to involve parents as far as possible, I seriously doubted whether Mr or Mrs Singh would be either capable or prepared to enter into the kind of partnership the school envisaged. Looking through the booklet the head had given them, I guessed that they would have some difficulty making sense of it. They would probably need help with sentences like 'Class teachers, together with the help of the remedial specialist, ensure that there is a detailed understanding of the learning difficulties of each individual child.' Terms like 'environmental work', 'a full curriculum', 'special programmes of work for language development' would all need to be explained to them. The school's expressed intention is that, 'Parents are helped to understand the nature of the learning difficulties of their child and are encouraged to visit the school frequently to develop that understanding and to continue that approach at home.' Neither Mr nor Mrs Singh have the confidence to take on such a role. Their own experience of schooling has left them unlikely to be able to contemplate the idea that they might, 'in partnership with the school . . . help their children acquire the knowledge, skills and attitudes which enable them to contribute to society and lead an independent adult life.' Families with both parents at work, a poor understanding of English, and no means of transport might be expected to find this a challenge that they cannot cope with.

March 12: explaining the procedure

I met with Mrs Singh and the educational psychologist in the head-teacher's room. Mrs Singh was very certain – she and her husband had decided last night that they both want Balbinder to go to Cedars. I tried to explore the problems Mrs Singh would have in attempting to be a fully participating parent, but the educational psychologist seemed to feel that this was a problem common to many Cedars parents.

The educational psychologist spent some time explaining the legal side of statementing, which is complex. He told us that it would take many weeks to sort out and would involve a variety of procedures, such as a medical, reports from the school, and visits. There would be twenty-nine days between the initial letter from County Hall and any action. The sheer amount of information seemed daunting. I arranged to visit that afternoon and to go through it with Mr and Mrs Singh.

When I arrived, they showed me the letter they had received from the Chief Education Officer that morning which explained the proposed 'statementing' procedure: 'The learning difficulties being experienced by your child were discussed and you agreed that your child probably has a special educational need which requires further investigation. Therefore it is proposed to carry out an assessment of your child's needs under the Education Act 1981 with your agreement.' The letter was at pains to stress the parents' involvement and their rights: 'If it is agreed that the Authority should determine the special educational provision for your child . . . your further rights under the Education Act 1981 will be explained to you.' An enclosed booklet gave further general information about the provision of special education with an addendum summarizing the legal rights of parents in relation to the assessment process. In this, the mysterious twenty-nine days were explained: 'Parents will have a period of twenty-nine days in which to seek further information from the Chief Education Officer and to make representations and submit written evidence.'

Since they had evidently made up their minds, none of this seemed important to them. Going through the Cedars' brochure with them, however, they were pleased to find a statement which they could relate to, namely that the school sets out to help children 'who are having problems in learning to read, find spelling and writing difficult, are unable to express themselves well, are unable to settle and concentrate . . . ' All these seemed to relate to Balbinder's needs as his parents saw them, and Mr and Mrs Singh were beginning to seem happier. As they understood it, after a short while Balbinder might be sorted out and returned to mainstream. I did not feel so optimistic. The brochure stated clearly that while some children transferred back to mainstream schools, 'the majority remain until they are 16 years of age'.

May 6

The headteacher told me that he had received the papers about Balbinder's statementing from County Hall.

June 3

Arrangements were made for a meeting at school between Mr and Mrs Singh and the educational psychologist. He had to go through the results of the tests. He has a legal obligation to explain these to the parents.

June 5

I visited Mrs Singh at home. She told me that she had been present when Balbinder was tested by the educational psychologist. Balbinder had had to do a lot of puzzles. The psychologist had said he was good with his hands. Mrs Singh said he would not sit down and kept walking about. She said he was the same at home, he only wanted to play with toys and watch television; he wouldn't do any 'work'. I was not sure what she meant by 'work'. She went on to speak of her worries about Jeetinder who still wasn't bringing anything home from school. She was having trouble with local harassment and was afraid to go out into her garden. Her husband was away in India for three weeks. People were throwing things over her garden wall and someone had painted on the front door. We spent a lot of time discussing this. In some ways, Balbinder seemed the least of her problems at the time. Perhaps it was a relief that matters were being taken out of her hands. We agreed to meet at school the following week.

June 10: making the decision

First, the headteacher went through the school report, details of birth, address, etc. stating that Balbinder was in a first year mixed-ability class. There was a brief account of professional intervention to date. Before starting school he had attended the child development centre, received speech therapy, and since had been seen on several occasions by the educational psychologist.

Second, there was a description of the child's functioning. He had taken a long time to settle into school, for example routine and order of the class. He had communication problems – speech and knowledge of English language were not good. He had difficulty 'sounding' because of this, and it was thought to be affecting his progress in learning to read. The headteacher attempted to explain to Mrs Singh how children have to learn the initial sounds of words and how having two languages can impede this. I *think* Mrs Singh understood. Balbinder has also had difficulty learning colours, numbers and sounds. His progress was slow because his retention was poor.

At this point Mrs Singh, looking concerned, said, 'You think there's something wrong with him inside of him?' The headteacher said, 'No, he's not *ill*.' Mrs Singh agreed that it must be the way he forgot things. The headteacher said 'Yes, he does have difficulty in remembering – particularly "sounding"', and felt that this could be because he was perhaps more fluent in Punjabi.

There were discrepancies in the report. On the one hand Mrs Singh was told that his drawing and writing were immature, that he was still drawing and writing like a very young child; yet later she was told that he was very good with a pencil and talented at art! Having said that he was very immature, the report added that there had been considerable improvement, but it had taken a long time (he had only been at school for four terms and had had a change of teacher). The headteacher stressed that what Balbinder needed was to be in a small group, not in a class of twenty-three. In order for him to maintain interest he needed to work in short spurts. In his present situation, his difficulty in concentrating took up a lot of the teacher's time. The headteacher then commented on his social development. Here they felt there had been much progress. Balbinder used to be 'wild', but he had learned to share and to take part in group work, despite still being a very lively child.

The headteacher then went on to describe the aims and provision of special education. Since Balbinder clearly made more progress in a small group where he could have a lot of attention, and where all children worked at the same pace, this could be an answer. The headteacher felt that the boy needed somebody permanently watching him. Also, he needed a lot of practice in English, as he was still not sounding words clearly. Further, he was a very active child, and needed specialist apparatus. They had all the necessary facilities and resources at Cedars. The headteacher was very persuasive at this point showing concern for the way Balbinder would react when (or if) he fell behind. As Balbinder was already behind in mastering the basic skills which lay the foundation for all further work, the headteacher felt that Balbinder needed a lot of help if he was to do justice to his abilities. And he said very kindly, 'That's our view of Balbinder.'

The educational psychologist took over at this point to explain the contents of his report. He felt that Balbinder's problems with language had needed attention before school and obviously the family had noticed the problem at an early stage. He stressed in his report that he was a very likeable little boy. However, observing him in the classroom he had noticed his immature behaviour. He ran about a lot, had language problems, and found concentration difficult. Despite a lot of improvement in pencil and artwork there had been none in reading and school work generally. He had noticed that Balbinder was not listening to the teacher and had to be given instructions. He was fidgety and in a dream world when being given instruction in a group. He often watched other children and then followed and copied them.

The psychologist commented that Balbinder had liked having a reading book and clearly wanted to read, but when it came to reading he did not understand what he was doing and relied on guessing. He clearly wanted to do well, and wanted to read, but needed a lot of extra help. When asked questions, he gave one-word answers, though he used two words on occasions, as in 'boys swimming', 'wet play'. In the tests given to him, he was better on puzzles and patterns, poor on those involving speaking and understanding.

The psychologist felt that Balbinder needed to work slowly and not be pushed – he needed more time and specific help to speak in sentences. At this point Mrs Singh said, 'They are not allowed to speak English at home.' She felt that he spoke better in Punjabi and that he remembered better in Punjabi. She referred to her own family, parents, brother and sisters, who all spoke English at home. She found this very odd. At the weekend when she had taken Balbinder to stay with his grandparents in Coventry, her brother had been trying to teach Balbinder to say, 'Can I', or, 'May I' instead of, 'I want to'.

The educational psychologist listened tolerantly to Mrs Singh's comments, did not respond to them, but simply reiterated that Balbinder needed to be with teachers who were experienced in working with small groups. Mrs Singh said that she felt that Balbinder would always do what was wanted if it suited him. The educational psychologist told her that one of the teachers from Cedars had visited Balbinder in school and had made very positive comments. It seemed that a place was available, but that all the complex procedures had to be completed before it could be offered to them. He still had to have a medical. The headteacher would speak to the school doctor that same day. The social services would write to Mrs Singh. The procedure was necessarily long-winded but it could be completed by the end of term. Mrs Singh expressed a worry about Balbinder refusing to dress himself and ordering her to get him ready for school when he could do this perfectly well if he wanted to. The educational psychologist said this was understandable while he was feeling rather unsettled. The headteacher said he would chase up the documents.

Mrs Singh seemed bewildered by the amount of information she had been given; she would probably need reassuring and some recapitulation afterwards. I promised to go and see her again on Friday morning. Throughout this interview Mrs Singh, who was still struggling to grasp the implications of what the headteacher and educational psychologist were telling her, attempted to contribute. Her anecdotes were treated courteously but no real response was made. It seemed that now the process was under way her contribution was not required.

June 12

I visited Mr and Mrs Singh. Mrs Singh and I talked Mr Singh through the meeting, point by point. He agreed with the headteacher's account of Balbinder's lack of concentration, which obviously worried them both a great deal. He listened to what I had to say about the procedure still to be gone through, and said he hoped that they would soon hear whether Balbinder had a place. I said that this was almost certain but that the process was rather slow. Mrs Singh agreed to tell me when she heard from the doctor. They both understood that this was a formality and that he was not thought to be 'ill'.

What particularly concerned me was their feeling that Balbinder seemed to understand and respond better in Punjabi. Mrs Singh expressed her feelings that it was very important for all her children to speak Punjabi and she was afraid that they might not do this if she and Mr Singh spoke English. Both parents were very concerned that he should get more appropriate help and were now convinced that this would be provided at Cedars.

June 22

Mr and Mrs Singh had received a letter offering Balbinder a place at Cedars. They had understood the gist but needed help. We filled in the acceptance form and telephoned the school about a visit. The school secretary said all the September intake would be invited for a morning before the end of term. Balbinder, who had been excluded from all deliberations about his future, had not seen his new school yet.

July 8

Mrs Singh telephoned to tell me that they had been invited to visit the school on 15 July.

July 15

Mrs Singh, Balbinder, and I set off. Balbinder was *very* subdued. His mother said he was not happy about the new school, and wanted to stay where he was. He had, after all, had five terms there; he would be 7 years old in December. He did not speak at all during the journey. Mrs Singh remarked what a long way it seemed. We were early and stood in the playground. Balbinder looked around but clung to Mrs Singh. We went in and were ushered into the hall where a number of other new children were looking at books of photographs of school trips and events. We were asked to sit in the third and fourth rows and the lower school children filed in. The headteacher introduced himself and handed over to the headteacher of the lower school. He had explained that the school had a lower/middle/upper division and the lower school headteacher briefly explained that the children were going to show the parents and new children what they had been doing. Each year group described a recent trip and showed photographs and work they had done. The classes were small, as were the number of ethnic minority children. There were one or two Afro-Caribbean children overall, and one or two Asian children in each group. Mrs Singh and Balbinder noticed each one and commented. It was hot and the demonstrations went on far too long, but it gave us all some idea of how caring the teachers were and was a practical illustration of what the school was trying to do.

The children were then asked to go out to play. Balbinder was very reluctant and clung to his mother. He had lost interest in the activities. There had been too much 'talk and show' early in the display, and he had been wriggling about and scraping his chair back, for which Mrs Singh reprimanded him constantly. It looked as if we would have to take him out, but an older Asian boy came and took him away, and he went quite confidently. The headteacher then told the parents about travel, uniform, swimming (once a week all the year round), the parent–teacher association, illnesses, notes for absence or non-swimming and, above all, that parents should contact the school whenever in doubt about anything. We were then taken to have coffee and the school secretary handed out official forms for the parents to fill in. Mrs Singh filled them in, although she had already expressed alarm at the number of notes she was going to have to write to the school.

Classes were allocated, and Balbinder was to be with a Mrs Allinson and a nursery assistant. Class 1 was small, with its own toilets and washbasins and an entirely private playground. Balbinder ran outside straight away, gesturing to me to come and look at it. In the playground they had a sturdy wooden house (a real summer-house) with a door and windows, climbing and swinging equipment, and lots of small bicycles and tricycles. In the classroom, photographs of the trip to the seaside were on display and there were small circular tables. It was all on a scale much more appropriate for children than the high vaulting of Balbinder's previous school and, of course, there was much more play equipment. This filled Mrs Singh with horror, as she was sure that what Balbinder needed was not more ad lib *play* but more discipline. She was worried by the way he roamed about touching everything, and during a long chat to Mrs Allinson she expressed her concern that he could not get on with anything, and could not write or read. Mrs Allinson was very reassuring. However, Mrs Singh clearly saw Cedars as a temporary phase. Earlier on in the playground, as Balbinder had gradually gained confidence and begun to explore and use things Mrs Singh had said, wistfully, 'I do hope Balbinder learn so quickly he will soon go back to his school.'

On the way out the headteacher knelt down to say goodbye to Balbinder, who was still looking rather mystified, but seemed much less clinging and was smiling more. In the car on the way home he sat alone, opened the window and put his head out. It was very hard to imagine what he made of what was going on. No one had consulted him and he didn't seem to want to talk about it. In all these transactions Balbinder seemed a shadowy figure. Decisions were being taken about his future which no one could explain to him. Over the last few months he had become rather withdrawn and mistrustful, a subdued version of his former self.

At Cedars Mrs Singh had instantly made friends with a young Asian woman (wearing trousers and a shirt) who had a little girl who was evidently a year older than Balbinder. She and Mrs Singh spoke in Punjabi but her English sounded local and I suspected that she preferred to speak English. However, Mrs Singh was pleased to meet her and generally liked all the teachers and what she saw. I wondered whether she had any misgivings. The distance will certainly be a problem. What *she* was making of this experience was also hard to imagine. Choice seemed to have been taken away from her, but some of her anxieties had also been allayed.

STATEMENTED

In September Balbinder started at Cedars. My contact with the family became much less frequent. Their circumstances had changed. Mr Singh had a full time job, they had taken a big step and purchased their council house, and Mrs Singh now felt that she needed permanent work herself. The job she finally acquired during the summer holidays meant leaving home before the children and returning after them. The coach which picked up the Cedars' children stopped about five minutes walk away from their home. Balbinder had to be seen on to it, and met at the end of the day. For the first few weeks of term this was a problem. Mr Singh could take him to the bus when he was on late shifts and collect him on early shifts. His brothers aged 8 and 10, whose school was a long walk in the opposite direction, had to be relied on to take this responsibility when their father could not. The whole operation caused Mrs Singh a great deal of anxiety. By half term, a local parent with a child at Cedars had offered to put Balbinder on the coach in the morning and let him stay at her house until he could be picked up in the evening. Mrs Singh had now effectively become cut off from her children's education just as Balbinder had been cut off from local peer group relationships. She occasionally contacted me, and for a Christmas present gave me a photograph of Balbinder taken at school and made into a calendar. This showed him sitting at a desk, pencil in hand: his mother's vision of what school should be about. She and Mr Singh had visited the school for a Christmas event and had been pleased to hear that

Balbinder was being moved into the second class. She had been worried that he was still playing too much and not learning anything.

From January to July my contacts with the family were infrequent and concerned the progress of the two older boys. My advice was sought on several occasions when the family did not know how to cope with quite serious problems concerning the behaviour of one of them. Balbinder was no longer a worry. However, in July Mrs Singh telephoned to ask whether I could go with her to Cedars' open evening. She wanted my opinion on Balbinder's progress. I was not able to go with her, but, as I was in contact with the school's Section XI teacher at the time, I arranged to visit on my own. The Section XI teacher, who had particular responsibility for Balbinder, said that he was the least of her worries. He had been moved to a higher class, seemed well adjusted and chatted a lot when she worked with him. His class teacher also felt that he was making progress. Both parents had come to the open evening and she had been able to talk to them. They had also come to school earlier in the year for the annual assessment meeting, a statutory requirement for children receiving special education.

Looking back to her first encounter with Balbinder a year ago, when she had visited him at his previous school, she said that she had been shocked. He had been on the periphery of a large class and little attempt was being made to involve him in what was going on. She had felt at the time that he was 'pretty borderline for special school'. It seemed that in a school where he was in such a minority, his language and ethnicity had been defined as particular problems requiring the rather draconian solution of statementing. His present class teacher and the Section XI teacher both agreed that he was a slow learner, but felt that he did not exhibit the behavioural problems nor degrees of learning difficulty that characterized many of the children in the school. This was borne out by observing him in the classroom, where he was sitting quietly working at a particular task. His concentration and social control were in contrast with the much less controlled behaviour of some of the other children in this small group. It was the last week of the summer term and they were talking about the different outings they were going to make later in the week. There was much erratic behaviour, and Balbinder seemed one of the most self-possessed and normal children in the group – a far cry from the behavioural problems attributed to him in the past. In this environment he appeared to have become a model pupil.

At the start of the new term in the autumn, the Section XI teacher told me about his smart appearance and new clothes on the day of the school photograph: 'Bearing in mind what he was like when he first came to us, he's a lot better now.' However, despite the small class and the specialist attention, he was still considered far behind for a 7-year-old. He could not read or write independently. His written work, like both his brothers', was neat and controlled, consisting of short accounts of daily events which the teacher had transcribed and he had carefully illustrated and copied. I did not see his number work. The question of return to mainstream schooling was not being considered.

Talking to his teacher after a year and two terms at Cedars, it seemed that Balbinder's conversational language was developing well; he could hold his own in a small group, often initiating topics of interest, describing, explaining, and enquiring. However, his teacher warned that proficiency in conversational language should not be assumed to equate with proficiency in cognitive or 'academic' language. In a written account of Balbinder's development she referred to the large variations in second language acquisition found in individuals (Cummins 1984). A sociable child may achieve higher levels of English in a shorter time than one who is less sociable or, as in Balbinder's case, on his own in a group where no one spoke his mother tongue. Assessment of such children, both in language and in more general development, can cause problems. In some cases children who have been statemented and referred for special education may only have needed extra support in language development within mainstream classes, provided by Section XI teachers or language specialists. In cases like Balbinder's, however, it is the stated policy of the local authority that children from the New Commonwealth and Pakistan who need special education do so because they have been diagnosed as having learning, and not language, difficulties.

Having said this, however, his teacher admitted that most of the children in special education who spoke English as a second language (ESL) would still 'need a good deal of input to improve their understanding of English and their use of expressive language'. Cedars, like many special schools, uses the Derbyshire Language Scheme (Knowles and Masidlover 1982). Children are assessed to discover their language level according to the scheme, and then work in small informal groups. The emphasis is on initial assessment and subsequent development of comprehension in as normal a language environment as possible, while maintaining structure through the use of games (Raban and Strutt 1988). At Cedars, the Lower School ESL children worked together as a language group with the Section XI teacher.

The teacher's account of Balbinder was very different from the record he had brought with him a year earlier when he was finding it hard to settle to any routine, to concentrate and to communicate, and needed constant adult supervision. She now felt that:

> Balbinder's behaviour bears no resemblance to what it was apparently like at his previous school . . . he concentrates well and is always happy to get on with the task in hand without too much

> direction. He is a pleasure to have in any group. His language skills have developed considerably . . . he is a very sociable and confident child who enjoys informal conversation and will relate events which happened some months ago. He will come into school and discuss his family and events which take place at home such as details of visitors or outings which have taken place. He was particularly excited at having been to see a pantomime at Christmas, and brought his programme into the language group, explaining details of the story and the journey by coach to the theatre. He has a good imagination, something which shows up particularly in his drawings, which always contain fine detail.

His language was improving but in assessing his development she was disappointed to find that he was still at the same level as when he was tested some months previously. He seemed to have difficulty remembering a sequence of more than three numbers or coping with three item instructions. But her feeling that his overall level of language had improved greatly over the past year seemed to be borne out by an example of his language in use. She had recorded a small group who were drawing Christmas pictures and talking to each other. In this conversation with his teacher he seemed to engage spontaneously with the problem of sequencing events and numbers, as he tried to explain the order of his family's birthdays, that is who was first, second and third:

BALBINDER It's my dad's birthday.
TEACHER Today?
BALBINDER Mm yes. And that, it's my brother's.
TEACHER Your brother's birthday as well?
BALBINDER Yes.
TEACHER They both have a birthday on the same day?
BALBINDER Yes, my brother's and mine, mine and my brother and my dad. My dad's birthday is 'day, my brother's next time and mine is last.
TEACHER Well, it's your birthday soon, isn't it?
BALBINDER Yes, I'm sec . . . after my brother.
TEACHER Yours is after your brother?
BALBINDER No, my brother's second, I'm third, my dad is first.
TEACHER Mm.

Out of mainstream education perhaps for the rest of his school career, Balbinder is no longer defined as a problem. His re-entry, however, either to mainstream or to the start of adult working life, may not be achieved so smoothly. The process of statementing has disrupted his normal development. It has not taken into account the evident disjuncture between the cultural norms of his home and community and those of the school. More recently, his mother still expressed her worries about him despite good reports from the school and the fact that 'he now speaks both languages alright.' Her lack of contact with the school, its distance, from their home and her full-time work made her feel helpless: 'I can't rely on myself – I don't know – working all the time – how could I know.' Balbinder would be eight at Christmas and she saw no evidence of the improvement in learning to read and write that she was hoping for.

Too late for Balbinder, the *Report of the Task Group on Assessment and Testing* recognized that 'there may be difficulties presented by those whose first language is not English', and felt that to record a low level of performance for this reason would not reflect a pupil's general ability. Furthermore, it recommended that 'assessment in other skills and understanding, particularly at age seven, should, wherever practicable be conducted in the pupil's first language' (Department of Education and Science 1988, para. 53). However, at the time that Balbinder was demonstrating his newly acquired confidence and his developing communicative competence, the conference, *Asian Children and Special Education* (ACE Bulletins 1989), was discussing issues of importance both to him and to other Asian children involved in special education: home/school relations; mother tongue information to parents; parental rights; and the need for independent interpreters. The recommendations that arose from this conference, for strengthening support and appropriate provision for Asian children with special needs, seem a fitting postscript to the story of Balbinder:

- to urge that every education authority with ethnic minority communities employ a number of bilingual liaison officers to inform and communicate with parents;
- to urge education authorities to provide information in mother tongue languages;
- to ensure that information, especially legal documents, be delivered by hand by someone capable of speaking the family's first language and of explaining the meaning of the document;
- to encourage the use of a pool of teachers in each school who have linguistic backgrounds and who can liaise with parents and maintain community languages in schools;
- to urge schools to communicate to parents using trained interpreters where necessary, before a crisis occurs, in an attempt to remedy minor problems at an early stage;

- to highlight the need for more research to be done on unbiased psychological tests for children; there was acknowledgement that while present tests are culturally biased, there remains a need for some objective measures to identify a child's particular needs;
- to encourage the use of bilingual professionals and the use of the child's first language in assessments;
- to urge education authorities to support independent advice centres, similar to the ACE project, in each city.

(ACE Bulletins 1989)

4 Becoming a junior

Pupil development following transfer from infants

I'm a dingle dangle scarecrow with a flippy floppy hat.

(Music Time)

In our school system the age of 7 is a critical one for many children. Like those of 5, 11/12, and 16, it represents a major transition in the pupil's career, in this case from infant to junior. Yet we know little about how this transition is accomplished (see Bennett *et al.* 1984), or what it means to the pupils concerned. We were particularly interested to see how this transition worked in the multi-ethnic context, so we made a special study of one particular transition in a school we shall call 'Albert Road'. This was a 7 to 11 primary school of some 200 pupils. It had a staff of ten, including two Section XI teachers. At the time of the study, the school had 44 per cent white children, and 56 per cent ethnic minority, consisting mainly of Hindus, but with some Muslims, and a few Afro-Caribbean, Italian, and Chinese. The school was one of special interest in the county, because of the area it served, its ethnic mix, its staff structure, and its relationships with other schools, especially all-white schools, which were by far the most numerous in the county. The school was therefore well situated to promote the line argued in the Swann Report (1985:363) that 'the fundamental change that is necessary is the recognition that the problem facing the education system is not how to educate children of ethnic minorities, but how to educate all children.'

In the course of our eighteen-month association with the school, beginning in the summer term of 1985, the researcher spent one day (sometimes half a day) a week, mainly with class 1. This was, then, actually two successive classes – the last term of the 1984 intake, and the whole year of the September 1985 intake (a class of some twenty-two 7-year-olds). There were two intake classes at the school, and, occasionally the contemporary groups were also occasionally looked at. Here, studies of all four groups are drawn upon, but mainly that of the 1985–6 class 1.

TRANSFER

The 12-plus transition of some previous research (Measor and Woods 1984) was found to involve not only crucial academic development, but also cultural, and to coincide with puberty for many children. It also operated at levels to do with: (1) the more immediate physical and emotional effects of the change of schools: and (2) the longer-term changes following transfer, worked out over the ensuing year. The former were attended by considerable anxiety, which the pupils handled to some extent with the use of myths. The 7-plus transfer also takes place on two levels but is not attended by the same kind of developments as in puberty (as is the 12-plus), nor the fragmentation involved in moving as only part of a cohort to a large, sectionalized, specialist institution. The younger pupils' anxieties on the first level, therefore, are on the whole more immediate, and more localized, and more susceptible to conventional treatment. They are, however, keenly felt, and there are shades of certain aspects of the later experience in the following accounts written by the pupils towards the end of their first year in the junior school.

The accounts focus largely on the teacher who will be at the centre of their school lives over the next year. Despite several visits paid to the infant school the previous term, she was not only unknown, but she could quite possibly be completely inhuman. For instance, Daniel was 'very frightened when I stepped inside the classroom. I was thinking that if Mrs Brown saw my behaviour she would just take [me] to the headmaster and get me a smacked bottom.' Dipak was told by his cousin that 'the teachers are bad and if we do a bit wrong we get smacks with a slipper. When I came in the classroom I was shaking, but my cousin tell me lies.' Sarah was also 'shaking', but received different advice which helped modify the concern: 'My sister said don't because Mrs Brown is nice, she tells you jokes. So when I came in I was still a bit scared . . . but not shaking.' According to her teacher, Sarah was 'a terribly nervous child, who had stomach aches all the first week and burst into tears one day when she thought her sister had gone home without her.' Caroline, on her first day, actually 'started to cry because I thought I might get hit . . . but I haven't.' Kaushik was also worried when he first came because he 'thought that Mrs Brown would hit me. Afterwards she said she only shot people's heads off. I thought she really meant it so when it was dinner time I said to my Dad don't tat me to that school. I forgot how to say take. He said he won't tat me to school but take me . . . . So then I went school someone had done something wrong, and Mrs Brown said she's going to shoot his head off. I didn't look but when I opened my eyes his head was still on so I wasn't scared any more.' It is within the bounds of belief, therefore, that your teacher can legitimately take the ultimate disciplinary measure! At 7 your new teacher can seem as alien as 'a creature from Mars and come down in a space ship' (David).

Things were a little strange. The school was 'big'; the whistle deafened Hemang. He had also been very worried about the older boys in the school. But these problems were quickly overcome. He found that on the second day, 'I felt a bit better but on the third I felt alright because I got used to all the boys and I started having great fun playing football and lots of other things.'

Older pupils were quickly seen as a resource rather than as a threat. They offered a broader base of friends on which to draw. Also, the size of the new school was not a problem. It was almost impossible, for example, to get lost. And their teacher was discovered to be human, and quite an asset, as we shall see later.

These first-order problems, therefore, though acutely felt at the time, seemed to be fairly rapidly resolved. One might argue that the anxieties associated with transfer, as long as they are not too great and prolonged, act as a catalyst for the deeper changes that are to come. Robail argues that such anxiety 'is a necessary emotion of learning about life, and perhaps a desirable emotion to provoke that will provide a landmark of growing up' (Robail 1985: 5). This, then, is the connection with the second-order changes involving the infant school child becoming the junior, which took longer to accomplish and involved a status shift equally, if not more, profound than that at 11-plus or 12-plus.

PERSONAL DEVELOPMENT

> One more step along the world I go
> One more step along the world I go
> From the old things to the new
> Keep me travelling along with you.
>
> (Assembly Hymn)

New skills

Over the year as a whole, pupils acquired new skills and knowledge, new behaviours and attitudes to learning, and promoted their identities in significant ways. This was not so much a result of linear progress as the pupil career unfolds, but rather of quantum leaps that both cause and reflect a profound shift in status, and provide a new platform from which to reach new heights of learning.

Taylor argues that 'literacy should become the stock in trade of primary education [and] must increasingly be recognized as essential to the development of thresholds of thought, feeling and action in many subject areas, not only of intellectual endeavour but also of social and moral insight in children' (Taylor 1986: 120–1). Taylor sees literacy as including understanding story and play, which 'involves rules, teaches self-distance' (1986: 121), and allows the objectification of action – all elements involved in the widening development from the egocentricity of infancy. Some important tools for the acquisition of this literacy are fashioned, arguably, during this first year. They help the child to 'decentre' and to appreciate the perspective of others – an essential element in the multicultural anti-racist education.

Capacities increased almost from the first day of term. Thus when Dipak wrote down his news, he 'almost filled up the whole page.' Gita used to do 'one or two pages and now I do three, four, five or six.' James said he could 'remember when I could not read when I came to this school. But I can read and write now with a pencil or a pen.' Looking back, Rajesh could see that they had been 'infants' in the other school, . . . doing baby work . . . [but] at this school we do some hard work.'

For Hemang, 'the thing that I've learnt very well is my hand writing because in the infants I used to write like this:'

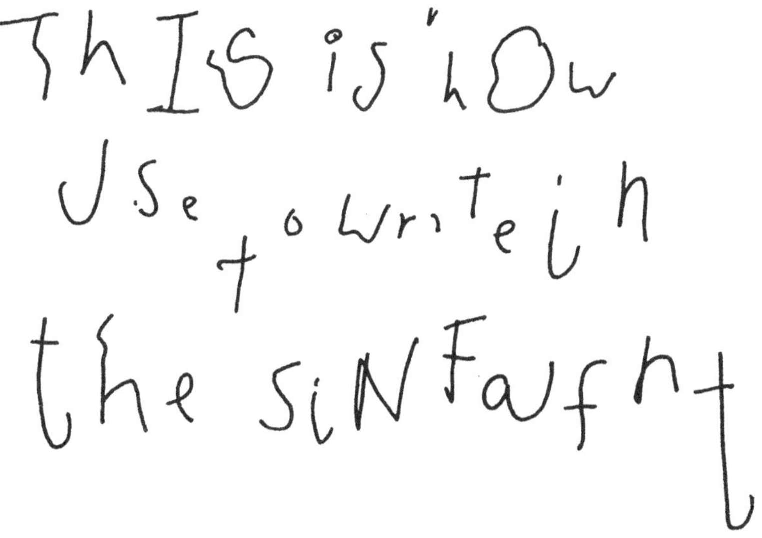

Figure 1

Amina liked it 'when we were learning joined up writing', a prominent symbol of having progressed to a new stage in learning. Like the second set of teeth (which most of these pupils were to acquire during the year), there is no advance beyond 'joined-up writing' – it is the ultimate. Daniel (a British Afro-Caribbean) claimed that within two months he had more than doubled his vocabulary and gained new fluency: 'Before I was eight which was in November I learned how to spell and read in fact when it was my birthday I knew about more words than I knew when I was at the infants school.' Daniel's new-found skills are illustrated in the following graphic poem:

HALLOWEEN is the spookiest date in the world
All the wiches come out to do spells and wicked things
Lots of ghosts and skeletons come out to scare people
Lots of wicked people turn from wiches to ghosts I hate them
Owls fly in the midnight hour they dont talk just hoot
Wizards and witches Ghosts and Skeletons come out and do tricks
Every ghostly thing scares people even some people are awake
Every wicked person trys to see a black cat to help her with her spell
Near Halloween so get ready to stay up till midnight.

Daniel was aided in the structuring of this poem by it being an acrostic – the first letter of each line spelling out 'HALLOWEEN'. However, if anything, he over-indulged his new talent, being much given to long, disjointed stories, full of *non sequiturs*, devoid of shape, simply following his thoughts as they jumped now here, now there. Perhaps this is what he meant when he said 'I may be stupid but I've got a clever brain.' He had ideas, fuelled by his new literacy, but just strung them together in a line – all beginning, no development, no middle, no end. By the end of the year, however, in response to structured and planned activities, Daniel's writing was showing another significant development that had taken much longer to achieve – mastery of form. He had learned the discipline of economy and structure. Together with his extended vocabulary, this makes a powerful springboard for the kind of developments Taylor speaks of.

Here, then, is an illustration of Daniel's prose writing towards the end of the year (there is no space for an earlier one!):

Our move from town to the country

Long long ago in a town there lived a family of witches and wizards who hated living in towns. Townies were so noisy not even their major powers could stop the noise. So one day the Chief Wizard said it is time to leave the town. So all the wizards and witches packed up, put their things in their car and drove it to the country. They had some

> adventures while they were on there way. It was 75 minutes after they had left their house when they all saw something very strange it looked like a cloud of yellow. When they got nearer they stopped and went out of the car and thought. It took them a long time to think soon they decided what to do. They went right through the yellow cloud. No sooner had they found themselves in space this yellow cloud had vanished, so they looked in their spell book. It was on page 708 but they just didn't look on that page. So they first drove in space waiting if they could think of a bright idea. Then they had a great idea. They called upon the God of Wisdom. We want to have the wisdom to know how to find ourselves in the country. No sooner had they said this they found themselves in the country. Then the chief of witches said What a relief!

Daniel's was the most obvious case to illustrate this achievement. It was one that others reached to varying degrees at various points throughout the year. Hemang showed early mastery of form (he told me a splendid story about 'Gnasher', which he invented on the spot and which grew in carefully cadenced evil to a grand finish where 'Gnasher' over-reached himself – a neat illustration of how these skills help the moral to be internalized). For much of the first term Dipak could not sort and order his thoughts, and his teacher was feeling quite 'demented because he had potential, but was not progressing.' However, after sustained work with pictures, muddled-up sentences, role-play etc., Dipak made a significant breakthrough in his ability to sort and order thoughts as late as the summer term. Others had not quite arrived at this point, or showed signs of it in some respects and on some occasions, but not at others.

Some of these young children occasionally made rapid advances almost in an instant. Invariably, something seemed 'to click', leading to a new level of understanding or unlocking of new skills. Steven, for example, according to his teacher 'had improved no end' since open day when his parents came in. Since then 'he has not looked back.' Rewards, as others have noticed (for example, Jackson 1968, Pollard 1985), played their part. Sarah had been delighted when she got her first piece of 'news' back to find 'it had a star and it said good try.' Sheela reminded the researcher, 'If you think I've done it all right you can give me a star!'

For Daniel, 'something happened that never happened in my life before. My behaviour thanks to Mrs Brown herself changed. I felt like a new boy ready to work its just like being a man in prison with a bad teacher.' Daniel thus felt liberated. He had been encouraged to develop the predisposition that facilitated the extension of vocabulary and writing skills mentioned earlier.

There were many such examples. Another form this progress took was the freeing of conceptual blockages and the unlocking of illogicalities. An example of this is the case of Karupa and the vase. The class were asked to draw and paint a decorated vase of flowers. While the rest got on with it, Karupa was unable to start satisfactorily, wrestling now with this line with her pencil, now that, with much rubbing out. When the teacher sat next to her to talk about it, the problem was discovered to be the convex shape of the vase. All the vases Karupa had known, including the one they currently had at home, had been concave. The breakthrough came when she was encouraged to trace the lines of the vase with her finger. Her eyes opened wide and she smiled hugely as she suddenly saw what was needed. Then she was off, going into the most intricate detail on the vase's decoration. She had some problems of technique here, the colours running together, but she soon learned that if she left one colour to dry, the running did not happen. She put in the green stems and flowers afterwards, filling up the paper, and showing good skills of design, perspective, and colour. It took time and she was the last to finish, but from a position of total blockage she had produced a masterpiece, which received a special commendation from the teacher and from the rest of the class. The finished product could not have been more at variance with the initial approach to the task.

There were several similar examples across the curriculum, and no doubt this is a common occurrence. Progress in these instances is not a matter of pupil training or ability, but a case of tracking down impediments and identifying switch-mechanisms. Pupils are aided in this by another fairly common feature of junior school work, which certainly applied here. This involved a move toward pupil-centred learning, and to acquiring the attitudes and dispositions needed for it to work. In this case, pupils had previously been taught largely by traditional methods. They were used to having knowledge transmitted to them, and to external forms of discipline and control. At the junior school, teaching in these classes was based on different principles. Knowledge is not defined solely by the teacher, but is reinterpreted and 'appropriated' by children as they relate it to their own concerns (Armstrong 1980, Rowland 1987). The case of Karupa and her vase illustrate the scenario and the unpredictability of learning very well. The problem was in her own limited world-view of vases, heavily influenced by the one she saw every day. How could they possibly be any other shape? The problem was overcome with help which did not tell her, but adopted her position and viewpoint through what Rowland (1984: 148) terms a 'conversational relationship'. The *chef-d'œuvre* was then threatened by lack of knowledge of technique which she was motivated to rectify. In this process she discovered artistic skills she had not previously demonstrated. The whole was governed by a rationality that many feel 7-year-olds do not possess.

Individual development was found to gain from taking place within a cohort undergoing transition. Moving up to the new school is a distinct mark of growing up, performed as a member of a group. It was a matter for particular note, therefore, among many in the class that one girl had forgotten to go to her new school on the first day and had gone back to the infants – a clear case of regression. Warish also wrote, 'In the infants i think we wasn't moving but we did move into this class I didn't know that we was changing.' The transition is that less profound than the 12-plus, to the extent that some had no prior knowledge of it!

During the year it was thought remarkable that Gita 'can't even ride a bike, she still has to have a three-wheeler', and that Ann 'still has baths with her father' ('I wash his back for him'). Mind you, Urmi's brother 'still does poos in his pants and he's 10!' Their new status is marked in so many ways. Robail reports a subtle but emphatic change of vocabulary: 'Kirsty, the majestic, the well-behaved Kirsty, had told the teacher in a loud voice that she was so upset she needed a "pee". With her sense of the occasion the infant "wee-wee" had been promoted to a junior "pee"' (Robail 1985: 6).

New attitudes

The move from infant to junior school is a considerable transition for young children to make. They have experience of only a small range of teaching approaches. Their adaptability, as yet, is limited. It is not surprising that, at the beginning of their junior career when first exposed to this new approach, they were for a time in a kind of limbo. They had lost the stern external controls of the old (perhaps their expectations of even sterner ones were behind their views of their new teacher as a monster), without as yet having developed the internal ones of the new. At the beginning of the year, therefore, this class was a noisy, rather indisciplined group, its members at times bursting and vying with each other for individual attention, and with very limited powers of application. During the first term their teacher said she was having to shout at them more than she would like. Basic instinct seemed particularly to prevail during that essential feature of the junior classroom – queueing up – where at times there was a great deal of pushing, thrusting, and chattering. The teacher had, on occasions, to remind them of their new-found status: 'Go away! Go away! That's infant behaviour again!'

Gradually, however, in the course of the year the class 'learned to learn' by these new methods, and internalized the rules associated with them (see Getzels 1977). They learned, for example, when to approach the teacher and when not; how to use their fellow pupils, books and other documents, parents, and themselves as resources; how to be more co-operative and less competitive in their work (the protective 'hands round their work' syndrome gradually disappeared); how to pace themselves in their work; how to relate the more informal, casual moments with the more formal into an integrated experience, instead of separate, oppositional ones. Rowland argues with respect to the class of 9- to 11-year-olds he studied that

> There were interludes in the work of many of the children when they would step back from their work, 'play' with it and chatter not too seriously about it. It was during such episodes that their work became more really their own, was placed in a more social and everyday context and was understood more deeply by them.
>
> (Rowland 1984: 95)

The basis for such constructive experimentation was possibly laid in the first junior year.

Identities

> As long as I live
> I shall always be
> Myself – and no other
> Just me
>
> Walter de la Mare
> (on classroom wall)

This is an important year for some pupils 'coming out' and establishing an identity for themselves with which they could both cope with the demands made on them, and generate and retain their self-respect and sense of personal dignity. It was an enormous advance, for example, to 'be allowed to go to school by myself', one of those unmistakable symbols of new-found independence after two or more years' subscription to the 'mothers' and toddlers'' club. During the year the teacher remarked on one child who seemed not to have made the personal and social advances that the others had, and whose mother still insisted on bringing her to school.

There were some remarkable gains here. Warish was very withdrawn at first, but by the middle of the year he was going to his teacher to ask for 'words' and eventually 'even getting a bit naughty.' She did not discipline him too much in case she 'put him back to square one.' Sarah had been very tearful at first and very dependent on Ann, but by the first half-term had broken free and 'was working well on her own.' Ann herself had been rather overbearingly egocentric to begin with, but over the year came to channel her need for self-expression more into drama. Sanita also found relief in drama, but as an aid to self expression. Withdrawn and unsmiling deep into the year, overburdened with the domestic responsibilities of five younger siblings, she came back from the last rehearsal of the year with delight all over her face. 'I'm a servant,' she told us. 'I like plays.'

A few of the Asian children, especially the girls, seemed to want an exclusively English cultural identity. Many of them spoke their mother tongue at home and were encouraged to do so in their parent culture, within strong and thriving communities. But Yogita, for example, preferred to speak English, and found conversation in the mother tongue 'boring'. While some were keen to have their names pronounced correctly, one girl preferred her English nickname. Others played games with English derivatives. Some called Shuli 'Sugar'. 'So we're going to call her [Saneha] "Semolina". Good in't it?'

One of the older girls had fought against her parents involving her in Hindu culture, throwing out all the make-up, refusing to wear the clothes. Another girl, asked by her mother to wear a sari for the Diwali ceremony, announced that she 'was not going to wear curtains.' Amina also, in class 1, fiercely resisted wearing any other dress preferring her jumpers and jeans. Another girl at the beginning of the project on 'Ourselves' described herself as having blue eyes, fair hair and white cheeks, and drew herself hiding behind her mother (although most of the Asian children coloured themselves pink). Kaushik reported that his family had told him that to go into the sun and get a dark brown tan was bad – it was good to be pale. When asked why, he replied, 'You know, just good.'

Others seemed to adapt to dual cultures more readily, taking a pride and delight in their identity. Meena, struggling to learn to speak and write English (which she would eventually accomplish), became almost a different person when performing an Indian dance. Some conversed or spoke in their mother tongue at every opportunity, clearly accepting their bilingualism as an asset. The opportunities for mother tongue speaking were, however, restricted by, among other things, the very number of languages involved. Of the two Muslims in the class, for example, Sanita was Bengali speaking and Shakeel, Urdu, and they could not speak each other's language. Dipak's description of himself led off proudly with 'I'm an Indian . . .' Such identities were readily accepted, and esteemed, by others. Some white English children were delighted to have 'Indian' friends. They took part in the Hindu festivals, as they did most other things, with enthusiasm and without inhibition, taking the roles of Ram, Sita,

Ravan and others, as did Chinese, Afro-Caribbean, Pakistani, and Italian children. There was a similar inter-ethnic mix at other festivals, such as Christmas, and the Chinese New Year celebrations.

This account points to the conflicting pressures operating on these children. There are several factors involved. Most importantly, some argue, in its social, political, and economic structure, society favours certain cultural forms (see, for example, Brah and Minhas 1985). Some families struggling for status and/or survival see 'westernization' as a strategy, and exert pressure on their children to conform to the majority culture. The greater the struggle, the greater the pressure, and sometimes the struggle is compounded by social, geographic, religious, and linguistic factors within the minority groups. Thus Amina, a Punjabi Hindu and an untouchable, did not consider herself part of the dominant Gujarati community, and reacted against it as her family saw better chances in conformity to western styles.

Gender identities appeared to be fairly well established, and to become further consolidated over the year. Friendships, in pupils' informed activities, and interests were gender specific. The most popular play activity amongst the boys was football, with a number of rough and risky variations (such as lining up against a wall while the one who was 'on' kicked the ball as hard as he could towards them to see if he could hit one of them). Several had become consumed by the whole football culture, their enthusiasm shown by such things as collecting insignia of the various clubs, and championing one in particular. Pradeep was particularly keen. Amongst his other football enthusiasms, he had a World Football Book 1986 which had all the countries in, details of which were on stickers that could be bought from the 'Sid' shop. He was proud of the fact that he knew all the countries ('I know all the countries, don't I?').

A 'craze' of the year among the boys was 'transformers' – machines or creatures which, with a few adjustments here and there, could be turned into another form, mostly in this case superhuman monsters. These toys indulged mostly in a great deal of macho posturing and mechanical wizardry, combining within them two of the most prominent elements of Western maleness. Perhaps it was this fact that made them so popular. Their influence was considerable. Steven, for example, over several weeks filled a whole exercise book, in his own time, with a story about Grimrock (who transforms into a *Tyrannosaurus rex*), Starscreen, Shockwave, Thundercracker, Megatron, and many more. Developing literacy skills and gender identity are used here to promote and consolidate each other. The same is true, of course, of other skills. For example, two pictures during the year to rival Romanna's vase were Tony's of the Iron Man – full of detail, with teeth, patterns on the arms, aeroplane seats, and passengers, wheels, and tail gunner, and Steven's wolf – fierce, aggressive, eyes malevolent, and fangs dripping blood. The following two examples from essays on 'Things I like doing best' point the contrast. Hemang likes:

> to play football because it is great fun and my best football team is Liverpool. I like riding my bike with Jignesh because we do skids and other stunts too. I like to break-dance.'

Ann likes:

> playing with my Sindy doll. I like playing with Sarah. I like to play with my doll's pram with my baby doll . . . I like to play school as well as ball. I like going for rides in my dad's car best of all. I like to knit as well. I am knitting a blanket for my doll's pram. I have a lot of wool to knit a blanket.

Television was universally popular. Boys watched programmes like *Streethawk, Airwolf, Star Wars, Lords of the Universe, The A team.* Mitesh liked playing with his train set, Melvin his BMX, Shuli liked her doll and 'helping my mummy to do the housework'. Boys were collectors – of model cars, badges, can tabs. For Christmas, boys wanted transformers, a watch, a sledge, a BMX, a 'Commodore plus', Grimlock, a B wing fighter, He-man figures, the A Team, Superman, a computer. Girls wanted fuzzy felts, a scalectric ('for me and my dad' – Ann), games, a book, a Sindy doll, felt-tip pens and a colouring book, a Barbie doll, a desk with drawers, the Hart family.

Here we see gender identities becoming more firmly established as boys are drawn into the football culture of the school and girls develop their own kind of interests. With the development of firmer relationships, as we shall now discuss, these identities become clearer as friends reflect and cultivate interests and selves both by their own increased and deepened natures, and by their increasing differentiation from others.

SOCIAL DEVELOPMENT

> Would you walk by on the other side
> When someone called for aid?
> Would you walk by on the other side
> And would you be afraid?
> There's a child in the streets
> Gives joy to all he meets
> Full of life with many friends
> Works and plays till daylight ends
> (There's a man for all the people
> A man whose love is true

May the man for all the people
Help me love others too).

(Assembly Hymn)

The first year of junior school is an important year for social development, in learning to relate to others in ways beyond the immediate, physical, rather selfish manner of early childhood. In so doing, the children gain a new conception of the self – from an interactionist viewpoint, developing a notion of the 'me' as well as the 'I', learning to see the self as others do (Mead 1934). Friends play a crucial role here.

Psychologists argue that there are two critical stages of children's friendships, one at age 3/5 when the focus is on momentary specific physical actions and physical accessibility, and the other at age 11/12 when friendships involve more psychological compatibility and longevity (Rubin 1980). Again it seems that the first year of junior school is crucial in the progress from one stage to the other. With the other developments already discussed and the general exposure to junior school culture, with its point of centrality on an age group above them, the 7/8-year olds are pulled towards deeper and different forms of friendship.

The junior school vastly increases the potential friendship range. Unlike the 11-plus or 12-plus transfer, there was no evidence here of a fear of losing one's friends (or of being bullied) in the new school. They fall quickly into the swing of things. Boys very soon established their membership of the 'male club' (Lever 1976). Hemang felt better on the third day because 'I got used to all the boys and I started having great fun playing football and lots of other things.' Another boy on the first day 'met a lot of children. But I knew they were nice children and they were. Then I said to one child could I play football with you and he said, you could play football he was good. But I was rubbish.' In the second term, Daniel 'made some second, third and fourth year friends. They were getting used to me.' Rajesh only knew 'one of the fourth years when I came and now I know lots of fourth years.' Girls also had more resources. Amina 'has got more friends in this school and I like it here the best.' She had friends in classes seven, six and five.

Main friends were, however, within the same class. Friends spent time with each other, helped and cared about each other, were 'kind', shared and gave each other things, found each other attractive, played, and had fun together. They provide physical, intellectual, emotional, and moral support (see also Davies 1982). Here we see elements of both stages mentioned earlier. Friends need to be with you, there is some emphasis on physical aspects, but also, in the caring, thoughtfulness, and reciprocality, some emotional and psychological emphasis. This was, perhaps, a little more evident among the girls than the boys. Already, the classic formulation of boys being members of a group with looser connections between individuals, while girls cultivated dyads with stronger ties, is apparent.

Rashan's friend was 'Karen and I like her so much. Her eyes are so beautiful. She looks so nice. She is kind to people. I go to her house to call for her at dinner. I go to her house to play sometime we have good fun. I play with her every playtime. She has hazel eyes and gold and brown hair. Her clothes are nice. She wears lovely shoes.' Andrea's friend, Rothna, 'tells me everything, she is kind', while Rothna thought Andrea 'sometimes looks pretty and we share sweets and toys.'

The boys used different terms, but they help each other, do each other favours, are kind to each other. Physical attraction does not appear to be a factor, but participation in the football culture appears a powerful thread uniting the boys. Malcolm's friends, Surdip and Rajesh, are 'both helpful, we all like playing football I know that if I fell over they would fetch the teacher'. Rajesh remarked that sometimes Surdip 'brings his football and he lets me play and sometimes he is happy and when I don't no a word he helps me and when he doesn't no a word I sometimes help him.' Warish likes Darren 'because he does not fight with me. I give Darren lollipops and he comes to my house', while Darren thought 'Warish as good as gold.' James always lets his friend Farooq 'play with my football and he always says you can come to my party.'

A more sophisticated approach to friendship is further illustrated by the development of degrees of friendship. For Caroline, 'Sangeeta in the other class is my first friend, Sheela in this class is my second friend, and Gita is my third friend.' Gita is of lower standing because she 'breaks friends when you haven't got something she wants, and when you're playing and pretending you're strangling someone she believes it and she's nearly crying.' Gita has not yet learned the rules of this more advanced form of friendship, is unable to reciprocate in kind, is still within the individualistic mode more typical of infants. Among most of the pupils here, there was more investment of self in the friendship and more consideration of the other. They are more able than infants to distance themselves from the relationship and to see it objectively.

Friendships were for the most part gender specific and multi-racial (see also Denscombe *et al.* 1986). Penny's best friend was Shirley (an Afro-Caribbean), Rashan was friendly with Karen, James with Farooq, David with Warish, Malcolm with Surdip and Rajesh . . . and so on. Mandy liked Rashan because she 'is pretty and she is indian. She is kind and helps people. We shares sweets and time together. We play with my ball we play tickie as well. Rashan has got black curly hair and brown eyes I like her. I like because she is indian and I have never had an indian friend before.' In some instances, therefore, inter-racial friendships were struck up as a matter of deliberate choice.

These associations were long-lasting, most of them surviving our eighteen month period at the school, despite occasional tiffs here and there. In their general interaction in class, there also seemed a high degree of racial interrelatedness. Michelle 'needed to know how to spell everything' and Rajesh always helped her, spelling the easier words himself and pointing out others on the board. One day when Winston was reading out an account he had written and began to struggle, Surdip came to his assistance, interpreting his untidy writing, making suggestions. Jonathan and Daniel held hands on an outing to the park, and so on – there were many such examples. This also illustrates the considerable resource pupils were to each other in learning. As Karen claimed when she was sitting next to James, 'I give him words and nudge him if he is not listening.'

In the playground, football predominates for the boys, and there is no apparent racial discrimination. As Pradeep said, 'it is all against all' (boys, that is) and that is exactly what it looked like! In one of the teacher's opinions, 'The children see no ethnic boundaries. It comes later from the home and the media, and prejudice builds up. At this age, they all get on together, they are quite uninhibited.' The teacher capitalized on this – indeed pupil co-operation was central to her policy. It can be seen that where relevance, reconstruction and problem recognition and solving in their own terms are considered important, pupils can be of the greatest assistance to each other. So they did a great deal of group work, paired and group reading, and joint discussions, and were encouraged to help each other generally.

Observations of and discussions with pupils in general bore this out. However, there were one or two pupils who seemed outside the general pupil society and had no friends. The only thing that distinguished them from the rest as far as could be seen was that they were of an extreme minority ethnic group or religion within the school. Kamlesh, a Muslim, for example, was an isolate, and when asked to write about her friend, could only write about her teacher. The same principles of friendship are evident, though unfortunately an adult cannot meet them all!

> My friends name is Mrs Brown. She is very kind. She looks nice as well. She helps me with words all the time. I can not play with her because she is an adult. Well she is a teacher as well . . . she can make me laugh all the time . . . she taught me about tadpoles as well.

Surdip, in one of his confidences, said once, 'Shall I tell you something? I said "Who likes Shakeel?" They all put their hands down. "I said who likes Andrea?" They all put their hands up (as they did for Shirley, Karupa and

Surdip himself). All of them put their hands up except for Shakeel.' Winston, an Afro-Caribbean, went through a period of what he and his mother felt to be persecution. Sarah was laughing at him because she said his picture of Father Christmas was 'rubbish'. Sheela 'nicked his rubber', Jonathan kept teasing him and accusing him of calling him 'Bogglass' when 'it wasn't him but Caroline'. These things happened to other children, but they seemed more able to cope. Winston was reduced to tears on occasions, and to complaints to the teacher. In desperation, the teacher placed him with Daniel, the only other Afro-Caribbean boy in the class, and there a kind of peace prevailed. Kulmeet, a Sikh, was also excluded, even from the list of Gita's friends which included almost the whole class. This was not through an oversight – rather, she included her through oversight, then deleted her: '. . .Caroline, Sheela, Sarah, Amina, Kulmeet – I mean not Kulmeet . . . Wayne, Hemang, Pradeep . . . and all of those.' Kulmeet, Kamlesh, Winston, and Shakeel seemed pleasant, happy, outgoing, friendly children – there was no evident reason why they should not have friends. The ethnic/religious factor was one of the things that distinguished them from their peers, but exactly how it operates must be the subject of further study.

There were also, from time to time, conflicts within the class. Sometimes there were just tiffs between long-standing friends. As Karen reported, 'Sometimes we have fights but we always make up again and for ever will be . . . we sometimes change seats.' This sense of longevity is important, and sometimes a disagreement can bring it into question, as when Stephanie fell out with Rebecca: 'She says she's going to get her brother on to me. I'll get my cousin on to her. I said "Right! I'll not be your friend for good now!"' But they were soon friends again, as were Urma and Andrea when they fell out (Urma spent much of the day on the floor under desks avoiding Andrea's dreadful gaze!).

Conflict was a particular problem at one time of the year with some of the girls – Ann against Gita, Gita against Sarah, Sarah against Caroline. They were spiteful toward each other, Ann actually hitting Gita in the stomach on one occasion. The boys, too, at times had fights. After the assembly on 'good friends and loving care', for example, two boys in class 1 were found fighting and 'calling each other silly names.' The principles of friendship are not always easy to live up to.

Pupils were encouraged to have a caring attitude towards each other, and certainly 'caring' was one of the prominent features of the school ethos. It was evident in pupil–pupil and teacher–pupil relationships. It was reflected in certain curriculum activities, and in the children's reactions to visitors such as 'Baby Elizabeth', the two baby lambs, 'Welliphant', and Susan, a handicapped girl. The children were very positive about Susan, not mentioning in their reports things she could not do, only those she could – how she ate, what she liked, how she got about, took a shower, went swimming, got cream cake ('naughty but nice') all over her face, wrote with a pencil in her mouth – all beautifully illustrated, the whole put over with affection and humour as they joined with Susan in her outlook on the world. On another occasion a relief teacher brought her 5-year-old son in with her because he had hurt his leg, and the class 'adopted' him. Ann did him a stencil of Roland Rat, Kaushik drew him a tall thin man.

Caring was celebrated, too, within the festivals of the major religions of children at the school. Diwali, for example, is a time for sharing in everyone's happiness, for distributing gifts as part of that festival of sharing – as is Christmas. In one typical letter to Santa Claus, Hemang generously wrote:

> Would you please get something for people in Ethopia because they are very poor because they can't grow lots of vegetables. This is because it is very hot thats why so could you please at least give two sacks of grain each for one tent. All I would like is one transformer.
>
> Thank you Santa.
> Love from Hemang

Winston seemed to think of everybody except himself:

> I am writing to you please can you get the ghanies a new home to live in and dont make this one burn down. And make them have some clothes and some shoes and toys could you help the Ethiopians and please get my sister a doll too.
>
> Love from Winston

In general, there is evidence here of significant development along three crucial dimensions identified by Rubin (1980: 42) – taking the other's point of view, seeing people in psychological as well as physical terms, and seeing social relationships as more enduring systems. There is still much of the former 'infant' state evident, but there are signs here of the basis having been laid for the development of more complex relationships.

CONCLUSION

The pupil's career has been conceived of as a series of steps or stages, consisting of points inspiring pronounced change, followed by comparative plateaus of consolidation and gradual development (Woods 1980). The transition from infant to junior at 7-plus, especially where different institutions are concerned, is one such stage. How general the changes documented here are, would be a matter for further research, as would the conditions under which they occur (for example, where infants and junior are taught in separate institutions or departments, labelled as such, taught by different methods by different curricular schemes, have access to different materials and situations, experience different school ethos or teacher personality). There would ideally need to be comparisons not only between schools and school-systems, but within schools, to establish whether these processes are indeed more pronounced here than at other stages in the primary school career.

The evidence advanced here points to the possible significance of such a move. Pupils' personal concerns at the time were real and keenly felt, but short-lived. At a deeper level, pupils began to undergo a profound change. Some acquired basic skills they had hitherto lacked, and/or significantly extended their knowledge. This equipped them better to shake themselves free from 'infancy' and take on the role of 'juniors'. It involved, in this case, learning to take more responsibility for their own learning, recognizing the need for the acquisition of certain skills, cultivating attitudes that facilitated the reconstruction of knowledge, becoming more independent – of parents, of each other, of the teachers – and forming new kinds of friendships. The new juniors became subject to the influence of older children, with whom they quickly began to form liaisons, and they began to be affected by the school in general with its ethos of work, caring, participation, and fun. Friendships crossed ethnic boundaries. Indeed, at this age this actually promoted friendships in some cases, although not with real minorities within these classes.

In the construction of pupil identities, pupils from minority ethnic groups adapted to the majority culture in different ways. Some actively promoted the culture of their forebears, others rejected it. No doubt there are variations in between. For these children this is a critical matter and a source of great tension as others fight for what they are to become. If, as is suggested here, the 7/8-year-old age group in the present social and institutional arrangements is a key one in the development of perspectives, in beginning to identify the 'me' and to acknowledge enduring systems as opposed to present practicalities, the form of their adaptations to members of other groups will also take a pronounced step toward consolidation.

So, too, will gender identities. Boys join a strong collective entity based on football culture, while girls begin to cultivate more personal and intimate friendships, both being consolidated by the further cultivation of specific matching gender interests. Rubin (1980) argues that neither boys' nor girls' development is complete where this occurs, and that they should have access to both kinds of social patterns. Life-chances are determined or constructed for many people in the early years. The channels of their educational potential which are realized at secondary school are already formulated before they arrive there. It has been argued here that the 7/8-year-old age group is currently a crucial one in the development of those attitudes, abilities and relationships that go toward the making of educational success at secondary level. In this sense, the transition is not only one of infant to junior. Like joined-up writing and the second set of teeth, there are other ultimates here, and they lay down the means for the next transfer to secondary, and indeed for later life.

5 Into the middle years

Transfer at 9-plus

We accompanied the study of transition of a whole class at 7-plus (from infant to junior) in one authority with one of a group of girls from different ethnic minorities at 9-plus (from lower to middle) in the other. There is more mobility and interchange at this juncture. Several lower schools may feed a middle school, and parental choice may result in children from one lower school moving on to different middle schools. It is potentially more traumatic for the pupils, therefore. Discussion with pupils, parents, and teachers suggested that one group with particular difficulties was that of girls from ethnic minorities. This chapter, therefore, provides information about another point of pupil transfer, to complement those studies at ages 7, 11, and 12, while highlighting the particular concerns of a certain group.

The method of research followed the usual pattern. The researcher held extensive interviews with twenty girls at three lower schools in their last weeks before they transferred to middle schools. She talked again to twelve of them after their first month at middle school and with five at the end of their first year. Twelve of the twenty were ethnic minority girls, nine from families of Asian origin, two Afro-Caribbean. The aim of the enquiry was to observe ways in which their perceptions of transfer differed from those of other children and to identify factors which may have made it more difficult for them to cope with this period of transition.

APPROACHING TRANSFER

One of the factors which seemed to affect their general understanding was their lack of knowledge about the procedures involved in moving to a different school; another was the language available to help them cope with this new experience. Several were recent arrivals in England and were not fluent English speakers. Many had already visited their new schools with their parents while still at lower school. Of those who had not, their unfamiliarity with the system and a lack of language to describe it gave them a more hazy impression of what their next school would be like. They relied on hearsay and rumour from siblings and friends. While those who had attended the open evenings held by all middle schools in the authority had often been quite overwhelmed by the size and nature of their new enterprise (science laboratories, home economics rooms, art studios, gymnasiums, playing fields), those who had not been able to go were prey to fantasies. Siblings could be unreliable sources of information. One girl said, 'My brother tells me you don't get enough dinner there.' Some were scared of the unknown older children:

CHARNJIT Big people.
MEENA Big people Miss, most probably be nasty.
CHARNJIT They might be horrid to you.

Others subscribed to more outrageous theories:

SANITA Miss, my brother told me there's a line at the school.
ANN And you can get lost there, my sister said.
SANITA And there's a line, right, and if anyone tries to come in, it's got electric on it, just trips up and the electric, he gets electrocuted.

Visits later in the term with their class teachers to meet their new teachers and look round the school during the school day should have allayed some of these fears, but, in fact, they replaced them with more real ones. One group of Asian girls had been alarmed to discover that they would have to have showers after games lessons:

KAMLA We saw the showers.
YASMIN Miss, we got to take all our clothes off.

Two of the lower schools had no male teachers. Several of the ethnic minority girls referred to their first encounters with men. 'There's a lot more man teachers.' These were often perceived as more threatening than women teachers:

NORMA Miss, I am scared because when we went yesterday, right, Miss, that teacher, that man that was going to show us some slides and when he took us to the class, right, and he goes and tells somebody off and I went scared and I was really scared, so I'm scared to go there.

CARLA	Miss, there's a tall man, nearly as tall as a door.

New rules had evidently been discussed, involving new rituals which were to be observed and new vocabulary which further mystified them:

GAZALA	If we late, we have to go to a lady and you have to get hit on the hand.
JUBEDA	No, you get a credit.
GAZALA	Conduct. . .
JUBEDA	No, not a credit, a conduct. . .
GAZALA	And then sometimes they hit you on your hand.

School rules which affect attendance and punctuality are often out of the children's control. For cultural and social reasons ethnic minority children may be poor timekeepers and school attenders, but at lower and middle school decisions about attendance are largely in the hands of their parents. Reasons for absence may involve family commitments, weddings, funerals, visits to relatives or to their country of origin. Religious observation, such as Ramadan, may keep children at home and for girls there are often domestic responsibilities. Conforming to the expected norms and values of the education system may involve clashes with their culture. One girl was worried about having to exchange her traditional salwar and kameez for the unfamiliar skirt, blouse, and tie demanded by her middle school. Others were acutely aware of the extra expenditure this would incur.

Language matters

Another factor which seemed to emerge and one which schools might wish to take into consideration when thinking about approaches to transfer at 9-plus was the very different grasp of what was happening that seemed to exist between children with English as their mother tongue and children who, although they may been born in this country, still had difficulty with English as a second language. Many apparently confident bilingual speakers may simply not have acquired the vocabulary and experience to cope with ideas about the way the education system works. Many of the ethnic minority girls feared the 'big people' and 'harder work' which they thought transfer would entail. Native speakers of English seemed able to contemplate change in a more informed way:

PARMINDER	You get harder maths books and you have to write more pages.

SUZANNE I don't think they're going to be harder, they're going to have to bring us up a bit.

Where teachers were seen as a threat and much more strict than at lower school, the more confident English speaker could think of reasons:

KATIE Because it's a higher school. You have to be more sensible there.

The expressed fears of the ethnic minority girls seemed as much to do with a lack of cultural knowledge, and understanding of the way the school system works, as with the language to express this. A white middle-class girl, exploring the kind of change she was involved in, could speculate,

> The middle schools tend to try and, in your first year, they make it as much as they can, as the school you've come from, to try and make it like, you know, and they make it different as they go up.

This explanation probably owes a great deal to shared talk with her parents at home. She and her parents would have discussed their expectations of the new school.

Several of the girls had only spoken English since they started school and it seemed that their more limited language resources affected their perceptions of transfer. They did not have the language or experience of the system which would enable them to make as much sense of transition as their white peers. Children from professional middle-class homes not surprisingly seemed able to articulate their expectations confidently. They had evidently talked about the transfer at home and had visited the schools with their parents. They were less likely to express fears of bullying, getting lost, and harder work. They explored these ideas but could propose an alternative version, looking forward positively to their new school. Thus, Lucy could draw an analogy with her previous experience:

> Things won't . . . just because you're moving up doesn't mean to say that things will be harder because they'll just be like having another stage, like moving up from the first year to the second year, you learn to write in handwriting.

She had an older sister at middle school and knew about science, French, and 'rough books'. In a similar way, Cathy and Rachel could refer to their previous experience for reassurance:

CATHY Well, we're going to be the small ones again.
RESEARCHER Will that be funny?

CATHY	Yes. We've already been the small ones in this school.
RACHEL	And now we're big here. When we get there we'll be small again.

They were looking forward to the move because it would be a challenge and a natural part of the process of growing up:

CATHY	We'll learn different things.
RACHEL	Then you'll think you are a lot bigger than you are now – you can learn different and instead of being in a small school, you can go in a big school.

The schools involved in transfer did not make it equally clear to all children and their parents exactly what to expect, however. This seemed to cause unnecessary anxiety and may have had further consequences for the way in which the children settled into their new environment. Having the appropriate language to explain things seemed an important priority. It was also evident that some of the most taken-for-granted aspects of the new school were not immediately understood by all the children. Coming from an integrated curriculum in the lower schools the idea of separate specialist subjects was hard to comprehend and continued to be a puzzle in their first weeks at middle school where terms like CS, SES, humanities, block, RE, and PE were mystifying labels. The idea of starting a new language called 'English' also seemed odd:

MEENA	I don't know what English is, like do they talk about English, like? But I really don't know.
RESEARCHER	Do you do English here?
MEENA	No.
SUZANNE	I don't know.
CARLA	Yes we do.
SUZANNE	We don't, that's reading and writing, yeah, we do.
MEENA	That isn't English.

A bilingual Italian girl who spoke and read Italian at home, acting as an interpreter for her grandmother, found written English difficult. She anticipated that at her new school she would have 'harder writing and you got to spell it out without the teacher spelling it in your spelling book.' A lot of the children sensed the possibility of having particular kinds of support withdrawn. They expressed a sense of moving on to a more adult world. As one put it about lower school, 'Here, everything's done for you.'

Choice of school

To a certain extent, the choice of a middle school was determined by the catchment area the children lived in. However, one Catholic school with no fixed catchment area drew a certain number of children from each of the three lower schools, and because of falling rolls it was possible for parents to choose alternative schools if they wished. In each of the lower schools a number of ethnic minority children had chosen schools which took them away from the one which most of their peers would be attending. In one lower school a number of Sikh and Muslim girls were going on to the Catholic school despite the obvious religious difference. When they spoke about their reasons for this choice it became apparent that other considerations took priority. In the case of the Sikh and Muslim girls, for example, the reasons for choosing the Catholic school were social. If the school was nearer to their homes it became the obvious choice, 'cause it's nearer and when it's dark nights and when I walk home it's going to be too dark for me because I've got to walk past that big park.' Two of her friends were envious but wondered about the school itself. There were things they did not understand about it:

PATSY	Yeah, s'horrible.
PARDEEP	And it's got crosses and everybody that's dead.
ANNIE	They have crosses when you're dead.
RESEARCHER	Where?
ANNIE	On the wall.

Another group of girls were aware of the differences and dismissed them:

RESEARCHER	It's a Catholic school isn't it?
KAMALJIT	Yeah, but I'm not going to be a Catholic.
RESEARCHER	Do you think it matters?
DEBBIE	Anyway, what's a Catholic?
YASMIN	It's a Christian, a Christian. . . .
KAMALJIT	Well, I think in assembly Catholics will go in a special room because they'll be talking about God and I don't know what we'll be talking about.

Not all parents chose to send their daughters to the Catholic school simply because of the security afforded by its proximity to their homes. One Sikh family chose to send their daughter on a particularly hazardous route from their part of town for rather different reasons. Kamla had taken one of the leading parts in a recent performance at her lower school and had received a lot of publicity. Visits to perform at their local middle school had not been happy experiences:

KAMLA	Well, what my Mum was thinking was that last time we went to do our dance up there, there's these people, they said that, they kept on talking about us, you know, rude things, so my Mum doesn't really want to send me there because, well they, the teachers are nice up there but the children are kind of making trouble and I don't like it. . .
RESEARCHER	What sort of trouble?
KAMLA	Well, when I went up there, they said that, yeah, look at that girl, look at her, showing off, look at her, oh my god look at her hairstyle, look at that, look at that. I'm getting fed up of these troubles and I don't like making trouble and usually in the class some children like making trouble but I don't. Well, if I'm with them, if they want to make trouble that's their fault. I don't and that's why I chose St Mary's.

Her reasons were complex. The boys causing the trouble in this case were largely Asian boys from her own community. In moving to a school physically and culturally distant from her home she would be making a deliberate break. She clearly had misgivings: 'I've only got a week left. I don't really want to leave this school and even though if I get use to it, I'll still start remembering this school and I won't have friends there.' She was also aware of it being rather different from her present school:

RESEARCHER	It's a Catholic school. What difference will that make?
KAMLA	Well, it's a kind of Christian school.
RESEARCHER	Yes.
KAMLA	So they don't talk much about Indians, Pakistans, Bengalis, they don't talk much really, all they talk about is Christians but they are quite, this girl she's a Christian, she can speak Indian, but she's a Christian, every person I've seen, I'm the only Indian that is up there.
RESEARCHER	Are you a Hindu?
KAMLA	No. I'm a Sikh. The only people up there are just Christian. There's no Indian person. They might think we don't know much about their religion. They might just talk about it and tell us about it.

Choosing one school as an alternative to another may rest on such arbitrary events. At the Catholic school Kamla's culture and identity as a Sikh will probably have to go underground; the school that she and her parents had rejected was committed to encouraging and developing pupils' awareness of their own culture and religion, reinforcing and continuing the multi-faith, multicultural policies of their lower school. Maybe better communication between schools and parents might have ensured that more informed choices could have been made.

Kamla's choice left her to make her way to her new school without the support of familiar friends. In another lower school, a similar choice had been made for seemingly equally arbitrary reasons. Parminder, one of a small minority in her lower school, would not be going on to the middle school chosen by most of her peer group but to an alternative school. She explained, 'Not many people play with me.' The other girls agreed that this was her problem and quite unselfconsciously explained Parminder's lack of friends:

ANNIE	No, she's always sitting down.
DONNA	Or she's trying to join in with the little children because none of us really play with her.
ANNIE	She's a different colour than us.

This was the first example of overt racism that we encountered during this project and it occurred in a school with a small ethnic minority intake and a larger than average intake of middle-class pupils. Her parents' reasons for choosing a middle school where she already had a cousin did not seem unreasonable in the light of this.

Friends

The more confident children could say, 'I think once you're there, you'll probably get loads of friends, like you have here', but many of the ethnic minority girls set more store by having members of the family around. One said, 'I won't really know a lot of people there, only my cousin.' Another said, 'I've only got Suresh up there and my sister, that's all.' But all the girls spoken to felt a certain amount of vulnerability: 'People might nick some of your best friends.' Friends would be important in coping with the unknown threats. 'They might help me when people get really awful to me.' Fear of bullying by older children was common to all the children spoken to. One said, 'I don't really want to go there because this boy said that when I go he's going to beat me up.' Girls' fear of boys was a recurrent theme, which did not die down once they were at their middle schools.

AT MIDDLE SCHOOL

The largest number of the girls interviewed had gone to the same middle school, and these were interviewed again after they had been at school for about four weeks. Before the start of term they had been speculating about whether they would be able to adapt to the new experiences. As one of them said, 'There are going to be quite a lot of different things. It'll be a bit weird for the first few weeks.'

The first weeks

Anxieties had shifted from fear of the unknown to coping with real life. In the much larger building – these pupils had come from a very small lower school – being late for lessons had become a major worry, and getting lost actually happened:

TERESA	You can't hear the bell very well from the first year playground.
ANN	I was worried about creative studies . . . there's different groups and they have to call your name out and once they didn't call mine out because I was in the wrong group.

Some still hadn't got their bearings:

SANITA	I couldn't find my way back to the classroom.
KATE	I once got lost on the, down to the place that the secretary came, I got lost downstairs and a teacher found me and took me back to my classroom.

Their fears about school work being hard were, at this moment, proving to be true:

MEENA	You get harder maths.
ANN	It's a bit hard.

They were still bewildered by different subjects and the names for these subjects, PE, SES, RE; the timetable was in itself a novelty and difficult to explain: 'We done one of those days, Monday, Tuesday, what we have to do.' A confident English speaker had no trouble, however and explained, 'Timetable, it tells you when you've got Maths and PE and stuff like that . . . and my mum's got to sign it . . . it's this special diary.'

They were meeting more teachers in a day than they had known in their previous school, but the teachers had proved to be less alarming than anticipated:

NATASHA	She's kind, she let you do . . . she doesn't tell you off that much, she marks your work.
KATE	Sometimes, some of the teachers are a bit bossy.

Predictably there were a lot of new things which they liked: netball, PE, hot dinners, having their own lockers: 'Look, inside you have to put your books and reading books . . . and I put my bag in.'

Assemblies at their old school had always been lively, participatory, and personal – often the focal point of the day, when the whole school came together to enjoy each other's company and share different experiences. They often set the tone for the day in particular ways, celebrating children's cultural diversity and emphasizing shared values. Now assemblies seemed less exciting:

SUSAN	All in lines.
CHARNJIT	It's a bit boring sometimes.
SUSAN	You have to sit there quietly.

They were finding their new uniform uncomfortable, particularly the ties. At their lower school many of the girls had worn traditional dress. Sikh and Muslim girls usually wore some form of trousers. In late September they were feeling hot. The long walk to school carrying heavy bags, PE kit and books was not popular, and for the Muslim girls often meant having father as an escort.

The separate playgrounds for each year group cut across family relationships:

SURI	I like to play with my sister and I never have a chance.

And caused problems for all the girls:

EMMA	See what the girls do, 'cos boys take up a lot of room playing football, is sit in little corners. It's where the building goes in, with benches and the girls sit on them.
KATE	The boys take up most of the playground, so we sit in the little corners.

Once again, it seems that boys were a threat.

Mathematics, about which all the pupils had been apprehensive, was not proving as alarming as they had feared, but nor was there the continuity that some of them had expressed a desire for:

> It's not like maths you do at your old school, it's different. Like sometimes maths is when you . . . we have to do maths like in our maths books and we have maths books but sometimes we do different maths, like . . . can't really think. It's a bit harder and a bit different.

There were different teachers for different subjects: English, art, music, science; and many subjects had mysteriously initialled names, CS, SES, RE. Some of the children were still confused by these:

CLARE	I was doing CS . . .
YASMIN	That's just to enjoy yourself . . .
CLARE	I don't know what it stands for.
YASMIN	Creative studies.
RESEARCHER	What does that mean?
LYNN	I don't know. It's a thing like that you can enjoy yourself.

At lower school they had had one teacher for all their subjects. Indeed, many of them had not really recognized the possibility that their experience at lower school could be divisible into specific disciplines. The confusion they had expressed at identifying a subject area as 'English' had vanished but had been replaced by confusion about the definition of subjects themselves. Further, where they had related closely to one class teacher, they now encountered a number of teachers and were not always sure how to relate to them:

MEENA	The teachers come too eggy, that's true.
CLARE	My teacher doesn't.
MEENA	The teachers come too eggy. The teachers are a bit rough. Say you did something wrong, some of the teachers say you haven't read it and we have read it.
RESEARCHER	And what do they do?
CLARE	They come eggy, I think.
MEENA	They tell you off . . . some teachers.

They felt differently about some teachers. One, for example, was 'a nice teacher, he doesn't come eggy with us.' However, some of the teachers were still anonymous and unpredictable.

Making friends

Their worries about making new friends had vanished. Sanita said, 'All our class is starting to make friends with each other now, we're quite, we're liking, starting to like each other now.' Nuzma, who had come from Bangladesh 'when I was a teeny weeny baby', was less relaxed; she wanted to be with her sister in the third year but was already discovering that she had to break rules to do this. She liked to play with her sister but 'never had the chance.' If she could get into the third year playground she played with her sister and her friends, 'Hopscotch or catching or just running ... sometimes I see some teachers so I have to run back.' She hung back to join her sister's queue at lunch time, waiting to eat with her because she felt responsible for the older girl who had only recently arrived from Bangladesh and needed help with her English.

THE END OF THE FIRST YEAR

Five of the girls were seen again at the end of the first year, by which time they were old hands, laughing at some of the things that had worried them at the beginning. They were all looking forward to becoming second-years. Of the three Asian girls spoken to early in the school year, two were absent. The school did not know where they were, nor did their friends. For them it seemed things had not changed a lot. The researcher asked where they were: 'Satinder? She wasn't here last week either.' 'Nuzma? She's always with her sister. She can't speak English properly, that's why.' 'Satinder's always trying to beat up people. She really is nasty.'

Two of them were receiving special help with the language. The Afro-Caribbean girl, who had said she had been frightened of coming to the school 'because I thought the work was all hard', now felt that it wasn't so much hard as different and only French seemed really difficult. Looking back, Meena said, 'Is Hills Road (her old school) an easy school? I think it is, yeah I think it's very easy. You didn't have a lot of lessons.' She remembered doing Indian dancing and being able to choose what they wanted to do – a very different world from their highly structured, time-tabled lives at middle school.

Playground socialization

All the girls complained about the way the boys still crowded them off the playground:

ANN Sometimes in the playground it's really horrible

	because the boys, um, won't let you play, you have to be stuck in the corner.
MARIA	And they catch your balls sometimes and throw them.
CHARNJIT	And then you walk over there and another boy picks it up and throws it and you have to walk back again.
MARIA	They threw mine right over there.

This had never been a problem at their lower school, but their particular class had had less boys than girls. Now they were having to develop strategies for coping with the boys' bad behaviour. They were developing evading tactics:

CLARE	Sometimes we sneak into the classroom.
YASMIN	Stay in the toilets sometimes.
KATE	The boys mess about too much, they're bullies.

Maria described the boys as having 'show-off jackets'. Clare told how 'third year boys, they go round slapping your heads and calling you slap head.' 'And bowl head,' Ann added.

RESEARCHER	What do they do that for?
ANN	Dunno, to act big.
CHARNJIT	As I walk past sometimes, they go like that.
RESEARCHER	Does it worry you?
MARIA	No, we just walk away from them.

Much of the conversation focused on this aspect of school. Now that they knew what was expected of them in the classroom, the peer group culture seemed to have become far more challenging. They all joined in an enthusiastic account of what the fourth year boys and girls were up to: 'Some of the fourth year boys are posers . . . This boy said to me do you want to go out with me. I saw him in town on Saturday.'

They admired the fourth year girls for the way they flouted school rules, wearing make-up, jewellery, and nail varnish, and vied with each other to describe examples of outrageous appearance and daring behaviour among the older pupils.

School reports

They had just received their first reports; not only were these a novelty but they were hard to understand with a mark for achievement of 1 to 10 and for effort, A to E. A brief extract from their conversation shows how little they understood this, and reveals the invidious nature of the comparisons such grading can lead to:

LAURA	I've got quite a lot of As.
MARIA	I've got an A too.
RESEARCHER	What are As for?
MARIA	That means you've done quite well.
LAURA	One's for effort and one's for whatsit.
MARIA	And E is really bad, you're not trying or something.
ANN	You know Hardeep, she's got all Ds on hers because she's really naughty.
LAURA	I got quite a few As.
SANITA	My cousin, well he had his reports and when we were round his house, right, um, he showed his sister, most of them were Ds and the only good one he got was 2B.

Through this kind of informal network the 'underachievement' of ethnic minority pupils seemed to become common knowledge.

Homework

At only 9-plus, homework already loomed large. However, different teachers interpreted the need for homework for first-years differently. Meena, from a large family, living an an area of poor housing, did not find it easy to settle down to work:

MEENA	Sometimes when I get home like, I don't be bothered to do any.
RESEARCHER	Do you have much homework?
MEENA	Our class has a lot.
ANN	They've got a teacher who loves homework. It's like our class doesn't have much.
MEENA	You're not supposed to really.
TERESA	Meena has to share her French book because she's lost hers.
MEENA	And I have to pay £5 but you know the teacher, she does always forget.
ANN	The first years are not meant to have homework at all.
LAURA	No, it says in the booklet you may be given some at

some times.
SANITA No, but only sometimes.
TERESA We get about three lots of homework a day.
MEENA Specially on Fridays, we get loads of homework then.
TERESA Yeah, because we've got the teachers again.
RESEARCHER Do you do it?
ANN Sometimes I make excuses, saying that I have to go out.
MEENA But Mrs X she always bosses us around, she says now, when we be noisy, she gets really angry and get eggy.

Already Meena, who was probably the least able in this group, was trapped in a self-fulfilling prophecy; she would probably fail to produce satisfactory homework, under these conditions. They recalled the more favourable arrangements at lower school:

LAURA Sometimes, I remember, I used to ask if you could take your maths home.
CHARNJIT Yeah but if you want to that is . . .

Lower schools tended to give the children more autonomy, more choice, and more control. One of the heads had feared that many of the children would lose their sense of their own worth and ability and their self-confidence once they got to middle school.

CONCLUSION

Recent research has shown that many 11-year-olds settle down at secondary school better than might have been predicted (Inner London Education Authority 1988). They seem to enjoy school more and like having different teachers for different subjects. However, the research also identifies a significant minority, children who experience difficulty with reading, who find adjusting to their new schools more problematic. Described as a 'vulnerable minority', they enjoy school less than other children, their attendance is more erratic, they do not like having different teachers, and generally do not join in the recreational side of school life – sport, clubs, and after-school activities.

If, as the ILEA research suggests, first-year *secondary* school classes should become more like primary classes and move towards 'a greater integration of curriculum areas in the first year', it would seem even more important for middle schools which receive children for the last two years of their primary schooling to strive to provide appropriate liaison and continuity. That they often do not do so at present is claimed by the head teachers to be the consequence of continuous under-resourcing, falling rolls and the failure of local authorities to see that positive strategies should be adopted to ease transfer, particularly for the 'vulnerable minority'. All the lower schools visited felt that liaison with their middle schools could be improved. Early identification of children who may be at risk and strategies to enable both the children and their parents to make sense of the transfer process would seem to be a priority.

The recommendations of the report of the Secondary Transfer Project include home links with more frequent, informal contact with the parents. Tizard *et al.* (1988) also stress the importance of these links, finding that children's progress in reading and writing was related to the amount of parental knowledge of and contact with school. They urge more open communication between teachers and parents, noting that 'parents are potentially the teachers' best allies; as we discovered most parents, especially black parents, value schools and teachers highly and are anxious to help their children' (Tizard *et al.* 1988: 180).

The parents of the ethnic minority pupils in our small survey had often not visited their children's new school. Lack of transport, shift work, and large families made attendance difficult for many parents. Meena, a child who had been seen as potentially at risk by her lower school – she had only returned from living with grandparents in India at the age of 5 – had received nothing in the way of extra help to make the transition more educationally satisfactory. She found it difficult to come to terms with the new school: 'Well, I haven't really, um, liked it, I've liked it but, er, I don't think it's still like our old school, very good.'

In mass processes like school transfer, the children in a particular age cohort are invariably seen as a homogeneous group in cultural and educational terms. This is unfortunate for those with particular needs that are not met by traditional provision. Children from minority ethnic groups have such needs, especially in the areas of language and culture. The ways of an English middle school are rather foreign to some of its children and parents.

6 Learning through friendship

The educational significance of a school exchange

A certain theory of teaching and learning running through this book becomes more evident in the examples in this chapter. It is an appropriate point, therefore, to say a little more about this theory before going on to give an extended illustration of it in practice.

MODELS OF TEACHING AND LEARNING

It is now generally recognized that the research into the efficiency of teaching styles has been inconclusive (Bennett 1987). A 'style' contains a number of behaviours, and it has proved impossible to ascertain the impact of any one teacher behaviour on pupil achievement. Differences within styles are often as large as those between styles; and, in any event, most teachers are a compound of traditional and progressive features (Bell 1981). The 'teaching for efficiency' research has moved on, therefore, and now involves more attention being paid to pupils, and the opportunities they have for learning. The focus shifted to 'time spent on task', and later, as this in itself was seen to be inadequate, to other factors, such as how a task is presented; the sequence, level, and pacing of content; the appropriateness of tasks to the children to whom they were given; teachers' levels of expectations of their pupils, and types of feedback from teacher to pupil.

A prominent focus within this work has been on 'matching' and 'mismatching', as these were felt to be key factors in successful teaching. Mismatching can occur at any point on this cycle. For example, Bennett *et al.* (1984) discovered, in their research involving sixteen teachers and ninety-six 6/7-year-old primary school children, a low incidence of cognitive match, that is, suitability of task for pupil. In number tasks, only 43 per cent matched; 28 per cent were too difficult, and 26 per cent too easy. The proportions were similar in language work. This produced problems for both high and low attainers. The latter

> produced very little work, concentrated on the production aspects of tasks, were slow to start, made extensive demands on the teacher and consequently spent a lot of time standing in queues . . . . In contrast, high attainers were often held up by the production features of tasks. For example, drawing coins as answers to money sums was frequently seen conducted by children who could do complex calculations in their heads.'
>
> (Desforges 1985: 100)

This research is important, but as it stands it is rather disembodied and decontextualized. There is little about the subjective concerns of teachers and pupils, their interests, and the influences operating on them (see Pollard 1985). The 'matching' is perceived on one dimension only – the cognitive. But teaching and learning involves more than this. Account needs to be taken, for example, of the social context within which teaching takes place, pupil–teacher and pupil–pupil relationships, and social factors bearing on teachers and pupils which affect their actions, and indeed how they think (see Doyle 1983). It also needs an affective dimension, for pupils will not learn if they do not wish to.

An expanded 'opportunities to learn' model includes cognitive and curriculum matching as developed by Bennett *et al.* (1984); and social matching as discussed above, including teacher–pupil interaction and relationships. It also requires a suitable learning theory. An increasingly popular one in this respect is constructivism, which emphasizes the progressive construction of cognitive representations through experience and action in the world (see Donaldson 1978, Richardson 1985). In one empirical study, Armstrong speaks of 'appropriation', the idea that

> from their earliest acquaintance with the various traditions of human thought, with literature, art, mathematics, science and the like, [children] struggle to make use of these traditions, of the constraints which they impose as well as the opportunities which they present, to examine, extend and express in a fitting form their own experience and understanding.
>
> (Armstrong 1980: 129)

These ideas have been carried further by Rowland (1984 and 1987), who stresses that much depends on the degree to which pupils control their own learning.

> There is a strong sense in which, as soon as they begin to tackle real problems, problems as they have constructed or interpreted them, then learning takes place and the knowledge which is gained is not merely a copy of our knowledge, but is a reconstruction of it. Such

> knowledge may view the same objective world and concern itself with the same facts, but will offer a perspective upon them which is individual, and to that extent unique and new.
>
> (Rowland 1984: 37)

Rowland is not suggesting leaving learning to children as they come to encounter problems and need, but a more considered view of the teacher as 'enabler', one who stimulates and helps children to reflect on their activity, to structure it appropriately, to identify needs and to help meet those needs. This has resonances with the work of Galton and others on the 'Oracle' research, where they found strong feelings among pupils over ownership of work (see Galton 1987).

Such a view of learning needs to be complemented by a consideration of the 'opportunities to teach'. This is necessary for a full answer to certain questions. For example, with regard to the mismatches in task mentioned earlier, we would want to know why they occurred. The researchers praise the teachers for their conscientiousness, and they were judged to be experienced and able. Nonetheless, they found the reasons for mismatching lay with them. The diagnosis took the form of identifying non-productive or counter-productive aspects of teacher behaviour, such as 'demanding concrete records of procedures rather than evidence of thought', and 'adopting management techniques which permit rapid responses to each child's immediate problems but leave the teacher ignorant of the child's confusions or potential' (Desforges 1985: 102). However, there appears to be an inconsistency here. If the teachers were experienced, able, and conscientious, how could they have such elementary shortcomings? We need to ask why these teachers acted in this way.

This is where an 'opportunities to teach' model is required, one that recognizes that such opportunities are affected by social factors such as the provision of resources, government policy, the requirements of examinations, the central dilemma of needing to select and discriminate among children *and* educating individuals to the peak of their abilities (Hargreaves 1988a). Teachers have to 'manage' such factors to best advantage. They have to seek to maximize their strengths – through influencing policy, through invention and use of natural resources, through pacing and timing, through joining forces with others to mutual advantage, and so on. They also have to be motivated to teach, and their interests have to be served (Pollard 1985). There is a great deal of 'self' investment in teaching. Like pupils and learning, teachers also have to 'feel right' in order to be able to teach (Riseborough 1981). If pupils are to appropriate knowledge, teachers must be able to identify the factors that promote and hinder that, which means both general theoretical knowledge, and particular understanding of their own classrooms and pupils. Thus if pupils are to control their own learning, teachers must control their own teaching. The two complement rather than contradict one another. Indeed, democratic co-operation and collaboration would be at the heart of such a pedagogy (Lee and Lee 1987), and would typically involve teacher participation in learning at certain points. Such a pedagogical mode requires teachers to have a degree of independence, space, and time for their powers of creativity to come into play, and freedom to act on initiatives which promise to promote children's learning on generally agreed criteria. In other words, 'opportunities to learn' have to be matched by 'opportunities to teach'.

Such a view of learning and teaching squares very well with interactionist theory (Woods 1983). This is important for the model, for through this lies the connection with its sociological elements. Interactionism sees people as constructors of their own actions and meanings. Those using this approach in classroom research, therefore, have been very interested in teacher and pupil perspectives, how they interpret the outside world, the mental frameworks through which these interpretations are made, and the social influences bearing on these frameworks. It will be seen that matching is necessary in this regard also. Teachers and pupils need to feel that they are engaged in the same enterprise.

MISMATCHING

A number of influences bear on pupils and teachers, producing different forms and levels of motivation, different values and aims, different cognitive frameworks and, in consequence, a range of mismatches throughout the various areas of the model.

As far as 'race' is concerned, black pupils tend to over-populate lower streams and ESN schools (Tomlinson 1982). The ILEA Junior School Project (Mortimore *et al.* 1988) showed that Afro-Caribbean children were placed by their classroom teachers in lower 'general attainment bands' than their scores on independent verbal reasoning tests would have predicted. The cultural problem is well illustrated by the classic study by Dumont and Wax (1971). They demonstrated how a white teacher could totally misinterpret the behaviour of a class of Cherokee children. She took their silence and docility as indicating well-mannered conformity – a model group no less. In fact, this kind of behaviour among the Cherokees was their way of indicating disapproval, and they learned through her methods rather less than she hoped. 'Race' can also compromise learning opportunities through pupil–pupil relations. While Denscombe *et al.* (1986) found this not an issue in the schools of their research, others have found 'race' a prominent factor in peer relations (for example, Davey 1983).

In all of this we can see a mismatching of interests and intentions at various levels. There are, for example, signs of a clash between teachers' ideal intentions (e.g. equal opportunity) and their actual intentions (pragmatic continuation of practices which act to preserve inequalities); and between what they claim to be doing, and what they have been observed to be doing. There is a gap between teacher and pupil intentions where the former are dominated by considerations of teaching and the latter by such things as 'race', social class, and gender interests. There are differences among pupils that obstruct learning, promoted by cultural exclusivity. Even where teacher and pupil interests match as, for example, in the study by Wright (1986) in that both were interested in furthering academic learning, there was nonetheless a *perceived* mismatch, teacher perceptions of academic attitude and potential being decided by their perceptions of pupil behaviour, and not actual academic attitude and potential judging by other criteria.

Even where teachers profess to be organizing their teaching with pupils' control of their own learning in mind, there appears, again, to be a disjuncture between professed aim and result. All the evidence suggests that experiments along so-called 'progressive' lines with its child-centredness, informality, and openness is a change merely in the technology of teaching rather than any radical departure from the 'transmission of knowledge' style of teaching (see, for example, Sharp and Green 1975, on keeping pupils 'busy' in a primary classroom; Atkinson and Delamont 1977, on 'guided-discovery science'; Edwards and Furlong 1978, on resource-based learning in a comprehensive school; Barnes 1976, on worksheets; and Galton 1987, on the failure of 'progressivism'). Other studies have detailed the cultural competence that pupils need to acquire if they are to learn as the teacher intends, involving a catalogue of rules about such things as how and when to answer teacher questions, how to signal responses, how to interpret teacher words and actions (Hammersley 1977). Learning about how to learn thus becomes the major activity, as it was with Abbas in chapter 2.

This takes us back to the 'opportunities to teach' model. It is all too easy on occasions to slip into a 'blame the teacher' mould. The pressures teachers work under, the resources they are given, the provisions for INSET, the conflicting demands made on them, the power of structural forces outside the school – all constrain a teacher's options and exert a heavy conservatism on the system (Ashton and Webb 1986, Freedman 1987, Hargreaves 1988a). Arguably, a change in the technology of teaching is all that teachers can accomplish in the circumstances. In many of these experiments, pupils were given a degree of control and choice that they had not had before. Otherwise, it was a question of teachers adopting strategies to cope with the various difficulties that assailed them.

SUCCESSFUL MATCHING

In an ideal form, the functioning of such a model where a wide range of matching occurs has been described by Pollard (1985: 239), in what he calls a 'positive cycle of teaching and learning'. Teacher initiatives lead to children enjoying a sense of their own dignity and value; they are 'stimulated by the curriculum or learning activities provided for them by the teacher' for they appeal to the children's own interests; they are fair, in the sense both that they are operating within negotiated frameworks and that the match between task and children's abilities and motivation is appropriate. Children will experience enjoyment and learning, since their primary interests are being satisfied. A further crucial consequence is that teacher interests are also satisfied,

> with the likely result that the teacher will feel able to inject further energy and care with which to again project the dignity, stimulation and fairness to fuel another cycle. A cyclical process of reinforcement is created which can then spiral upwards into a higher and higher quality of learning experiences.
>
> (Pollard 1985: 239)

If this seems rather idealistic, teaching in primary schools at least, as Pollard points out, sometimes goes like this. A good example occurred in Albert Road Primary School (see chapter 4). The focus was on an exchange between two classes of 7-year-old pupils, one from Albert Road, the other from an all-white rural village school, that we shall call 'Garfield'. The teachers were keen to explore whether the differences between the two schools could be used to mutual educational advantage across the whole range of the curriculum, though the promotion of racial harmony figured large amongst the aims. There was a considerable amount of preparatory work, including the establishment of relationships between the two groups concerned, involving the exchange of letters between the children. This predicated the activity on the affective relationships established between the two sets of children and the two sets of teachers. They then spent a day at each other's school.

The Garfield children visited first, travelling by minibus with two teachers, the main events of the day being (apart from meeting their friends) a visit to the nearby Hindu temple, which was introduced to them by the headteacher of Albert Road, and for which they had worksheets. These worksheets had been devised by the teachers as part of a larger project to raise awareness of the Hindu religion among junior schools generally, using the temple as a resource; 'playing on the apparatus' in the afternoon (they had none of this at Garfield); and meeting and playing with their friends. A fortnight later, Albert Road children returned the visit with two teachers and two parents, travelling by public transport. The outstanding features of this day were the bus ride, a walk round the village and over the fields, a visit to the church (where they were welcomed by the vicar; there were worksheets for this also); and meeting, with increased excitement, talking to and playing with, their now-established friends. The visits were the high point of the project, but there was much activity inspired by them before, in between, and after. What, then, was the educational value of the exchange? What follows is based on observations made on the two days of the visits, of the work produced in association with them, and on talks with the pupils and teachers involved.

English

The main need, especially for Albert Road's children, was seen to be language development, and particularly enrichment of vocabulary. For many of these pupils, English is a second language, not spoken at home. Everyday phrases outside schools are in the mother tongue. Thus, while they had picked up 'the language of the playground and the basics, they lacked the vocabulary necessary to express themselves.' The Albert Road class teacher, Jane Esmond, estimated that the project had enabled her to introduce over 300 new words. More important than the number of new words, however, was the meaningful context in which they were used, which had beneficial results for pupils' general understanding. Farooq, for example, had 'virtually no English language' beforehand, 'though he could understand what the teacher was on about.' His class teacher described him as 'like a boy behind a wall, peering over. His eyes are gleaming with what he is going to do, but he can't say anything. He is totally frustrated.' The trip to Garfield was the breakthrough. 'On the bus going over he wanted to know every two minutes when they were getting off and would his friend be there? Would he recognize his friend? And for him to actually come out and say those things . . . is almost incredible! . . . . The speech has come, and the written work has come, beautifully presented, and a fair command of English, for him.' If Farooq was the outstanding example, they all gained, even Ifzal, who was the only one not to go. He had never been on a bus, and had been desperate to discuss their experiences with the other children.

There was detailed planning of the vocabulary beforehand. For example, Garfield have a part-time teacher who lived in Bombay as a child, and who took saris and other Indian clothes in, and told them what different parts of the dress were called – and then they dressed up in them. Though some of the boys told me wryly 'we made right fools of ourselves', they were well prepared for seeing them in context and better able to appreciate other aspects of the cultures of northern India. At Albert Road also, there had been lengthy planning particularly on words they would actually use, even to phrases like 'a half return fare to Mill Road', simple vocabulary like path, pavement, road, street, specialized vocabulary that would be used in the temple and the church, and all the little idiomatic phrases that go between. Prior formal knowledge of the words aided identification and expression on the day, and facilitated discussion and reading afterwards. For the Garfield children, one of the main outcomes was learning skills of discussion. Their teacher said, 'They've done some discussion, which for children this age is quite hard. They can talk but they can't discuss. Now when they were talking about reactions, there was a bit of "why do you think they reacted like that? Why do you think Cherry jumped around screaming when she saw the chicken? Why do you think they were so surprised to see sheep and geese?"' So they were looking behind behaviour and doing some analysis.

The project also provided considerable motivation in writing. Notable here were the letters exchanged between pupils before and after visits. They 'actually learned how to write a letter in a much more enjoyable fashion than writing a practice letter.' They were writing to real people for a real purpose, and, more than that, the letter was going to a friend, somebody they cared about, and who would write back to them. They were consequently more worried about errors, about getting it right, about 'doing their best'. They learned about spacing and layout, capital letters and full stops. And, as John noted in one letter to his friend, they used their 'best writing'.

The first letter typically referred to their own looks, background, families and interests, with expressions of anticipation and friendship, and were illustrated artistically.

> I know I will enjoy the day with you. Dipak. The Hindu Temple is exciting and I like your name, I am looking forward to the apparatus. I am nearly eight. I have brown hair and blue eyes.

> We have a farm at Garfield which has sheep in. You can stroke No. 17. My hobbies are swimming, catching butterflies, collecting money and stickers I have one dog his name is pip his birthday is on may 22nd. Please write back soon. Good bye for now.

Letters were also exchanged afterwards. They did not only write to friends.

They also sent 'thank you' letters to teachers. Even Farooq, who found writing very difficult, managed one of these:

> Dear Mr Harrison and Miss Andrews,
>
> We like your school garden and we need your garden because it is nice and we have not got a garden. We need a tree please. Thank you very much for letting us come.
>
> From Farooq

There were follow-up letters in the last week of term. Sheila and Gita had struck up a good friendship and were developing this and their learning from each other:

> Dear Gita
>
> I hope you have a nice birthday did you get your birthday card?. . . I am looking forward to the summer holiday because you will be coming to my house . . . I would like to know what you eat in English . . . I like your mum very much.

Some, it must be said, were not so hopeful ('this shall most probably be the last time I'll talk to you so good bye'), but others wanted telephone numbers, urged replies, and conveyed expressions of genuine friendship. A Garfield child, for example, had palled up with Farooq. He found writing very difficult, but he made a big effort to get his point across on this occasion: 'I like you a lot Farooq I wot you to come a gen with the school please come a gen we went to the Hindu Temple.' There were other written pieces. Some of the Garfield children, for example, composed poems about their experiences. This seemed the most appropriate medium for some of the sentiments roused on the day of the Albert Road children's visit:

> Waiting at the bus stop
> Waiting for the bus
> Clapping and cheering
> Waving and Smiling
> Bus comes along some on bus
> but they don't make a fuss
> We have a good day
> Until the end
> but first we go to the Church
> we see the graves and say a prayer
> Then to go home
> Waiting at the bus stop again
> Nearly missed it nearly missed it
> but this time we don't make a fuss.

And of the day of their own visit to Albert Road, one wrote this:

We all went to Albert Road
It was very fun
We went on the Apparatus
And then it just begun
Swinging running climbing Jumping
riding balancing rolling bumping
and some of us was falling off
some of us were diving high
doing somersaults in the sky
but time went rolling by
leave the hall
and go back to Garfield school.

The children found new pleasure in their *own* areas. Garfield children described their visit to their own church (a new experience for most of them!), referring in quite rich vocabulary to things they had found interesting like 'the creepy scary stairs', 'the key to the door which was as big as my hand', 'the dead mouse and two live toads in the graveyard', 'the bread table', 'the stained glass window with colours of red, purple, blue, yellow, pink and green', 'the old pump for the organ', 'the weather vane and lightning conductor'.

Albert Road children also wrote accounts, some, like John, feeling inspired to poetry:

Garfield Church
I like going to the church
Because I go to church
The church is big with three altars
And the big pulpit
And the place where the choir sings
And the big bibles
The rector opened his organ and
Miss Andrews played the organ
She played it very well
We went up the tower
It had a few steps
The tower was small
There was a font where baby gets christened
I enjoyed going there.

Mathematics

If language both spoken and written was seen as the area of study which stood to benefit most, this was because of its central importance to the rest of the curriculum. It is in some ways inappropriate to itemize contributions made to other curriculum areas, for a distinctive aspect of the exchange was the way in which it promoted a sense of holistic, integrated, experiential, pupil-centred curriculum. As one of the teachers remarked, 'the whole is more than the sum of the parts.' However, it is convenient to look at some of these areas, while bearing in mind that they are part of a 'greater whole'.

There was a certain amount of arithmetic involved, subsumed within the activity. The Albert Road children, for example, did not know how to buy a bus ticket, or how to count out the money. They did not recognize the coins even though they made frequent use of 'pretend' coins in the classroom. They knew they had to get it right on the bus, and that made the difference. They also had to study the clock and consider distances, and 'how long it would take'. They had to make out a route to Garfield and mark it on a map in their folders. On the map were questions asking them to calculate certain distances between key points in the vicinity. They also made a sundial, inspired by one they had seen at Garfield church, one their teacher had brought in, and one they had seen in a book. 'Normally this was quite a difficult thing to introduce', but because they had seen one at Garfield, it meant something concrete. This went into the playground when the sun came out, and the children were seen actually measuring the time sections and the shadow.

Environmental studies

The whole project might easily be described as an exercise in 'environmental studies' as in anything else. The town children, particularly those from ethnic minorities, lacked experience of the countryside. The village children had not been in a town, especially the kind of urban area of the type where their friends were situated. The most notable feature of the trip to Garfield for Albert Road children was the 'school garden', and they were very impressed that the houses 'all had big gardens round them', and were all 'different'. They were very appreciative of the countryside, the sheep, the chickens, the geese, the trees. As we have seen, there were pleas for 'gardens' and 'trees' in their own playground. On the walk round Garfield, the children had pointed out to them, among other things, a thatched roof, a combine harvester, 'The Old Bakehouse', a burglar alarm, a notice reading 'A school for poor children', and Garfield House. At the bottom of the village they climbed over a stile and walked across the fields, rehearsing here and there the country code, and admiring the sheep and chickens. The Garfield teacher, Susan Andrews, was keen to show her pupils a contrast to their own area, and to cultivate skills of observation. She teaches them to look and learn from their immediate environment and surrounding areas so that when they reach their secondary school they will have the necessary skills to cope with more academic work in 'history' and 'geography'. What did Albert Road children observe? One noticed the quietness: 'We walk round Garfield/It is so quiet you can hear with ease a sound. . .' Kaushik 'liked the little village and the houses'. And the thrill, novelty and educational experience of the bus ride is evident from his account, 'I liked the bus. I sat on the top and I looked out the window and I saw trees and when you go on buses you look as if you are going to crash.' Another child who sat on the top floor of the bus saw 'a flat house with straws and there was a net on the house then we saw a boy sitting on a gate.'

Physical education

Undoubtedly the greatest attraction at Albert Road for Garfield children was the apparatus. They have none at their school, and they had been told about the frames, ropes, boxes, horses, benches, bars and mats that filled the hall at Albert Road. So deprived were some of the Garfield children in this respect that one child asked her teacher 'What is "apparatus"?' They had 'a few balls, a few hoops and a few skipping ropes' which they could only use 'if it was fine'. Consequently 'their co-ordination was dreadful'. If they went to Albert Road for just half-an-hour on the apparatus, that would be well worth it, according to their teacher, because her children 'don't get any PE'. Her juniors are going up to secondary schools not knowing what a rope is. One Garfield child wrote:

> Going on the apparatus was a lot of fun largely because
> we have none.
> Climbing up the rope and sliding down burning your
> hand but at least you get down.
> Climbing up metal going to the top,
> looking through classroom windows,
> Watching them work and stop
> Walking across the beam and trying not to fall
> When you look around you soon fall off
> Going on the apparatus was a lot of fun
> Shame you could not come along

Nor was the visit to Garfield without benefit to Albert Road children in this respect, for Garfield School's great asset was the walled, grassed garden, with a large tree in the middle. As we have seen, this figured large in their memories of the day, as did the games and activities it facilitated. Here Cherry 'learnt to do cartwheels.'

Religious education

This was an important area, especially in view of the 'racial harmony' aim of the visits. The exchange proved a sound basis for a comparative study in religion at the children's own level of thinking. They were encouraged (through brief introductory talks, worksheets, informal guidance, and considerable freedom) to explore the special features of these places of worship, to discuss them among themselves, and in doing so to reach out towards an understanding of a culture which in certain respects was markedly different from their own.

In the temple, the children were particularly impressed by 'God's Bell', the removal of shoes, the gods, the colourful and intricate decorations, the swastik, the food offerings. They had the advantage of some prior work and some worksheets to guide them round. The teachers themselves were provided with notes on the temple's chief features and history. The children later wrote:

> Ting ting the bell – ring it ring it hear it go – Lets go in – But wait we can't get in we have to take our shoes off. But why. Well because they are made of cow's skin. Yes and they are not allowed to touch or eat meat what's why.
>
> Going to the temple was a lot of fun . . . we went into a room where they played some of their own sports which had rather funny names . . . they had statues called Ganesh the God of wiseness and good friends, Shiv, Durga the Mother of the Universe . . . all these statues are very bright and colourful . . . there were seven bhavans, the Gods houses. It was very enjoyable in the Temple area.
>
> I like the colour in the Temple with shapes and God Fruit and oranges sweets and apples. They are juicy and they give Indian food in plates. The god was dressed in wonderful colours with necklaces and rings.
>
> I liked the horses on the wall, and the bell.
>
> I like doing the work sheets Miss Andrews gave us especially I enjoyed going to the Temple and seeing all the Hindu gods. The bells were loud but they were like god's doorbells.

Susan Andrews (the Garfield teacher) confirmed that they had enjoyed the temple, 'particularly the artistic children. They really did enjoy the colour.' In their classroom they had pictures, photographs, prints of the temple and Indian garments on the walls. They were able to explain what they were, 'Swastiks, Hanuman, Ganesh, Vishnu, Sari, Choti, Chemise, Scarf, Skirt.' They had remembered them well from a fortnight before.

An unexpected occurrence at Garfield Church heightened the significance of the visit for the few Muslim children from Albert Road. Scratched on the end of one of the pews Shakeel and Farooq found the Muslim star and crescent. No one knew why they were there. That 'brought such a lot of delight and pleasure to them, and they linked straight away ... that sparked off quite a lot of work when we actually came back'. There was 'a lot of comparative work' afterwards. The phrase 'Holy Book' became commonplace in the Albert Road classroom.

For the Garfield children, the RE project for the term was about 'the family and the rules we abide by, and the bigger family of the world, and looking at the people from different cultures.' The teacher 'carried that on and introduced them to the idea of children who had different colours from them, had different foods, spoke different languages and what *they'd* feel like if they were suddenly thrust into a school where the children spoke a totally different language from them . . . And they all talked about it, and said it didn't matter what colour people were. It was what the person was like that matters . . . And really it was quite new to all of them, this idea of mixing with other children.'

The sense of common cause was heightened by the discovery that the temple had certain things in common with church. There was a 'holy book', 'gods', interesting stories, prayers, singing, bells for organ or piano, the same kind of moral messages as, for example, symbolized by the swastik, and the fact that much of the information in the temple was in English as well as Gujarati increasing the sense of 'openness'. This was increased yet more by the welcome and hospitality afforded the visitors.

At times, some of these activities (sampling other cultures, visiting temples, etc.) have elsewhere been criticized as mere tokenism, compounding the racist nature of society rather than tackling it. The references above to the Garfield children's appreciation of the artistic merits of the temple might be interpreted by some in this light. But there are a number of answers to this. Firstly, the artistic features are an important component of the Hindu religion (as of many others). As Haigh has argued, 'there are many points at which the boundary between arts education and RE become blurred, just as worship and artistic expression often seem part of the same whole' (Haigh 1987: 19). Secondly, in any event, the children's interest represented the integrated nature of the whole activity. Thirdly, even if the Garfield children had visited the temple on their own, and done nothing else, it might be regarded as a very useful introduction to the Hindu religion and culture, given their almost total lack of prior knowledge (one would, however, look for it to be followed up, and developed). Fourthly, the activity was not decontextualized, but grounded in the affective relations of the multi-ethnic group of children. Finally, it is clear that these young children had grasped some of the basic comparative religious elements (gods, a holy book, the use and meaning of signs and stories, the 'binding' nature of religion). Their ability to do this also supports those who argue against an invariant developmentalism in children's cognitive abilities, and for their readiness to entertain abstract concepts and some quite difficult principles (see Pollard 1987, Short and Carrington 1987, Lee and Lee 1987).

Social and personal development

'Mixing' was arguably the greatest achievement of the project. This was certainly so for the Garfield teacher, for her children 'find mixing difficult', having had few opportunities to broaden their experiences in meeting other children, let alone those of a different ethnic group. They were also unused to mingling with much larger numbers of people, as they would have to do some day when they went to secondary school. At Garfield, there were only eighteen juniors. When they arrived at Albert Road, there were another twenty-two to play with, and at lunchtime nearly 200 – 'And they did play with them all . . . I mean, none of them sat around looking lost.' The fact that many of these children were to go to the *same* secondary school was another gain, establishing links across what can often be a difficult transition (Measor and Woods 1984, Delamont and Galton 1986). From the very first, these two groups of children developed a strong sense of friendship. Individual links were forged through the letters, which received added sparkle through the work being done on the planning for the exchange. These friendships, therefore, *mattered* within the context of their lives, and of the total framework of the curriculum. And some of the excitement of the special events arranged was shared with these associations.

These individual friendships gained also from being involved in the meeting of two larger groups, indeed two communities. The fact that these pleasures were being shared with others dispelled shyness and reservation, heightened anticipation and excitement, and helped to promote a sense of inter-regional and inter-ethnic community. This in turn reacted back on relationships within their own group, for 'it broke down a lot of barriers within the classroom, the little cliques that had formed, the little groupings.' There were three processes in train, therefore – the personal bond of one-to-one friendships, the culture and identity of the group as a whole as the two classes came together, and developments within individuals.

The latter can be illustrated by one or two of the more astonishing examples, for example, Darren. At Albert Road, the Garfield children had planned to stand in the doorway and say their name. His teacher thought, 'Darren will never manage this, he will die. You know, stand in a doorway with twenty children looking at him, because he's no self-confidence at all. But no! "I'm Darren" he said, and he walked in. Now for him to walk across that room with all those eyes looking at him was marvellous, because I really didn't think that he could cope.' Even Carl, who 'can't mix, and doesn't know how to play, even sort of stood and talked to them. He didn't actually stand on the outside and do nothing.'

One girl, aged seven, who was the only girl in that particular age group at Garfield, may have given the impression of being backward, 'not very academic, struggling, and can't read . . . And she had a whale of a time the day they came over here because she'd got all these little friends, and she is a friendly little girl. I've never seen her so happy in the playground among her own kind, she came out of her shell, had a field day.' My own memory of her is watching her skip around the playground with two of her friends from Albert Road.

They were worried about one boy from Garfield who on one occasion had asked a teacher 'Are you a Paki?' They worried about what he might say to a child, if he could say such a thing to a teacher. His friend was Larry, an Afro-Caribbean, and they were very wary of each other at first. But in fact when they got back from Albert Road it was that child who said, 'Can I write to Larry?' Larry himself could at times be 'a most difficult child, and yet when he went over there he was super ... he's remembered everything. He's a child who doesn't mix much but he thinks a lot and there's an awful lot of work come from him.'

The extent and nature of friendships was evident from letters, conversations, behaviour. The arrival of the bus from Albert Road was a high point. Friendships proffered in the letters, consolidated on the trip to Albert Road, now blossomed, free of reserve and constraint, and secure in the knowledge that feelings were reciprocated: 'When we went to the bus stop I was very excited . . . I couldn't wait to see my friend.' The Garfield children were equally excited. As they waited, Darren remembers, 'I was excited. We went to the bus stop waiting for a bus you'd better hurry up its ½ past 10 in the morning.' And Amanda, expressively described this scene in verse:

Waiting at the bus stop
Waiting for the bus

Never seems to come
Suddenly pop up
Shy and happy faces. . .

At the end of the day: 'Gosh! the bus is already there, Miss Andrews is running to catch the bus. She caught it and we wave our sad goodbyes.' Privileges were freely offered: 'We have a game called chuckie egg and I will bring it to school when you come. You will be aloud to have a go on chuckie egg.' Hopes *and* fears were expressed:

> I will be looking forward to seeing you . . . do come soon or I might forget what you look like and I collect the same things as you . . . I have got 1000 key rings I had 20 pound once and I bought all key rings with it but my mum wasn't too pleased and you can imagine that.

Promises were made: 'I am drawing you a big Donald duck.' Presents were exchanged: 'My friend gave me a bracelet.'

Sheila and Gita were perhaps the best example of 'hitting it off', which they had done immediately on meeting at Albert Road. The Garfield children had had 'such a marvellous time, they didn't want to come home. Sheila got out of the minibus looking so miserable . . . and her mother said that she talked from the moment she got in non-stop the whole evening, about the temple, the apparatus, her friends, the children she'd met and how marvellous it was.'

Sheila and Gita exchanged gifts at Garfield, held hands and arms, gave each other piggy backs, and talked incessantly. They phoned each other between visits, arranged for other, independent meetings in a truly blossoming relationship which spread to their families. Gita's mother accompanied them on the trip to Garfield. 'Sheila's Mum said that she would like to go to the temple', and they were trying to arrange it. The effects thus spread at certain points into another generation.

Cultural integration was all part of the mixing. There were no apparent barriers. The Garfield children took a delight in their friends' names, expressed with genuine pleasure: 'I know I will enjoy the day with you, Dipak. The Hindu Temple is exciting and I like your name'. The Albert Road children who spoke English as a second language signed their names in English and in their mother tongue. Some taught their friends at Garfield how to write *their* names in their first language. Amina Begum actually sent a song in Bengali 'to the children of Garfield school', though its translation would have to wait until a future visit! Their teacher reported that 'One or two of them who got given the white children got a bit sort of peeved really, especially the older children, they wanted one from a different country, please.'

This shows not only their enthusiasm, but also the extent of the Garfield children's ignorance, for most of the black children from Albert Road had been born in Britain. Such a mistake is perhaps typical of schools in the 'white shires', but it was soon to be rectified. The 'ethnic minority' friend was something special, sought by these children through a feeling of comradeship. Apart from the relationships forged, there is considerable educational potential within the children as culture-bearers. Most of these were second or third generation British, but some still have strong family connections in India, Bangladesh, and Africa, whom they visit regularly. As one teacher remarked, 'As they themselves acquire more command of English they could tell others about visits to Bangladesh or India or wherever, and if they hear it first hand from a child, that is going to be far more valuable than reading it up in a boring book.' An interesting corollary to this is that Sheila could understand Gita's English far more easily than she could Gita's mother's. In general, one clear educational function in these new relationships was evident in the amount of help the children gave each other in the worksheets. The Albert Road teacher was 'fascinated by how some who were normally reticent helped others.'

The community spirit was evident during lunch at Garfield. This was taken in the playground, as fortunately it was a sunny day, and notwithstanding the privation of sitting on hard tarmac, it became a considerable social event. The children had brought picnics, and sat down with teachers and parents, and talked, ate, and shared their food. The sharing was an important expression of friendship and another aspect of 'mixing'. Gita's mother had herself brought some sweetmeats, which she handed round.

After lunch there were games, and running about in the 'garden', playing 'tig', races, and the 'A team', or playing with toys in the playground (one group, their bottoms up in the air, huddled around some 'space invaders'). At Albert Road, too, they had indulged in uninhibited play. The boys had been fascinated by the pond in a corner of the playground, looking for tadpoles, bounding up and down on the board, climbing up a rope. It seemed important that the days included these 'letting off steam' sessions in each other's company, and taking advantage of the other's resources, allowing time to work off energies and excitement as well as to cement relationships in the joyous hurly-burly of play. As one teacher, reflecting on an alternative programme for a future occasion, commented 'Perhaps we could ship them off to somewhere like Roman Fields where there are some swings and just let them have a play. Just literally play together, because I mean that is a lot of it, playing with each other.'

The two days of the visits were very full, exciting, demanding, and exhausting. Atul sums it up in simple style: 'When we went home I was tired. I like the day. I was really tired. It was good that day.'

CONCLUSION

This exchange provided a great educational boost to these children, and to their teachers. It was a cathartic event, inducing a high level of awareness and motivation, sparking off developments across the curriculum, but in ways closely integrated within the person of the child and strongly related to the child's own concerns. It rose above the institutional level of the school, placing all the activity firmly within the context of everyday life. It made use of resources readily and cheaply available in the everyday world, and within and between the people involved. The establishment of friendships and the degree of freedom allowed for these to develop ensured that all was anchored in the children's worlds. From this basis, several reached new heights of achievement, understanding, and appreciation in the work associated with the project – the development of language, writing, mathematics, religious education, physical education, environmental studies, etc. But the main achievement was the platform itself – the personal and social relationships established. New identities were forged as barriers were overcome, confidence established, abilities harnessed, so that several children were seen to do things they had never done before, that some, indeed, suspected they were incapable of doing. This was coupled with the social development involved in the forging of links across regions, across generations, and especially across cultures.

Such an exchange might be seen as the high point of quite a long educational process – a catalytic event which sparks off a number of educational developments both before and after. The teachers, for example, were preparing for it six weeks in advance, and the follow-up afterwards might take a similar period. This took several lines, including, at Albert Road, capitalizing on newly awakened interests and ensuring that library books were available on such things as churches and temples.

It will be seen that many of the ingredients of the model elaborated earlier are present here. There is cognitive, social, and affective matching. Teacher and pupil interests and intentions coincide. The aims do not outreach the available resources. There is stimulation, enjoyment, fairness, and learning. There is a measure of pupil control over their learning, the teachers acting as facilitators. Their learning tackles the constraint of 'race', and the influence of gender and social class do not appear to have acted as impediments in this instance. But this project was not only pupil-centred; it was teacher-centred also. It had been their idea, and had arisen spontaneously from an informal social visit by one friend to another.

Before the idea itself, therefore, there was a personal bond between the teachers. They planned the venture in further informal visits. They thus had a strong personal investment in the project. Apart from planning, there was also a sense of teacher participation in learning, for example in the new environments, especially in the temple and the church, and about their own children. It was also an exercise in team teaching. As always, when this works well, the three teachers concerned 'sparked each other off', maximized their strengths, created new ideas and possibilities, took problems and potential weaknesses in their stride. As one teacher remarked, 'I think the teachers doing it have got to be on good terms themselves and have similar ideas as to what they want out of it. I think there has to be a lot of give and take, because, I mean, it is a bit of a squash, it disrupts everything the day you meet.' It could, in other words, be disastrous.

The teachers thought it essential for this project to be within the school's programme of studies, and not just a one-off social event. The careful planning, therefore, ensures that the motivation and high level of enthusiasm aroused is controlled and geared towards the achievement of basic objectives. It is possible to 'go overboard' on such an event and end up with nothing but happy, and perhaps riotous, memories. For these reasons one such exchange a term was thought to be the maximum since, if more frequent, they could disturb routines counter-productively, instead of servicing them.

The teachers had plans for a further exchange of visits the following term, perhaps to attend their different religious festivals – Diwali at Albert Road, the Christmas Carol Service in the church at Garfield. Apart from the value of the enterprise itself, the reinforcement of certain aspects, like handling money, and the numerous other educational spin-offs, the series of exchanges could be a useful resource in meeting the objectives in the schools' specified programmes, especially in social and educational studies. For example, in both schools, 'buildings' were to figure large in these programmes the next term, and there are obvious possibilities in this area within such a project. Susan Andrews hoped her older children would be placed in the same class at secondary school as those from Albert Road (these exchanges could clearly help to alleviate some of the personal and social problems involved in the 11-plus transition). And a number of informal contacts by telephone, letter, and visits were maintained by some of the children themselves.

Having said all this, a reservation has to be noted. Closer and longer study would be needed to ascertain the degree to which knowledge emanating from this project was conserved over time within the children's perspectives. Time also did not allow for the children to be interviewed at length on aspects of the visits; this would have been highly desirable.

Without such interviews, and indeed without more detailed ecological and temporal contextualization, it is impossible to say whether such an activity transcends or merely masks the structural influences of gender, class, and 'race' (Brah and Minhas 1985). This account has relied on observations, study of the documents involved (letters, poems, accounts, artwork), and discussions with teachers. These materials suggest that this was an implicit operationalization of the 'opportunities to learn and teach' model, and that the chances are that pupils had a degree of control over their learning, and appropriated much of the knowledge involved in some quite difficult areas. For stronger claims to be made, more detailed and longer term work would be necessary.

However, the project does provide strong support for the findings of Denscombe *et al.* (1986), that in some primary schools at least there is a considerable level of friendship and integration between pupils of different ethnic origin, in contrast to the results of previous sociometric studies. Indeed, in the eyes of their teachers, it was these very inter-ethnic relationships that were the catalyst for some quite exceptional work and development. For the promotion of racial harmony, and for learning in general, therefore, such exercises appear to have much to offer.

7 Pupils' perceptions of religious and cultural diversity

> The multi-faith school, at every age, is potentially a place for growth and enrichment of a kind never before experienced in Britain.
>
> (Owen-Cole 1981: 194)

> First-hand experience of celebrating different festivals should help the children to learn about festivals in a variety of religious traditions and to understand something of the significance of each festival to the community which celebrates it.
>
> (Gregory 1986: 24)

Celebrating different religious festivals has become an accepted part of the sharing of cultural diversity advocated by the Swann Report (1985). March 1987 was 'Religious Education' month, in one of our LEAs, and among many activities being organized was a multi-faith evening intended to reflect the religious and cultural diversity of the area. Three lower schools, a middle school, and an upper school contributed to an event, 'Celebrating Together', at one of the community colleges.

We wondered what sense pupils made of these experiences. Was their understanding of religion advanced? Did they come to a new appreciation of faiths other than their own? How did such an enterprise advance their knowledge, understanding, and skills for living in multicultural Britain? The heads of two of the lower schools taking part were interested in the enquiry. The researcher accordingly made plans to talk to some of the children before, during and after the event. Conversations were recorded, and a report based on these was written for the teachers at the two schools. This was intended as a discussion document, which, together with the transcripts, might help the teachers draw their own conclusions. The schools, referred to here as School E and School F, had different catchments and started from slightly different perspectives, but both showed a concern to know about the different backgrounds and cultures in the wider community.

This chapter is an edited version of the report presented to the teachers, and is in two parts, consisting of observations based on listening to groups of children from both schools before and after the event.

BEFORE THE EVENT

School E

School E is a lower school in a village on the outskirts of the town. It has four classes and is full to its capacity of 120 children. These come from the semi-rural village and the local authority and private housing on the edge of the town. It has a small ethnic minority and a socially mixed intake. A month before the event, a group of third- and fourth-year children, 7- and 8-year-olds, were working on Judaism. Their contribution to the multi-faith event would draw on this. They already knew quite a lot about the Jewish way of life, and they were learning some songs and a dance, and rehearsing a play about a Jewish family's traditional celebration of Shabbat.

Thinking about Judaism

The researcher visited the school a week before the event and was able to talk to fifteen of the children, in groups of three, who were going to take part. They were looking forward to going to the Community College for a rehearsal in four days time. They discussed Shabbat:

VICKY	It's a family meal and celebration.
MARK	It starts on Friday in the evening.
VICKY	And finishes on a Saturday.
MARK	At sunset.
VICKY	. . .to celebrate, um, Shabbat from . . .
MARK	I know, because there was a story about . . .
VICKY	Because, um, Pharaoh. . .
MARK	There was a story about. . .
VICKY	. . . the Israelites.
MARK	The Israelites.
VICKY	When they were slaves.
MARK	When they were slaves.
VICKY	And, um, Pharaoh wouldn't let them go.
MARK	. . . and they got let go.
VICKY	And so they celebrate that day.

This impressive co-operative and economical account suggests that these children have grasped the essential information needed to explain why Jewish people celebrate Shabbat. In this example they are referring both to the play they are going to perform and to the knowledge about Judaism which explains this play. In focusing on Judaism these 8-year-olds are having to learn about a different religion at second hand. There are no Jews in the school so they are being told about different traditions and ways of worshipping and looking at and using related artefacts without a point of reference. They may have been familiar with some of the stories:

KATE	We heard the story of how Moses saved the Jewish people from Pharaoh.
WILLIAM	Like when they was, when the Israelites were slaves in Egypt.
CARLA	They had to do slaving and Moses got all these, did all these good things for them and sent all the ten plagues and the land that they went to was called the land of, I think it was sugar and honey, I'm not sure. . .
WILLIAM	Milk and honey.
CARLA	We know they went into captivity again . . .

Many of the children have a Judaeo-Christian frame of reference, however slightly grasped, which gives what they are doing a context and starting point for making assumptions. The traditions they are learning about may not seem difficult to understand:

NATALIE	On the seventh day, there's a special day they don't even work.
RANI	That's the Sabbath.
ADAM	Yeah, because Jesus . . . *Moses*, said that they shouldn't work on the seventh day.

It is interesting that none of the children explicitly related the Jewish Shabbat to the Christian sabbath, although they were using both terms.

'They only had the Old Testament'

Learning about Judaism involved becoming familiar with new ideas and new vocabulary. They talked confidently about synagogues, the Torah, Matzo bread, Hebrew, and the Holy Ark and were keen to explain what they were. They had not been taken to a synagogue but one group explained:

REBECCA It's a kind of church
STEVEN They pray there . . . they're just the same as churches.

Another group referred to special garments worn for particular occasions:

ROBERT When they go to the synagogue, only the men and boys wear things on their head and they have a sort of half a hat, not a full hat . . .
JENNY They have to have these special hats on their heads . . .
MARK Skull caps. . . men and boys wear them.
JENNY And a scarf, a special scarf, and when the people, on the seventh day they go to the synagogue.

Slowly, as groups explained, they seemed to be building up what they knew. Sometimes they were not sure: 'I think it's to keep the sun off their heads or something.' The local Rabbi had visited the school to watch their play and check its accuracy: 'We've had the Rabbi in twice . . . She came to help us with the play and tell us whether we got the words right as well . . . She's a priest.'

In their play they were going to read from the Torah. They explained this by referring to what some called the 'English Bible' and though 'it's only the first five books', or as one child explained more precisely, 'We've been finding out about the books of the Torah, like Genesis and Exodus and Leviticus and Deuteronomy and also Numbers.' They seem confidently knowledgeable:

ADAM It's a book what you read.
RANI Not a book, it's a Old Testament.
ADAM Old Testament, and you have to read it in the synagogue.
RANI Yeah, and the Rabbi reads it all, like the priest reads it.

Another group can describe what it looks like:

ROBERT It's a sort of big scroll with Hebrew writing on it and it takes over a year to write out.
MARK It's like it's in a scroll.
ROBERT And you have to read it backwards.
JENNY They read a part every Shabbat.

They knew, too, that it was a precious book which had to be read with a special pointer: 'If you follow it with your finger it would smudge it, it would ruin the whole thing and you'd have to write it out again and that would take a year.' They were less sure about the Holy Ark, but knew that it was to protect the Torah:

NATALIE	It's kept in the ark .. where it's kept safe.
ADAM	It's kind of like a safe but it's got a light at the top.

'They eat Matzo, we've had that'

All the groups had enjoyed trying Matzos:

MATTHEW	We tasted them, they were like bread, they were Matzo things.
VICKY	Matzo . . .
MATTHEW	. . . bread, we tasted it.
VICKY	It's like biscuits.
MATTHEW	We tasted it with marmalade, jam.
VICKY	Lemon curd.
MATTHEW	Cheese, and the one that we all like most of all was jam, that was the most popular.
WILLIAM	Alan said he didn't like it.
MICHAEL	I don't like it.
VICKY	I liked it with the cheese and the jam.

Other groups thought they were like bread, biscuits and crackers, but none of them attempted to explain why Jewish people ate this kind of bread. The religious and symbolic significance may have been discussed in class but was not explored in our conversations.

Shabbat: 'They're not allowed to do nothing'

Their play was about a family celebrating the start of the sabbath. They were impressed by the strictness of the rules:

WILLIAM	They celebrate on Friday evening and on Saturday until it's evening and that's called Shabbat and they are not allowed to do any work at all. If they do then it's said they become evil.
CARLA	When the mother lights the candle they can't do anything, not even go and put something on the table or anything.

Thinking about this provoked one child to conclude, 'Well, they're a bit more, sort of, they give you, it's sort of like the impression, I don't know whether they are or not, it's like they're more sort of religious than English people. They've got their own way of doing things.' There was a general feeling that Jews were not 'English'.

What being 'Jewish' meant was something they were not certain about. They talked confidently about the play itself, described exactly what they were going to do, could recite their lines, re-tell the bible stories related to the event, and use the vocabulary of Judaism, without being sure who all this applied to. They seemed confused. One suggestion was, 'some people who have got a Jewish mother and father and they are born in England, so that will make them a little bit Jewish and a little bit English.' Another person thought, 'some come from here, some come from Egypt, some people come from Israel.'

For many of them, the problem seemed to be that terms like *religion, faith*, and *belief* were hard to explain. They have quite a lot of knowledge about Judaism, but little understanding. Some thought that Jewish people came from Israel but they only understood Israel in biblical terms, 'how they wouldn't let the people go . . .' They were not sure whether there were Jewish people actually living in their town. Some thought that perhaps there were, 'but not many though.'

The songs they were singing as part of their performance were in Hebrew. One group reported that Hebrew was 'writing and you've got to say, *language*.' Another group said it was 'the language of the Jews' and were fairly sure that most Jewish families spoke Hebrew at home. Another declared 'they talk differently':

MATTHEW They talk in a different language and they write differently, they write from . . .

VICKY . . .left to right.

'Do they believe in God?'

No one seemed absolutely sure what Jewish people believed in. One girl said that she was a Christian and that this meant 'we believe in God.' Someone else agreed: 'I do, I'll see God in the sky when I'm dead, if you believe in God.' One said she thought so, another was certain they did. They thought about what being a Christian meant. Most of them thought you were only Christian if you have been christened. One girl said firmly, 'No I'm not a Christian', while a boy was not sure. A girl who had been baptized was quite sure why, it was so she would be good and would believe in God. Having talked about what they did not believe in, this group, and others, still found it hard to draw parallels with Judaism and there was uncertainty, and disagreement about what Jews believed in: 'People say that they don't believe in God.'

Some were clear that they were joining with other schools for some sort of celebration:

NATALIE	To celebrate . . .
RANI	Shabbat.
ADAM	The Shabbat, as they told us, we think that, um, the Jews think that it took seven days to make the world.

Other groups thought it might be a competition:

MATTHEW	To see who's the best, what you have been learning.
VICKY	No, to see what you could learn and what other schools do.
MATTHEW	And to see who is the best.

'We have been doing quite a lot on Israel'

Certainly 'what you could learn' had been a very important factor for these children. They acquired an impressive amount of information. They all knew the story 'of how Moses saved the Jewish people from Pharaoh'; they found out about the early books of the Old Testament; they did a lot of writing 'about how they escaped and about the plagues'; they wrote 'a diary of an Israelite slave, what we think it would be like'; they acted out one of the most common rituals of Judaism and were impressively word perfect as actors and narrators; the choir mastered several Hebrew songs which they sang really well. The extent to which they could link all this with a twentieth-century living faith is questionable, but some of them had a clear idea of what they had been doing: 'We do more historical than modern 'cause we do things that are to do with when they were slaves and we find out things, we look back and find out what started them off.'

School F

School F, with approximately 190 children, is a racially mixed town-centre school in an area of late nineteenth-century terraced housing where a considerable proportion of the local population has recently arrived from the Indian subcontinent. Several different churches, a gurdwara, a temple, and a mosque are all close to the school and bear witness to the religious diversity of the local community. As so many of the children have English as a second language, literacy and communication are priorities. For the children here, participating in the multi-faith event would not involve a new perspective; the school already had a policy of 'making festivals a focus'. Their contribution would be drawn from their experience of celebrating in this way: a dance drama to celebrate Holi, a group performance of a stick dance for Diwali, and a play in collaboration with the local middle school, telling the story of Mohammed. The material they were using was drawn from cultural experiences which were already familiar to most of the children. Thus, the focus was different from that of School E where a new topic, albeit one with some familiar points of reference, had been introduced and new information and understanding had to be acquired. This did not mean that the participants found it easier. For both schools, participation in the event meant hard work for pupils and teachers. The children at School E were spending every lunch hour practising their play; some found this boring and felt it was unfair. School F were rehearsing equally remorselessly.

Rehearsing the Holi dances in school

Two weeks before the event, the researcher observed a group of girls rehearsing a dance based on a story about Krishna and Radha. This would celebrate the Hindu spring festival of Holi. Before break the goddess Radha and her handmaidens had scripted the choreography of their dance, discussing every move with their teacher, creating the notation of each sequence. After break they practised in costume – ankle-length, pale cream robes with loose circular sleeves which hung in an arc from wrist to ankle as they moved with arms outstretched. They walked their dance to a count of four, not simply being directed, but actively involved in working out the best way to do it. 'Hold on, he done it two times,' said one and they all gathered round to check their scripts to see whether 'Sir' had got it right. The goddess practised her entry with another teacher. Long sticks in her sleeves allowed her to describe a complete circle as she raised her arms above her head. She seemed composed, discussing each of her moves with the teacher. 'Head up, you're a proud goddess,' he encouraged her. The boy who was to play Krishna would join them later. A week later, the handmaidens were dancing to taped music, the stage had been marked out, and they wore elaborate golden head-dresses. They had a little time left before another group arrived to use the hall. 'Come on. Starting positions, and let's see if we can do it all together,' said their teacher. There was a sense of urgency now that there was only a week to go.

In the larger hall, the middle and lower school children rehearsed the story of Mohammed. Two boys opened the drama reciting from the Koran, children improvised the story of Mohammed's life, and narrators read from cards. On their second run-through, the improvisation seemed more confident. A teacher asked the two boys who were to recite to check with their Imam that they were not making any mistakes. The dancers arrived, to go through their routine again. They were all tired and losing concentration. The teacher was tired too. 'No! People aren't listening, now try listening all of you.' The Indian music was very difficult for them to follow, and they had to count their steps all the time. The teacher decided to make it more fun, jazzed it up, joined in and they all skipped round with a temporary renewal of energy. 'Was it getting boring?' they were asked as they were getting dressed again. 'Yes, all dancing, all morning, nothing else,' said one of them. 'Krishna's a boy,' said another and all the handmaidens giggled. They were wondering about the event at the Community College; how they would get there and whether their parents would come to watch. Several said their parents would be at work. 'Radha' said hers would be busy in the shop. Another said her mother worked from 6 in the morning to 5 in the evening at the pizza factory so she did not expect her to come either. They were all looking forward to the Monday afternoon rehearsal at the college.

The final rehearsal at the Community College

School E and F children were arriving with all their props, School F with boxes of costumes and head-dresses each in a labelled polythene bag. They had shared a coach with the middle school. The backstage room was cluttered and crowded. A girl's changing room was rigged up by putting a table across a corner. The girls dressed swiftly, needing little help putting the clothes they had taken off into their bags. The head-dresses were tied on. Radha's looked very uncomfortable – she had got her ear caught under the headband. They were all ready too soon, as they had to wait for School E to rehearse their contribution and then sit through a lengthy photography session while the local press grouped the entire cast on stage. Once they were dressed, the girls said they felt shy and lined up, giggling nervously.

School F's props were complicated but their costumes at this stage were restricted to headware – skull caps for the boys, scarves for the women. The actors, overwhelmed by the size of the place, were rather quiet, but the singing was confident and good. They joined the audience to watch the other schools.

The handmaidens, daunted by the much larger space, were predictably uncertain. Their teacher shouted joking encouragement and criticism. Radha looked more and more miserable. One of the School E children said, 'I wish our teachers talked to us like that.' It is obviously a novelty to encounter other people's teachers. There was much prompting. Krishna seemed rather embarrassed, particularly at the point when baskets of streamers had to be thrown at the dancers and the audience (it should have been paint!). The younger children, some only 6 years old, performed their stick dance delightfully. It was confident and well rehearsed – a remnant from last term's celebration of Diwali.

The researcher went behind the scenes to help the girls to dress and to talk to them. Now it was over they were playing clapping games to let off steam, or sitting and chatting. The noise level was high, despite pleas to be quiet as the story of Mohammed was still being performed. Radha said she was very hot in her costume. They all said that they had been nervous.

School E had seemed confident but were having difficulty with the number of different props involved in their play – candles, bread, bread-board and knife, the Torah, which took on a life of its own when removed from its holder, and assorted hats and shawls which they were not used to wearing. On the night they managed to control all these remarkably well.

Talking about Holi

Taking part in the rehearsal seemed to give the dancers at School F a much better idea of what to expect and what the event was all about. Even so, when they were asked whether they knew what was happening, at first they seemed doubtful. They had been puzzled by the place itself. It was not what they had expected: 'It didn't really look like a . . . but I thought it was going to be a stage but it was a flat stage. I thought there were going to be three hundred people but there were only those kind of seats about.' They were a little disappointed that it didn't seem very different at first:

TERNDEEP	Like a sort of a school hall, like our hall . . .
BUCKSHOW	A bit little, about the same size.
NICKY	But, the only thing is . . . it feels like a stage then . . . it felt more different.
TERNDEEP	And I was nervous . . .

It was a big event for them, meeting with other schools in a strange place and having to fit what they knew into a programme of events. They had found it much more difficult having to concentrate on 'doing the right things'. The rehearsal had brought home just how much responsibility they had to take for their own performance:

NICKY	When you turn round . . .
TERNDEEP	Especially when, you know, when I turn around and

do that part, I get confused because um, especially when I walk down low, middle and high I get confused as to have I done it another time instead of doing it two times, I do it one time and get confused.

NICKY There's one part where I get confused in the starting part when you have to go out because we don't really know when we have to go out, it's, we just have to think in our minds when we have to go out. We don't really know so we have to choose the right time, but I think it's best to know the time when we should come in because if . . . Today it was OK because we didn't get a you know, what's it, the other boy who is doing the reading because if he is doing the reading we would have to wait to come out, so I think it's best to have someone to tell us, 'take part'.

RESEARCHER Don't you come out when he's finished his bit of reading?

BUCKSHOW No, when he says 'moonlight, dances in the moonlight'. Then we come out but she (*Pointing to Terndeep.*) stays inside.

TERNDEEP I get put off by these lot (ie. the handmaidens). They turn round . . . and instead of going up there, they go up here . . .

It was hardly surprising that 'Radha' had lost her confidence and looked so miserable during the rehearsal. It had clearly been a more than usually stressful experience with an additional factor that had almost gone unnoticed:

TERNDEEP I was nervous because I didn't have a petticoat. I thought we were just going to do it with these clothes and a costume on top but it wasn't like that, so Mrs Daniels said take your clothes off and I said I haven't got a petticoat and she said I'll get you one and when we got . . . I was kind of nervous because I didn't have a petticoat underneath.

Petticoats were not the only problem. An added stress had been parental approval. Terndeep's mother had not been happy about her daughter being involved in a play about Krishna:

TERNDEEP I don't know, I can't give mum a welcome, it keeps getting on your mind because mum said that you're not allowed to do the dance. I said it's a Sikh and Hindu festival, and mum said, at first, it's with a boy. And I said it's not going to be dirty parts and all that, and I said I hope not. And I said if there is anyway, I don't do it and mum said alright, you will do it, so long as it's *not that*.

This troubled explanation suggests something of the tensions and constraints which underlie young Asian girls' experience of schooling in this country. In order to take part in a fairly routine activity, she has had to both reassure her mother and negotiate for permission in a way that seems unusually mature for an 8-year-old. Her English friend (in the extracts below) has to struggle to imagine what the problem could be. As she sees it, the only 'rudeness' occurred when Krishna threw the coloured streamers over Radha. In discussing this she seems to have helped Terndeep to see how she had already controlled the threat:

NICKY Anyway, there's nothing really, you know *rude*, about it, it's just you having, it's only . . .

BUCKSHOW He's the one who starts Holi first.

TERNDEEP The first time, guess what happened, you know those flick things (*Streamers*), he bunged it all over, I was about to go like that, but he kept on going up and up, and I was trying to take it off and I said, *next time you better not do that* (*She speaks in a very stern voice.*).

NICKY Cause, there's nothing really rude, it's just when she just runs to snatch the bowl . . .

Asked whether her mother felt happier about her doing it, she said confidently, 'My mum's *really* happy,' and had agreed to come to see the show. The other Asian girl in the group wasn't as lucky:

BUCKSHOW I said to my mum, mum are you allowed to come and she said no I can't come. She's got a lot of work to do and my dad can't come because he has to open the shop.

NICKY Who's taking you then?

BUCKSHOW My mum's going to take me and she's going to come back home and do some work.

It seemed sad that she would not be able to see her daughter dancing so seriously and so well. By now the children at School F were full of the sense of themselves as performers and were looking forward with excitement and trepidation:

TERNDEEP	I can't wait to go to the (*Community*) Centre, really . . .
BUCKSHOW	I thought it was last night.
TERNDEEP	I thought it was Wednesday. I couldn't get to sleep all night.
NICKY	I'm excited, I actually can't wait.

No doubt, by now the children at School E were feeling much the same.

All kinds of religions

Although the rehearsal seemed to have given the group at School F a better idea of the purpose of the event itself, they were still confused about the content of the programme in general:

TERNDEEP	. . . there's going to be a Sikh festival and a Chinese festival. We saw lots of girls and kind of, boys dressing up as Sikhs and Hindus and Bangladeshi, all of them, all kinds of religions.
NICKY	Because all of us who are different religions are going to go in another religion, so, so I'm not Holi I'm not a Holi person I'm just English and T's not an English . . .
BUCKSHOW	It doesn't matter really.
NICKY	It doesn't matter who you are, it's just what you do and when you do it, really.
TERNDEEP & BUCKSHOW	Yeah.
BUCKSHOW	And how you do it.

Perhaps because they are confronted with a range of religious differences in their local community and because their school exploits and explores these differences, the concept of religion is one they are at home with. Moreover, they seem to be actively thinking about these differences and about sharing. Asked whether Holi was a Hindu festival, their response typifies the way this group explores ideas together:

TERNDEEP Hindu and Sikh, yes, both . . .
NICKY Anybody can do it. English as well.
TERNDEEP No but Sikh and Hindu, special people, but anybody can as well, you know join in and do all that.
NICKY Because they join in to our religion. . .
TERNDEEP Just pretend the Englishes joined in ours and we wouldn't let them, it's not fair like that, it's fair that we be kind to each other.
NICKY Say like, so we say, 'you can join into our festival' and they say, 'you can join in ours', so we both just share everything we have . . . because if they come into our, into England, they should share, should learn our religion and if we go in their country we should learn their religion.
BUCKSHOW Doesn't matter really.

Where they are particularly fortunate at School F is in having children for whom Holi is a real festival and who can bring it to life in particular ways. The two children who spontaneously and vividly described what Holi is like in India are unlikely to have experienced this themselves but can draw on family stories. They were asked, 'Do you celebrate Holi at home?' The researcher meant at home in England but the children interpreted it more broadly:

BUCKSHOW Holi? Yeah we do.
TERNDEEP Holi, yeah! Especially at India. Oh, it's lovely at India. I wish I was in India right now, they'll be celebrating with colour and all that lot, all, every single . . .
BUCKSHOW They chuck it at people, and any people they know.
TERNDEEP Yeah, every single people in their village will be outside and throwing stuff . . .
BUCKSHOW Mm . . .
TERNDEEP Powder. Oh it's lovely, and there'll be water powders too . . .
BUCKSHOW It's all over your clothes, red, yellow, green, everything . . .
TERNDEEP But they wear white there.

Listening to this, the one non-Asian girl responded thoughtfully. 'It's fun that. We do something else different, they do something different.' Perhaps it is easier for children to be swept up by their pleasure and excitement, and to sense something of the quality of Holi as a festival of spring and of renewal when members of their peer group celebrate it as part of their culture. For the children at School E to experience and understand the solemnity of the Jewish sabbath will be harder:

RESEARCHER	Holi is about spring?
NICKY	It starts the spring.
TERNDEEP	And Krishna, the, er, god of spring, and wherever Krishna used to play the flute Radha every time used to dance around and play her sitar.

However, while they find it easy to describe what happens they are probably not yet ready to think about what it stands for.

AFTER THE EVENT

School E

SEAN	I liked the whole evening, all the different things.
RENA	Did you stay until the food?

Talking after the event was much more relaxed. The children had a better idea of what it was all about and wanted to share their experiences. The talk was much less focused; although they had all experienced the same event, individual reactions were different . Their performance had taken place in the context of a range of experiences and different aspects seemed important to different children. One had felt sick, another needed the toilet, another had been embarrassed by the top refusing to come off the wine bottle he had to open. Finding mum in the audience, getting home late, watching a video, talking to children from other schools, and eating food at the end, were all as important as taking part in the play, although this had been quite stressful. Most of them admitted to being nervous:

CLARE	'Cause when you go on to the stage, there's like this big audience and when you go . . . you think yourself as though you're going to . . .
JAMES	Muck it up.
NICOLA	Yeah, muck it up and do something wrong.

Their talk was a patchwork of impressions from which it is possible to trace patterns of perception and find clues about what they were making of the event.

Personal responses

HEATHER — I was nervous at the end because Carol didn't feel very well. She felt sick.
RENA — She went to the boys' toilet

General questions like, 'How did you enjoy it? Tell me about it . . .' were the cue for anecdotes and observations of an immediate and personal kind:

> My friend was sick.
> We were allowed to eat the bread.
> We were lucky, we watched a video afterwards.
> When we came home a little bit late my mum got really worried.
> I had to wait to the end because my mum was working nights.
> Susan's friend needed the toilet. I was trying not to laugh it was so funny.
> There was food at the end . . . it was ever so nice.
> I could see my mum.
> Carol went into the boys' toilet.

The last episode assumed epic proportions and was described in detail by every group as one of the most significant events of the evening. Carol herself was conscious of having been a star and said modestly of the boys' lavatory, 'Well it was better than nothing'; however, two boys who told her to 'push off' had added dramatic effect. To a certain extent this incident seemed to allow them to express the stressful aspect of being involved in an event of this kind.

'I thought it was funny'

Laughter had been another outlet for stress. They all laughed a lot as they told me about the boy who needed to go to the lavatory during the play itself. 'Everybody was watching.' His discomfort was evidence of the nervousness they were all feeling. Some described how they tried hard not to laugh when the top would not come off the wine bottle. This need for something to relieve the tension could explain their overwhelming enthusiasm for one particular incident in the middle school's contribution 'Celebrating Easter'. One lighthearted episode briefly involved slapstick comedy:

CLARE — I liked the Easter one.
JENNY — The funny one. I like the one where the boy was carrying the big box and bumped into one of the

readers and goes, 'Hey! Watch where you're going.' That was the best bit.

Children from five groups described this incident with evident pleasure:

Oh that one was good.
They were really good.
I liked the way the cover of the book came off.
He went *dee*-licious, *dee*-licious.

An episode describing the pre-Christian pagan origins of Easter, however, had completely mystified them: 'There were these girls who came on and there was these people and all the lights went down, a soldier and some kids and woman . . . But I can't remember what it was celebrating.' What they all remembered and mentioned was that they did not get one of the chocolate eggs being handed out. 'It's not really fair because I was right nearly at the top . . .' Familiarity with aspects of Easter and some comedy had helped them to enjoy and remember the 'Easter Celebration'. They referred to it as one of the highlights of the evening. Getting them to talk about some of the other events needed more prompting.

The story of Mohammed

Not all of them had seen this but those who had, either at the rehearsal or on the night, had found it confusing: 'The one where they built that temple sort of thing?' One group had gathered that 'they wanted to kill him', but had then construed the building of the Mosque as 'a thing so that if he had a gun he could shoot them.' The best attempt was, 'Well, there's Mohammed, and there was these other people, and they built this sort of building and they were looking for Mohammed 'cause he had been causing trouble.' Their unfamiliarity with the story had made it hard to understand what the play was about.

The story of Khalsa: The origin of the Sikh religion

For similar reasons they did not seem to have understood what was happening in the play about the origins of Sikhism. There was much confusion. Some thought it was about 'a hangman, you didn't see.' Another group seemed to have sorted out the story but not what it meant:

HEATHER Er . . . there was this one at the end, where this man had some people and he asked them to go out and bring some people to him. About seven I think it was and he asked them who was willing to take their

	life because his sword was thirsty . . .
RENA	Yeah . . .
HEATHER	And all, some people came and went behind the curtains and he was said to be killing them all.
RENA	Yeah.
HEATHER	But at the end, um, all the people came back again.

Another group were able to take it a bit further; in trying to make sense of the story they began to construct a plausible explanation:

CLARE	That one was good. Well, it was about this prince, sort of man and he wanted some people's heads, 'cause he said that his sword was thirsty. And these people had their heads . . . and at the end there was this, what happened, all of them came out dressed like him.
JAMES	Because he wanted them, sort of into new people and he changed their names.

When I asked them whether they could remember which religion this was, they had no idea.

Indian dancers

At the rehearsal the organizers were not sure whether it would be two or three girls on the night. One of the girls still had not been able to persuade her father to give her permission to dance in public. All was well and the three upper school girls were very popular:

NATALIE	There was three girls in Saris and they done some nice Indian dancing. They done two dances and their saris were lovely.
RANI	They weren't saris, they were jackets, shirts . . .

One of them had seen something similar on *Asian Magazine* which she watches every Sunday and said, 'I liked that one and I like the music on the tape. It was lovely.' She remembered School F's stick dance which she had also enjoyed.

Dances for Holi

There was very little comment about this on the night. But some people remembered watching it at the rehearsal. What had impressed one group was the confidence of the child who had introduced the dancers: 'Did you see that little boy, standing at the microphone. He did a speech. I wouldn't have done that if I was him.' One girl had remembered how the goddess, Radha, oppressed by the responsibility of leading the dance, her lack of a petticoat and the teacher's last minute shouted instruction, had come close to tears:

RENA	That girl, there's this girl and she's dressed up like a god and when we was practising it, we saw them, and there's this girl, her face was really sad, like that (*Imitates expression.*). She made me a bit laugh because she was really upset.
NATALIE	She was meant to be a queen when she danced.

No one at School E had heard of Holi before.

Understanding the purpose of celebrating together

Now that they had taken part in the evening, I wondered whether they had a better understanding of what it had all been about. I asked each of the groups what they thought. This was not easy but they seemed much more ready to try out ideas:

CLARE	Celebration.
RESEARCHER	Celebrating what?
JENNY	Religion.
CLARE	Different religions.
RESEARCHER	What do you mean by religion?
JENNY	It's kind of something . . .
CLARE	. . . they believe in,
JENNY	And, um,
CLARE	Their gods, they've all got different gods.
JENNY	Yeah well, I have . . .
CLARE	Well, the Jews don't think Jesus really came down but the Christians do, I know that's the difference between them.

'To show you all different faiths . . . like I'm a Buddhist'

They were using words like *religion* and *faith* with much more confidence and seemed to feel that the evening had been to do with finding out about things they did not know before and about difference:

> Because if you didn't know about Hindus and what happens about them, well you could find out, when they do it.
> It was about religions and what people done at different times of the year.
> Because some people might not know about the faiths.

They were able to be much more specific in their references than they had been before:

HANNAH	Different religions.
RICHARD	About Jewish and Indian.
HANNAH	Hindu . . . the story of Mohammed.

Making links with their own experience

Owen-Cole suggests that through celebrating festivals together 'differences will come to be accepted positively as interesting and important, providing variety long before their particular significance can be understood' (Owen-Cole 1978: 192). But he warns that one of the difficulties peculiar to teaching in the multi-faith school lies in the potential for divisiveness: 'Muslim and Sikh children are still being given false information about one another's faith in the mosques and gurdwaras and their own homes' (ibid: 189). Prejudice is not the property of the host country and the dominant culture alone. There is a danger that events like 'Celebrating Together' could be seen to be inspired by a romantic idealism based on vague affective-type goals. These may stress self-expression and self-fulfilment, while ignoring evidence of the early onset of racial awareness and attitudes in the way young children are socialized into prevailing norms in their homes and local community (Milner 1983).

Two examples of the problems this can cause for young children emerged spontaneously in discussion with children from School E. One girl had not been able to stay for the rest of the evening and explained why her mother had taken her home after she had performed in the Shabbat play:

RENA	There was Sikhs right up the back of the, that's why my mum couldn't, wouldn't stay, 'cause they're Hindus.
RESEARCHER	Are you a Hindu?
RENA	Yes, so I don't like Sikhs, they're horrible.
RESEARCHER	Why?
RENA	Um, because they ruined India . . . it said on the news that Sikhs were ruining India.

RESEARCHER How?
RENA Oh, they're killing people and stuff like that . . .
NATALIE What about religions? Was it anything to do with their religions?
RENA No, they wanted their country back.
RESEARCHER It's nothing to do with religion?
RENA No but Rajiv Gandhi, he wouldn't let them have the country back so they went stabbing people and killing the Hindus.

This 8-year-old is handling quite sophisticated political ideas in her attempt to explain, and the child who responds seems to begin to suggest that these powerful feelings could be something to do with religion. They are both involved in discourse which might well be thought to be beyond the understanding or interest of such young children. In this particular context, perhaps, both have been enabled to express and begin to speculate about ideas that might be thought to be above their heads.

Just as the girl who played Radha had to take on board and negotiate with the cultural norms of her parents, so this one has concerns which seem strange to her non-Asian peers. Two girls ask her to tell me about something which clearly interests them very much:

NATALIE Rani, tell her about your mum chooses the right person to get married. What was it you were telling me about?
JAMES Your mum's got to choose the right person . . .
RANI Oh yes, my mum said that, um, if I be like this, playing with boys this age, I might get divorced when I am big . . . Well my mum said, she might let me get married in India not in England, so she says she doesn't have any trouble but she's going to invite my god to the wedding and then . . .
NATALIE What's your god's name?
RANI I don't know.

Gregory (1985) suggested that ordinary human experience and everyday life are the raw materials of primary education. Listening to these children suggests that we should not make too many assumptions about what constitutes ordinary and everyday experience in the lives of children whose cultural traditions are very different.

School F

A group of boys from School F talked excitedly about their experiences in *The Story of Mohammed* almost a week after the event:

SARFRAZ — I was a builder.
MELVYN — Miss, we all were the builders, only he was a rich man.
RESEARCHER — Can you tell me about it?
SARFRAZ — Miss, first me and a boy said a prayer and then they told how Mohammed escaped and the rich men of Mecca wanted to get rid of them and then the rich men send their sons to kill us, when they found us, we were in a cave and a spider web was there and they just thought the spider web . . . that we weren't in there, so they went away then we went back to Mdina and then builded the mosque and then they said a prayer and then we . . . and then it finished.
RESEARCHER — That was it?
MELVYN — Yes, we were Mohammed's followers.
SARFRAZ — By the cave there was a pigeon nest too.
RESEARCHER — Why were the nest and the spider's web so important in the story?
SARFRAZ — Because Mohammed was hiding in the cave.
MELVYN — Therefore it takes about two, one week to make for a spider to make, spin his web and so he can't be . . .
NAZEEM — Under the pigeon nest.

Having taken part in the play they can talk and explain the story, just as the participants in the Jewish play were able to talk about Shabbat. Their familiarity with the story, however, is different. Three of them are Mohammed's followers in real life. They have not had to learn about Mohammed, they already know.

SARFRAZ — He was a good man.
NAZIM — He taught people good manners.
SARFRAZ — They wanted slaves and Mohammed said they couldn't and they tried to kill him.
NAZIM — And the people in Mecca, they liked his teachings and they built a mosque.

In the same way, Holi is a familiar festival and they express their pleasure, like the girls spoken to before the event.

RAVINDER	Holi is a time when people have fun and parties and play games.
RANJAN	And throw powder.
MAJID	Yea, powder.
RANJAN	I like Holi, it's fun.

The task for the children at School E had been to find out about Judaism and present their information to an audience. The children at School F could draw on their experience of being Muslim or Hindu, or of having many friends who were, to help make sense of what they were doing. Their perception of the event and the meanings they might make of it would almost certainly be different. A boy from School F, when asked what the evening had been for, said, 'A celebration for all the world'.

'We done plays of different countries, English one, we done Indian one, Easter one . . .'

Looking back on the event itself, both schools had much in common. The children at School F, like School E, had mixed feelings about their own performance:

MELVYN	Miss, it was exciting.
RAVINDER	You feel badly shy.

They, too, had enjoyed themselves once it was over:

MAJID	It was good. I enjoyed it.
AZIZ	Eating biscuits and that lot . . .
MAJID	After the play. . .
AZIZ	We had biscuits . . . and we also had a film.

Unfortunately, they had not been able to join the audience and watch the other schools performing.

NAZEEM	It was boring waiting and when we done the play, we were very shy and then when we came out of the play, Miss did give us chocolate biscuits, shortcake biscuits and orange and we kept putting our hand up and getting orange . . .
SARFRAZ	And then we went back . . .
RAVINDER	Home.

Like the children at School E, they had experienced an intensely nervous time while they were actually performing followed by a release of tension, characterized by enjoyment of food. For both groups the excitement of the event had alternated with periods of waiting and boredom.

Mohammed's followers

At School F one group seemed to want to talk about related experiences as well as the event itself:

NAZEEM We read this book and it's called the Holy Koran.
SARFRAZ And Miss, you have to learn it, then you have to show it to a special man, if you have got it right or not, and then he gives you more things each time.
NAZEEM First you learn something by heart in the Koran and then you have to learn all the Koran.

They were far from being daunted by this prospect, although 'there are thousands of pages', and the three Muslim boys claimed to enjoy Mosque school. One admitted that he only sometimes enjoyed it: 'Sometimes you feel sleepy, then you don't feel like going. Sometimes when an hour passes, it looks like you have been in the Mosque for four hours. You get bored sometimes.' The other two found it less boring:

NAZEEM Miss, we fight about upstairs.
GULAM You play about.
IBRAR Fight . . .
NAZEEM We do sometimes.
GULAM Sometimes we do.
IBRAR We jump about and fight and we take people's hats off and chuck them round behind the windows.

But however mischievous they are, they know that the Holy Koran is to be treated with respect:

NAZEEM You usually take your own. Sometimes you're not allowed, sometimes there bes too much mess, and then people keep on pushing and the Korans fall down and then the special man hit you.
GULAM Miss, it's too precious that's why.
IBRAR We leave ours at the Mosque.

The children at School E have been taught that Jewish people consider the Torah to be a precious book and the children at School F know from experience that they have to treat the Holy Koran with respect.

The influence of a sacred text

Two Muslim boys from School F gave some idea of the power of the Koran and the extent of its potential influence on the language and thinking of young children. Heather Mines has written about the literacy skills which young children may be absorbing at Mosque Schools:

> Koranic teaching is part of an oral and literary tradition, indeed the word *Koran* means 'that which is recited'. It is a religion of the Book, the sacred text ... At its simplest, learning the Koran may be rote-learning but important lessons are still being taught about literacy: the meaning of print and layout of a page. Furthermore the book relates to the rest of life.
>
> (Mines 1984: 17)

When she talked to some boys about Mosque schools, she also found that they enjoyed it, joining in a group activity where they all chanted together, giving themselves up to the rhythm of the text.

Perhaps it is possible to see something of this powerful oral and literary influence at work in the talk of the two Muslim boys at School F as they shared their experiences with a Sikh from the Punjab and a Hindu from Nepal:

AZIZ	There's a million reasons you must not swear God, I got this book about this and it told you that you mustn't do it. You go in a snake, a snake you know, a snake room and God put in the snake room fire ... and you burn for a million days. It says on the book.
RESEARCHER	It says in your book?
AZIZ	It's got all the story, all of it, of Mohammed in it.
RESEARCHER	In your book. What's the book called?
AZIZ	The Holy Koran.

The individual interpretation, elaboration and poetic retelling, which Mines (1986) refers to, already seem to be part of these 8-year-old boys' linguistic repertoire:

BOY	If you be good, and if you be very good in the wide world you don't swear, you got marks every time

> and you must pray every time and God will give you anything you want. He'll give you gold, anything you want to be, because to be nice and not to swear, that's why he says on the Koran.

Perhaps this owes more to the rhythm of the Koran than to any other source. It is impossible to do justice in a transcript to the intonation and pace which gave this account such dramatic effect and poetic force. It is all the more remarkable since the speaker has not lived in England for long and arrived speaking no English. Despite his limited English he seems amazingly fluent in a narrative mode, describing aspects of the way his religion affects family life and his own world view. It is also significant, perhaps, that his father died fairly recently. His reference to God in this context provoked one of his listeners, a Sikh, to ask, 'Miss, where is God?' and change the direction of their discussion:

RANJAN	Miss, where is God?
MAJID	In the sky in heaven.
AZIZ	Yeah.
RANJAN	Where is heaven?
MAJID	I don't know.
AZIZ	If somebody dies, yeah, and they bury them, God comes with men, yeah, you can't see them and they take their, the man, whoever dies, he takes him to heaven and they be live again.
MAJID	Miss, he takes the soul but leaves the body.

Again, Majid and Aziz speak with authority. Majid is inclined, however, to alternate between the Holy Koran and his mother as his source of authority: 'My mum said they take all the body up.' When challenged he will reply, 'Yeah, my mother said.' His account of what would happen to a person who damages the Holy Koran is powerful and poetic:

MAJID	If you rip the Koran, you are going to be in bad things, you will be in bed first, and go in fire, then be everything, you won't come to this country for ever, and for a million days you have to stay.

He shares with the other Muslim boy in the group a narrative style which seems to reflect a culture that values story, in particular stories which transmit religious beliefs and moral ideas. Retelling stories they have heard at home, they seem to have a means for making sense of the world. As Fred Inglis has written:

> If we are lucky, some of our earliest cognitive memories, our memories that is of thinking, will be of listening to stories told or read to us . . . the more stories you remember, the richer and more various they are, the better you can understand what is going on.
>
> (Inglis 1987: 10–20)

A story told by the other Muslim boys seems to illustrate an underlying respect for the power of the word, a recognition of the importance not only of being able to tell stories but of being able to *read* them:

> My mum told me about one thing – there's a Mosque man and . . . he could go up to God, and he, she said that she was born then, and he wanted to see all around the world. And then he said, God said, don't go in the wrong place. He said he wanted to go and he went and God said, you have to cut the first person's head off and when he looked, he had cut all the stuff that we need to read and the Mosque man said, 'I can't cut his head off because he reads everything', and then God said he had to and he cut it off and snakes and dragons came out . . .

The two boys vie with each other in their accounts of the supernatural and miraculous:

AZIZ	In our country there's ghosts, yeah, kind of a spirit, yeah because the spirit goes in the palm tree and every tree . . .
MAJID	My mum said that this really happened, someone put something in the water.
AZIZ	Yeah.
MAJID	And they put on all their, you know, and they go to the courtyard and they get this bottle and say this prayer and all the spirit go to the bottom and they dig it in the ground. And if you open it, all the spirits go again and you'd be sick, and you'll be, you know, you'll be mad and you'll be very sad.

The story continues, unfortunately almost inaudibly, but is rounded off with an accomplished story-teller's expertise: '. . .and that's why they put these bottles and dig in the sand.'

Negotiating and sharing cultural information

The two Muslim boys did not dominate this group discussion. All the examples above were part of an impressive interaction between four boys from different backgrounds – Bengali, Pakistani, Nepalese (Hindu) and

Punjabi (Sikh), and had arisen during a discussion of the multi-faith evening.

The Sikh boy had played the part of Krishna in the Holi play. The reason for performing this had been obvious to him: 'Because it's the same religion as us', he had observed, to be countered by another member of the group, 'But I don't believe in the same religion', and explained by a third member of the group, 'It wouldn't be fair if only one religion had done it . . . because then they wouldn't learn about other people's religion.' In the first moments of coming together as a group they had already begun to explore and explain the purpose of the event. Throughout the ensuing discussion, they listened intently to each other as they exchanged experiences and points of view, often asking questions which moved the discussion into related areas that reached beyond simply accounting for the event, to speculating about the underlying issues. The Hindu boy, fairly newly arrived from Nepal, asked crucial questions at intervals throughout the discussion, which often provoked the others to question and try to explain some of the taken for granted aspects of their lives:

What is Mosque School?
Where is Mecca?
Did you go to Mecca?
Why don't we eat cow?
They eat cow?
What is the Koran?
Where is God?
Where is Heaven?

Sometimes, he made statements which, by their speculative nature, also pushed the discussion towards new boundaries.

'Miss, God is the, God is the Sun,' he says at one point, and then apparently having thought about this, interrupts a conversation about when people go to Mosque school and initiates a new train of thought:

RANJAN	Miss, I like God . . . because he is the one that gives you everything.
SUKJINDER	Miss, I think because he don't know much about his own God . . .
AZIZ	Miss there's only one God.
RESEARCHER	Do you think you all share the same God?
RANJAN	Yeah.
SUKJINDER	Yeah, Miss we believe in different kinds of things.
MAJID	We believe in different parts of it.

AZIZ	Every time we listen to, you know, prayer at the Mosque, we pray because we believe in different parts.

They may not seem to be paying much attention to the events of the multi-faith evening itself but to be exploring quite difficult, often abstract, ideas. As they talk together they seem to be looking at each other's religious differences and similarities from their own perspective. They discuss Krishna:

AZIZ	He is a king.
RANJAN	He is a god.
SUKJINDER	He is a god . . .
MAJID	God.
RANJAN	He comes from Nepal and India.
AZIZ	He is Hindu.
RANJAN	Yeah, Hindu, I am Hindu.
SUKJINDER	Not me, I am a Sikh.

Their talk, however, stems from their shared participation in the multi-faith event; the perceptions that emerge do so in the shared social activity of their discussion. As Bruner wrote:

> I have come increasingly to recognize that most learning in most settings is a communal activity, a sharing of the culture. It is not just that the child must make his knowledge his own, but that he must make it his own in a community of those who share his sense of belonging to a culture. It is this that leads me to emphasize not only discovery and invention but the importance of negotiating and sharing – in a word, of joint culture creating as an object of schooling and as an appropriate step *en route* to becoming a member of the adult society in which one lives out one's life.
>
> (Bruner 1986: 127)

8 Multicultural mathematics

A whole-school approach

One school provided a particularly good example of whole-school, collaborative teaching, incorporating a multicultural perspective. The school had an unusually balanced ethnic intake. There were seventy-nine children on the roll (September 1986); thirty-eight were white English, six of these coming from travellers' families; four were white and Italian in origin; thirty were from the New Commonwealth, including fourteen Indian, ten Bangladeshi, four West Indian, and two Pakistani; and five were children of mixed parentage.

The headteacher took the fourth-year class of 8/9-year-olds. She had three other class teachers (5-plus, 6-plus, and 7-plus). In addition, there was a full-time Section XI teacher and a teacher who had the responsibility for the travellers' and the mathematics' unit. Two mother tongue (Bengali and Punjabi) speakers helped with general activities, and mathematics, on a part-time basis. The size of the school, housed in a roomy building built in 1893, contributed to a family atmosphere and made possible some of the initiatives which were taking place there. There was a strong sense of multi-ethnic awareness and responsibility – and a respect for and acknowledgement of individual differences. The curriculum took children's ethnicity into account at all times.

The researcher's role was to become involved in the way the whole school met the challenge of cultural diversity. Her usefulness would depend on the extent to which she could maximize the potential for collaboration in the school and find ways of reflecting on the processes they were engaged in. The reflective teacher, 'one who constantly questions his or her own aims and actions, monitors practice and outcomes and considers the short-term and long-term effects upon each child' (Pollard and Tann 1987: 5) also needs a sounding-board or forum in which to question and to generalize; a research assistant on a semi-permanent or short-term basis could possibly provide support of this kind.

From the start, it was evident that the teachers were already engaged in ongoing action research, and that all of them were 'reflective'. As one of them wrote, 'I would say that active research describes what is happening here. It is a continuous ongoing process.' Communication in the school was highly developed; in the staffroom teachers readily discussed their ideas, sharing practical and strategic skills, constantly questioning and evaluating what they were doing. The small size of the school contributed to a continuous concern for professional development. In discussion, the Section XI teacher talked about the way the school promoted the exchange of practical and theoretical ideas:

> New ideas are welcomed, discussed, and encouraged. The staff, as a body, are supportive and are prepared to offer positive criticism and to support possible areas of expansion. Due to the flexibility of teaching methods and approaches, the children adapt readily to new ideas, provided the framework in which they are presented is secure and well structured.

Such confidence, enthusiasm, and openness made this an ideal environment for exploring teachers' ideas and approaches to multiculturalism in action.

THE PROJECT 'MATHEMATICS FOR ALL'

This chapter is an account of a collaborative enterprise based on observation and recording of everyday life in the school during a half-term project. This had been planned in response to parents' requests to know more about how mathematics was being taught. The staff had felt that they would not do justice to the way they worked at an evening meeting, as they wanted to show parents how the subject permeated every aspect of the curriculum. A half-term project would give them a chance to do this. Planning had involved selecting class topics which could be exploited for their mathematical potential. The fourth-year topic was 'Transport' and they were to work on space and shape. The third-year topic was 'The Jungle Book', and they would concentrate on multiplication. The second-year topic was 'Toys', and they would work on graphs. The Section XI and maths support teachers were to contribute in a number of ways, both with small groups and alongside the class teacher, and they produced some of the most imaginative resources and displays. For the youngest children in class 1, the topic was firmly located in their own everyday experience and was to prove a most exciting introduction to mathematics. As the document *Mathematics from 5–16* notes, 'The early stages of learning mathematics are of crucial importance ... when the early stages of learning are firmly established subsequent progress can take place much more quickly and confidently' (Department of Education and Science 1985: 36).

The researcher spent one day a week in the school for a term, and became involved in activities and conversations with the children and teachers as she collected material. In her report, written as a discussion document for the teachers, she documented the way stories, wall displays, and games were used to introduce and reinforce mathematical concepts in a cross-curricula approach. An account of some of the work undertaken by the reception class was written in collaboration with their teacher. It suggested how mathematics became the focal point for all activities. The teacher spoke of her belief that, for the youngest children, practical and everyday mathematics must be made meaningful. By the second week of term every child in her class had made, or been helped to make, a shoe-box-size house, covered in red paper, with chimneys, door, windows and the child's name stuck on. The two travellers' children in this class had been helped to make a trailer site with trailers, outhouses, and a fence. The houses stood in a double row in the hall outside their classroom, and a 'road' which children could walk down ran between them. It was marked with numbered squares ready for a dice game. Outside each house were the children's families, small card figures some of which had authentic turbans. During the weeks of the project more detail was added, such as a church, drawings, writing, and worksheets. Everything could be handled and moved, as this was essentially a game and invited participation.

Two 5-year-olds, Paul and Dalbir, were recorded as they played this game, observed by their teacher:

PAUL — You have some people and you throw a dice and if you get a six you go, one, two, three, four, five, six . . . then another person has a go, then it's back to the first person.

TEACHER — Is the person who gets to the end first the winner?

DALBIR — No, someone else can 'cause they can take over and if you go to the sweet shop you have to go all the way back and go to the dentist.

Their teacher explained that it was important for the children to walk down the squares themselves rather than move counters or models. At this stage, she felt that as children often have trouble with the physical representation of numbers, moving from square to square as they count helps to develop their sense of progression and linearity, and turns an abstract concept into a real experience; and as they throw the dice, they develop an understanding of probability. She had created this game in response to the actual needs of a particular group of children, believing that the teaching of mathematical concepts should start 'near to heart', in the home and the family.

She described how a course she was taking at London University had opened her eyes to the greater diversity and potential of practical activities which relate to the children's own experience. The idea for the street grew from this; 'I just thought, well, start off with something that's very meaningful to them, really . . . I didn't think it was going to be quite so big as it is, then gradually, I sort of adapted it to meet the mathematical needs of the children . . . they all seemed to like their little families . . . I didn't really force it on them, they enjoyed doing it.' She felt the 'little people' were part of the hidden curriculum, much as the travellers' trailer site was for the two travellers in the class. The travellers' children had been helped to make the site by their special teacher, and it had become a focal point for all the travellers in the school. Traveller mothers collecting children gathered near it and explained that the permanent buildings on the site were not 'sheds' but 'chalets'. The older children found it reassuring too. 'One day, it was during the dinner time . . . and these travellers don't like going out to play, there was Rene, sitting with her legs crossed, just beside it and there was a book about travellers' children and she was sitting there . . . reading the book.' Much influenced by her course and the work of Margaret Donaldson (1978), the teacher saw the street as real mathematics, 'You've got to translate from the child's experience and everything's got to be meaningful . . . that was really what made me think we've got to do something that's very relative to the child.'

Every child in the class could therefore find a point of reference in the street: the pub, the sweet shop, and the dentist were all part of their recognizable local community. Talking about it, Paul and Dalbir were using the language of mathematics as part of their normal discourse:

DALBIR	My house is near the sweet shop, just next to it.
TEACHER	Who lives there?
PAUL	Hundreds of people.
DALBIR	No not a hundred . . . twelve.
TEACHER	There's you?
DALBIR	Yeah.
PAUL	And his brother, and his baby brother and his sister.
DALBIR	How do you know . . . cause I told you, did I?
PAUL	And I saw your paper brother. (*The model he had made.*)
TEACHER	Who else is in your home?
PAUL	His grandad and his grandma.

DALBIR And my other grandad, I've got two grandads, um, my uncle and my other uncle, my dad and my mum . . . I got four uncles. That's all I know.

Using the street

> Conceptual understanding is more effectively developed through the use of mathematics in a variety of contexts . . . practical tasks or activities.
>
> (Department of Education and Science 1985: 17)

The early mathematical concepts illustrated in the dialogue between two 5-year-olds bear out their teacher's hypothesis that children make the transition to theory from real-life experience. These concepts are developed in the worksheets which she has designed to accompany the street. The first of these asked the children to count how many people lived in each house and to write these down, first as tally marks, and then as numerals. It listed the houses: Paul's House IIII 4; Motivr's house———. All the children had to do was to locate the house and count the people outside. A parallel worksheet asked them to find out who lived at a particular number. This time they had to match numbers and copy the names: ——— lives in number 9. Some involved more complex reading skills, but similar activities. They were asked how many people lived in a house, and had to record it as a numeral: ——— live in Michelle's pub; ——— live in Taleb's house. A more advanced worksheet dealt with the ordinal values. This one was not so easy for some children. Their teacher felt, 'It's quite difficult, particularly for some children whose . . . English is a second language. Very difficult for some, so you need lots of practice with it and practice in lots of ways other than this.' Evidence of this practice going on was visible in the classroom and on the walls of the hall – items and pictures labelled '1st', '2nd', '3rd' to teach the concept of ordinal numbers.

On the worksheet the children had to be able to recognize and use ordinal numbers in order to fill in the appropriate names: ——— lives in the 8th house/2nd house/5th house etc. Not many of class 1 were ready for this yet. Afterwards, when we were discussing the worksheets, the teacher felt, 'This is not a very good sheet because when I tried it out on the children there's too much questioning on one sheet, I should have had single strips, it's too difficult for little children.' But this was part of the teacher's learning process; 'Until you try things you don't know whether it will work. It's part of your training and finding out.'

The next worksheet involved counting on: 'I stop at Filomena's house and I go on three houses. What house do I come to? 6 count on 3 is ———

house'. The teacher commented, 'That's counting on . . . they could stand on 7, or put one of those little people on and count on two more, where do you land? number 9. This is a challenging one, it's a refinement of adding up really. It's a step they learn but it was nice with those people and them actually standing on the road, which is very meaningful.' At the time only two of the class could confidently do this, but most of them were managing the other worksheets. Even when they involved quite a lot of reading, children worked out ways to do them. 'They can look at the first letter and do a bit of deduction,' their teacher felt.

Making worksheets to suit particular groups of children at particular times and in particular contexts was something that all the staff were doing throughout the half-term of the project. On the activities afternoon at the project there were folders of worksheets to show parents the kind of material the children had used to reinforce work on capacity, number, money co-ordinates, time, and weight. However, it is typical of the very careful thought that had gone into the presentation of their approach to mathematics teaching that the teachers had ensured worksheets should be seen in the context of their use. Besides a display of different kinds of equipment used for measuring and accompanying worksheets, there was a warning note:

> The worksheets show how mathematics topics develop across the levels. The sheets are just a part of the work achieved. They are preceded and accompanied throughout by many and varied practical experiences. Only when these experiences become meaningful will a child tackle the appropriate sheet.

The advantage of this approach, particularly with the very youngest children, is the freedom and flexibility this gives teachers to try out and to adapt worksheets to suit individual needs. The street worksheets had not all been successful. Next time they could be different: 'They'd be a bit simpler, not so much on them.' The street could be different too, responsive to a different group of children, 'There might be special experiences that could crop up, that makes it more meaningful . . . you don't know what's going to happen. There might be more reading on it another time, it's what's needed at the time. I did use it for one of the slow groups. I put some writing on it, I used it for one of those groups that's very slow and needs a structured approach. It just depends on the children's needs really.' As HMI suggest, 'The value of an activity is that the differentiation is determined largely by the abilities of the pupils and their achievements within the activity itself and is not pre-determined by the teacher' (Department of Education and Science 1985: 28). Moreover, throughout the mathematics project, use was made of a wide range of resources and activities so that all areas of the curriculum were involved.

The use of story to introduce and reinforce mathematical concepts

Throughout the school, story is used as the basis for a great deal of cross-curricula work. During the project stories were used extensively. The story of *The Gingerbread Man* had begun as a third-year assembly and was subsequently used for multiplication activity to calculate the number of legs in the story's chase! As HMI suggest, 'at all stages the teacher needs to stress the translation of words into mathematical symbols' (ibid: 10). In class 2's room there was a mathematics story:

> One day a toymaker came to work. '*What can I make today*'? she said.
> If she has 10 eyes she can make 5 teddies because 5(2) → 10
> If she has 16 wheels she can make 2 pairs of roller skates. 2 (8) → 16 and 2(4) → 8.
> If she has 14 big wheels, can she make 4 trains?
> Does 4 (4) → 14?
> What if she had 15 eyes?

Stories like this, and class 3's 'spider maths tell us the story of eight', where sets of spiders illustrate the eight times table, seem to be doing this. For the younger children there were 'taking away stories':

> A farmer had 5 hens.
> He sold 2.
> How many had he left?
> Write the number in a sentence.
> 5-2 → 3

Other stories that were used for all kinds of mathematical work were *The Fantastic Mr Fox, The Very Hungry Caterpillar*, and *The Jungle Book*. Class 1's street topic was another story, the story of the children themselves: 'The most meaningful thing to them at that particular point in time; it's what they're interested in, they're not really interested in anyone else but themselves or their friends and family'.

> TEACHER Who lives in your house, Paul?
> PAUL Me, my sister, my mummy and my daddy.
> DALBIR I've got more families than you . . . I've got two cars.
> PAUL I've got *no* cars.

Later on in the term many of class 1 had to visit the dentist at the local clinic. This inspired another mathematics event, and another story. 'There were a whole lot of them needing dental treatment . . . you might as well use what they're interested in.' A dental surgery was set up complete with an anglepoise lamp, a bowl and beakers, towels and mirrors – all the equipment for looking into people's mouths. In the mornings before school and at various times during the day, children sat in the 'waiting room' nearby, the 'receptionist' made appointments, and a 'dentist' in a white coat examined teeth. The role play was impressive, the mathematics an unexpected bonus. As their teacher said, 'I mean that dentist was all mathematics, there was loads of mathematics in that.' Worksheets with sets of teeth were used for addition, one for one correspondence, for matching and tallying. The children recorded their own teeth on tally charts; for instance, zero = no fillings. Bad teeth were filled in on a worksheet specially designed for this purpose. 'There was a game I devised with dice . . . for addition you threw a dice and if it landed on 3 you drew in three bad teeth and then you threw the dice for the bottom teeth and then you said "How many bad teeth has that person got?" and counted them up, so it was real addition in a meaningful way. There was a zero on the dice which was useful, and just small numbers, so they didn't go high because it was just the beginning of addition.'

While all this was going on, some of class 1 were also working with the Section XI teacher using Eric Carle's story *The Very Hungry Caterpillar* to reinforce their understanding of sets. Their work displayed in the hall involved all passers-by. It asked, 'Can you find a set of long, wide caterpillars? A set of short, wide caterpillars?' The story was also being used to reinforce the work the class was doing on ordinal numbers. As their teacher said, 'You need lots of practice, and to practise in lots of ways', and happily this story provided material for this sort of practice, first the very hungry caterpillar eats one apple; second, two pears; third, three plums; fourth, four strawberries, and so on. Apples, pears and plums were grouped in sets and in the classroom John Burningham's story *The Shopping Basket* developed the theme with the contents of the basket on display: one packet of crisps, two doughnuts, three oranges, up to six eggs. Mathematics is an abstract subject and yet class 1 were experiencing it as tangible and visually present, and in terms they could understand. This seems to be in accordance with the recommendation that, 'Whatever the age or ability of the pupils, the [mathematics] content should not be a collection of unconnected items. Instead it should be designed as a structure in which the various parts relate together coherently . . . a whole network of relationships' (Department of Education and Science 1985: 29).

The use of wall displays to introduce and reinforce mathematical concepts

The Very Hungry Caterpillar display was typical of the way displays were being used. Their purpose was not to illustrate the end product of an activity, but to initiate further activity. There were interactive displays which could be used by other classes, groups, or individuals. *The Jungle Book* mural in the entrance foyer was one of these, incorporating a number of tasks at different levels – measuring, counting, and using the pictures. Questions asked children to count the animals' legs and ears, others involved multiplication: '4 monkeys have 4 legs, how many legs altogether?' The answers were under a flap: 'Are you right? Lift to find out.' The Jungle Book theme originated in the BBC's *Time and Tune* television programme, which was being used for dance and drama work during the project.

The second-year's topic was based on *The Fantastic Mr Fox*, by Roald Dahl. This provided work in addition and subtraction. Numerous worksheets were based on the activities of Farmers Boggis and Bunce and Mr Fox. Mr Fox's theft of hens, ducks, and geese was simple subtraction:

Farmer Boggis had 4 hens.
But Farmer Bunce had 2
4 take away 2 leaves:

Farmer Bunce had 3 geese.
But Fantastic Mr Fox ate 1.

These exercises were repeated in many ways, the cards having simple illustrations to help the children visualize the hens, ducks, and geese. Another activity explored the idea of holes: 'Mr Fox lives in a hole called a den.' The children used a workcard to help them collect and sort things with holes in them:

Holes to put things in.
Holes for things to go through.
Holes that separate things.

The examples were a jug, a keyhole, and a sieve, but many other items were displayed: shells, spoons, buttons, a funnel, a length of pipe, a tube, and a bucket for children to handle and talk about.

These examples illustrate only a few of the ways in which stories were found to yield mathematical dividends. Not only did they provide resources for the development of particular skills but they contributed to the children's linguistic and narrative experience.

THE USE OF GAMES TO INTRODUCE AND REINFORCE MATHEMATICAL CONCEPTS

> Mathematics must be an experience from which pupils derive pleasure and enjoyment.
>
> (Department of Education and Science 1985:7)

While stories offered a framework for different activities, games provided an opportunity to put theory into practice. From Class 1 to 4 they had an important role. By the third and fourth year the children were inventing games of their own. Suresh, a fourth-year pupil, made a complex three dimensional game which would help him to remember the names of geometric shapes in two and three dimensions. Annette and Laura, third-year pupils, had constructed a fish tank out of card and tissue paper and filled it with numbered felt fish and the symbols required to make sums. They made their own sums on the carpet:

ANNETTE Fish four.
LAURA And now you've gotta try and catch a sign as well.
ANNETTE No you don't have to.
LAURA I'm going to catch another fish to make this sum.
ANNETTE I'm catching a little fish – Ah yah!
LAURA I'm trying to catch the big fish. Ah now look what you've done.
ANNETTE This is good.
LAURA It's good when you don't have your fishing lines tangled up . . . oh dear . . . done it, done it again.
ANNETTE Oh dear . . . done it, done it again.
LAURA I'm trying to get number two, number, number, number two. There's two twos.
ANNETTE Do you know how to do your two times table?
LAURA Any day! one, two, three, four . . .
ANNETTE No! Two times table.
LAURA Two, four, six, eight, ten.
ANNETTE No! Not that.
LAURA What?
ANNETTE I mean one twos two, two twos four, three twos six, four twos eight, *those*, do you know how to do those?
LAURA Yes.
ANNETTE Easy isn't it. Do you know how to do your eleven times table?

LAURA	No. Ooh, caught a fish. What the number of your fish?
ANNETTE	That was two . . . all right – so that's four add two, six. There isn't a six though.
LAURA	No you have to – there is some outside, there's a number six for you, that big long one. Ow, I got it! This is the one I made.

This is a recording of spontaneous play, they were not aware of the tape recorder and were completely engrossed in the game. It is interesting to notice how Laura's casual remark, 'There's two twos', moves their attention from their 'sums', simple addition, to multiplication, the third-year topic. There are several things going on at once. They are playing a game they have made themselves and feel that they own. They are using numbers and signs to make sums. They are sharing recently acquired mathematical skills and knowledge. The game is a shared, collaborative activity in which they do not compete with each other but help each other. 'Any sixes hanging around in there?' One of them was making a long sum; 'We're both battling to get a six,' she says. 'I know how to make it easier for both of us,' says the other. 'It makes it funner.' They are learning social as well as mathematical skills and fulfilling another of the aims outlined in *Mathematics from 5–16*, that the subject should be interactive, less of a solitary experience: 'Collaborative activities contribute to the mathematical development of the pupils through the thinking, discussion and mutual refinement of ideas'(Department of Education and Science 1985: 6).

Two fourth-years had made a board game: a funfair with roundabouts and rollercoasters. They explained how the players spin a pointer to discover how many moves they can make. Some squares say 'Pick up a card.' These have instructions like, 'You are on a merry-go-round. Miss a go.' Many of the fourth-years designed and produced games like this one. The planning and production of these involved language, design, and mathematical skills. The end product in every case had been the result of considerable collaborative effort.

Games out of doors and in PE also became mathematical. Circles numbered 1–4 were drawn on the playground, and the first two children to reach the number called out won each round. This was made harder as the numbers were not always called out in English. Suresh explained:

SURESH	Then I done it in Indian.
KATE	We weren't even told before, we had to guess.
SURESH	No! They were all standing and Meena, Sheila and Mohibor just ran . . . I can count up to ten in Indian.

Consolidation and practice

During the project all the children also worked individually every day. The fourth-years were a splendid demonstration of the Cockcroft Report's (1982) belief that mathematics should be taught 'little and often' (Cockroft 1982). Whenever they were offered a choice of activities, usually at least once a day, they tended to choose to use their Nuffield Mathematics workbooks. This structured approach allowed them to work individually, developing and reinforcing basic skills at their own pace. They often chose to work with someone at the same stage, so that they could consult each other, share apparatus or request assistance. Much remedial teaching was possible at these times – for all children, at whatever stage they had reached.

During the half term the fourth-year also undertook a number of class topics. Kate and Suresh talked about this.

KATE	We did loads of fractions.

Suresh cut a square of sticky paper into a hundred triangles. He and Kate did measuring, learning the approximate nature of all measurement and the importance of estimation:

KATE	We did dinosaurs. We measured that out in the hall. A 15 metre one is about nine James's long – we measured it in people.

They also measured a wall notice board in 'paces' and 'children'. It was $8^1/_2$ paces, or nearly four children. They did graphs to show how children travelled to school and, using the computer, they used the data they had collected to make up mathematical questions of their own.

KATE	People did some bits on the computer and so we did our graphs out and made them look extremely nice.

The television programme *Junior Maths* had stimulated work using tracing paper to make overlapping shapes:

KATE	We got a square of tracing paper, or two squares, we cut it in half or cut it so it was quarters and then we moved them round to make a sort of picture.
SURESH	Overlapping picture.

They described some of the pictures people had made and explained, 'Everything has to overlap, doesn't it, to connect on really . . . it was looking at the overlaps, that's why.' There were large and 'tiny triangles' and where the paper overlapped it looked darker because there were two pieces of paper. They also made patterns using the overhead projector to enlarge small grids made by pin holes in paper. As *Mathematics from 5–16* (Department of Education and Science 1985: 20) suggests, children should be encouraged to look for patterns which can often produce interesting visual effects.

An ongoing practical activity for the fourth-years was the daily recording of dinner numbers. A detailed breakdown by class was on the wall of an entrance foyer. Two children were responsible for collecting, displaying, and calculating totals:

KATE Every day it's me and Suresh, we're the secretaries this week, so we have to go and change the bits round, so we're trying to work out how many people come each day – having hot dinner or packed lunch, and how many people go in the dining hall.

SURESH Mrs McCarthy gave us the numbers so we have to write the numbers and put them on – add the numbers all together, except for the packed lunch, and put the packed lunch numbers – then we add all the total up.

KATE There are seventy there in the dining hall today, 'cause we got all the numbers written out – fifty-four hot dinners and sixteen packed lunches, different classes have different amounts. There's always less packed lunches than hot dinners.

It was also their job to write out the menu for the day.

An activity afternoon for parents and children

Parents and younger brothers and sisters arriving through either door that afternoon could see examples of ongoing work, the recording of school dinners on one side, *The Jungle Book* mural inviting them to stop and participate on the other. Both were examples of the way the school drew equally effectively on everyday experience and imaginative fiction as resources for mathematics. The hall was full of exhibitions to look at and activities to participate in. An overhead projector magnified solid shapes on the screen, passers-by could shift them and make patterns. The computer was in constant use. Graphs everywhere recorded real experience as data, the colour of clothes, chest expansion, methods of transport. Parents could make their own graph to show the frequency of certain words in a text.

Class 2 had made a day clock to help them learn the time and another to show daily weather.

A group of class 1 children were sorting dolls' clothes, putting them in sets and then washing and hanging them out to dry. Each child chose different garments, and washed and pegged them on a line while a teacher sang a nursery rhyme, 'Sophie was in the garden hanging out the clothes when down came a seagull and pecked off her nose', jokingly showing the children their noses between her fingers and seriously offering parents a model for the kind of home activity which can become a learning experience. On a table nearby children and parents could use pastry cutters to make different shapes in play dough. Some of class 1 were playing the dice game on their street. Later, the younger brothers and sisters would have a small sports day with potato and spoon races, cheered on by the bigger children as they learned about being first, second, and third.

Stuck on the hall floor at one end were various lengths and all kinds of measuring equipment. There were suggestions as to how these could be used: 'See how many footprints measure a metre stick.' 'Now measure a metre stick in handspans.' The third-years' work on *The Gingerbread Man* was displayed; work cards and games showed many different ways in which children can learn about the concept of place value, whereby houses could be added to roads, windows to houses, spoons and eggs put into boxes. On the floor, honeycomb mosaics could be turned into intricate designs by children and parents as they passed. A mixed-age group played a board game, throwing the dice to see which number house or trailer the cardboard postman could deliver a letter to. In the mathematics room people could weigh pots of sand, marbles, beans, and lentils or try out any of the *Fantastic Mr Fox* problems which covered the walls. In every classroom there were very detailed displays of the work the children had been doing throughout the term. The second-year work on 'Mandy's toy shop' had used multi-ethnic toys borrowed from the Multicultural Education Resource Centre. The toys had been weighed in bottle tops: 'The Jamaican doll balances 24 bottle tops'; 'The Chinese clown balances 17 bottle tops'.

Parents seemed impressed by the activity and were asking questions. Class 1 ended the day by acting out the story of *The Wolf and the Six Little Kids*.

EVALUATION

All of the above was included in the report, which was entitled *Mathematics for All*. It included an evaluation of the project by the teachers themselves in response to a short questionnaire prepared by the headteacher. All the teachers felt it had increased their awareness of mathematical possibilities in many areas, and of cross-curricula links arising from a mathematical theme. It had given the subject a higher status, and had increased their interest. It had helped them to define aims and objectives and all felt they had learned from each other.

As far as the children were concerned, the teachers felt that it had also helped them to recognize the mathematical aspects of different things. They seemed to become more aware of why they were doing things and began to understand the mathematical purpose behind the games they played. It had become fun and they began to be able to talk about what they were doing and presenting. The quality of presentation also seemed to have improved. For the younger children, the project had been very child-centred and at the same time very unthreatening and pleasurable.

Everyone felt that it had had a considerable effect on the general ambience of mathematics in the school. There was an increased and much-improved use of display as teaching and learning material, and much more consideration of multicultural development. It had promoted discussion among the staff as ideas were thrown around, added to, and polished up. Thinking about the mathematical potential of any topic became second nature. Everyone valued the sharing of work experiences throughout the school – there was a feeling of 'team spirit' between staff and pupils.

It seemed that all these effects continued after the project. The subject had become less of a mystery for everyone. Since they had all been learning from each other, staff had become more aware of what different age-groups were doing. The experience was remembered by the children, who seemed to be reapplying the knowledge and skills they learned during the project. Everyone recognized the value of practical everyday mathematics as portrayed by the displays and demonstrations, and parents' comments show that they too had a better understanding of the feeling of the subject.

A collective view

Once the report had been read by the staff, it generated a great deal of discussion. Various issues were raised. One of the teachers, who was currently attending the LEA Section XI training course, questioned how far it had been an example of multicultural mathematics in action. She pointed out that this was crucial since this is a school in which children are positively encouraged to share aspects of their different ethnic backgrounds, and where the stated aims include 'an awareness of the value of the multicultural nature of society' and of 'the value of multi-sensory, multilingual, multicultural cross-curriculum studies'.

In subsequent discussion the staff seemed particularly aware of the problems of a second language when they are communicating mathematical concepts and of the danger of assuming that the subject is a-cultural. They talked about the way it is heavily dependent on visual perception and visual aids, both of which can also be heavily culture-bound.

Encouraging teacher reflectivity

The report had provided a chance for them to reflect on their recent practice. During the summer term we held a staff meeting to discuss the report. The researchers raised a number of questions. Had there been an evaluation of the pupils' learning? Could the multicultural aspects have been brought out more strongly? Could we detect differences between boys' and girls', and different ethnic groups', experiences during the project. One of the teachers volunteered to explore these issues. In a written response she said:

> The paper 'Mathematics for All' is illustrated with examples from most sub-areas of mathematics and also from all age groups within the school. This was not a blow-by-blow account of how to teach or how to learn each area of mathematics. The school's aim was more to show the ethos and methodology behind maths-learning at the school, and I think the paper reflects this.
>
> The paper is very readable and, I think, communicates the driving ideas behind our mathematics – child-centred, skills and concepts interrelate, maths is fun, maths is practical and then expressed abstractly. These can be used as general guides in any area.

Considering whether we had looked at attitudes and expectations, she replied:

> Within the school there was no formal discussion of this at the outset; our aim was to communicate the best of what we do in maths to parents.
>
> As the half-term progressed there was some comment on 'attitude' to mathematics (both teachers' and childrens'). Mainly that the topic had made attitudes generally more positive. However, there was no thoughtful assessment of differences of attainment, attitude, approach to mathematics, of different groups of children.

The paper did touch on the area of attitudes and expectations but perhaps did not make this explicit. In her response she attempted to do this:

1 Work in maths should be at the child's level, child-centred in content, non-threatening – does this imply that we expect no more

of children than they have already proved? – By taking account of children's mother tongue cultural backgrounds are we expecting less? I thought the section on multicultural maths was very pertinent.

2 Children's attitude to maths is modelled by teaching methods, e.g. whether maths is about getting the answers right, or whether maths is about solving problems.

> Within the school, evaluation of children's (mathematical) learning is tackled in various ways. Probably slightly different at different ages.
>
> The most important element is knowing the children very well and closely observing them at work. R (one of her colleagues) is brilliant at this and I think this is probably the only way with such young children.

The report contained some tape transcript of children at work, with some analysis by the researcher. She commented on the usefulness of these extracts;

> Reporting comments from children as well shows that they have a sharing investigative attitude to maths. They analyse their own learning.
>
> If work has already been done on mathematics attainment by girls and ethnic groups I feel we could benefit by looking at this. I know there are statistics that show that certain groups in the general population have low or high attainment.
>
> To answer the question 'Were there any differences between boys' and girls', and different ethnic groups' experiences?' I'm sure there were, because although all children had access to all physical elements of the project, work is planned to meet what we hope are the immediate needs of individual children. Therefore a child who (for example) speaks no English would be offered different tasks to one who had a vast English vocabulary. Similarly I (at least) try to plan activities for a group dominated by boys in a traditionally girlish field and vice versa, e.g. boys dress dolls, girls build with lego.
>
> So we evaluate children's learning by maybe asking them a question in a different way e.g. children doing 'take-away': 'I've got 7 pens, you've only got 3. How many more have I got?'
>
> The paper shows how children talking express their understanding. Dalbir's reply [see page 173] didn't really answer the question but shows great understanding of sequencing.

> Talking to R about the worksheets she made shows how working closely with children reveals gaps in understanding. Listening to Laura and Annette (see page 180–1) shows Annette does really understand tables (or has some externally applied idea about them!). Two, four, six, eight, ten is the two-times table but Annette doesn't recognize it.

Her response to this report which had been shared and discussed by all the staff indicates the extent to which the teachers were prepared to become collaborators in the research. Both at the level of the whole-school project and in the day-to-day activities of school life, they were all always keen to discuss and evaluate their experience. The extent to which a researcher could play a useful role depended on looking out for shared concerns or particular interests, and discussing any leads which might be followed, so that the teachers could have a chance to stand back and look at what they were doing.

Reflections on collaboration

Recording and discussing the mathematics project had been a beginning. Later in the year the staff were asked to comment on aspects of the year's collaborative research and to reflect on how it had contributed to their thinking and practice. They all felt that the school was generally engaged in a process of action research. There was a framework for this kind of collaboration provided by regular curriculum and general staff meetings. The presence of a part-time researcher had also contributed to this. As one person put it, 'All teachers here, whether working individually or on a collaborative staff basis, are constantly engaged in up-dating, consolidating, and assessing their teaching strategies and techniques.' Everyone seemed to agree that the school was a good place to talk about and try out practical and theoretical ideas. This was in part due, they felt, to the small size of the school:

> Practical research is easily implemented because it is a small school. The pupil–teacher ratio and support teaching enables class teachers to structure more individual group work with classes. The general ambience and work style of the school facilitates practical work, all theoretical ideas on varying aspects of the school curriculum are shared and are discussed readily.

Generally, they felt that the exchange of theoretical ideas was promoted by input from the different courses that most of them were or had been attending; they cherished the freedom to investigate and explore their new ideas, only wishing there was more time to share ideas about day-to-day classroom practices. Sharing ideas with colleagues was seen as crucial. As one put it, 'the positive way in which this is done is probably what I value most working here. I value the insight my colleagues give me immensely. They also give me positive feedback to my experiences.' Another added, 'I always feel completely relaxed with everyone on our staff and, consequently, I feel that I am always able to discuss, share, suggest, and enquire about any aspects of my classroom and curricular practices. Everyone is always very supportive and professional.'

What had started out as an exploration of multicultural issues was moving towards looking at the different ways in which staff relationships were making this possible. We were becoming aware of the 'organizational culture' (Nias 1988: 86) of the school, the jointly held beliefs and values of the teachers. What was emerging was evidence of a 'culture of collaboration' (Nias 1988: 86), which enabled them to work in the way they did.

9 'Living and growing'

Developing a multicultural perspective in a Church of England junior school

IMPLEMENTING CHANGE

This chapter is based on one school's experience of implementing a multicultural policy. It is of particular interest as the school was virtually all white. Multicultural education in all-white schools is a topic of some concern. Most local authorities, have produced policy statements which urge schools to engage in fundamental change, in recognition of the fact that 'the problem facing the education system is not how to educate children of ethnic minorities but how to educate *all* children' (Swann Report 1985: 363).

Parkside, a Church of England endowed junior school in a small English East Midlands town, had received the County Council's *aide-mémoire* on multicultural education, a worthy but wordy document that used phrases like, 'the curriculum must take into account the fact that...' 'the curriculum should be designed at every stage to promote racial harmony between those of different races, cultures and creeds', 'positive strategies should be employed in order to instil attitudes of tolerance'. The discussion guidelines, which were intended to help teachers to develop a curriculum which reflected the needs of a pluralistic society, asked a series of questions which seemed to threaten rather than assist 'teachers about to embark on curriculum change'. Questions like, 'What steps has the school taken to discuss in depth its aims and objectives in developing a multicultural perspective in the curriculum?' seemed to be asking teachers to undertake a rigorous scrutiny of their own value systems in order to decide which side they were on in the area of multicultural and anti-racist education. They were being asked to change their behaviour and practice and to question taken-for-granted assumptions, often on the basis of very generalized statements from their LEAs and advisers. While they might not disagree with the rhetoric, they were unlikely to find it helpful in planning appropriate curricula.

Like all schools, Parkside had its own framework of values and beliefs, its 'institutional bias' (Pollard 1985). The negotiated and shared order within the school was not immune to outside influence, but it would significantly influence any action on the part of the teachers. The headteacher realized that a multicultural curriculum could not be imposed from outside but would have to be constructed in collaboration with the teachers. He also believed that LEA pressure would be less effective than learning through doing. If the teachers in this monoethnic school were to be persuaded to develop a multicultural dimension to their work, then challenging their self-concepts and personal value systems at this stage was likely to be counter-productive. Parkside, in common with most primary schools, faced increasing class sizes, diminishing resources, and a barrage of new edicts from government. The headteacher might have been forgiven for filing away the *aide-mémoire* from County Hall and carrying on as usual, but instead he responded to a letter in the bulletin outlining our project, and invited a researcher into the school to monitor and report back to the staff on the extent to which the school's multicultural aims and objectives were being carried through.

Although only 2 per cent of the children at the school came from different ethnic backgrounds, the town itself had a sizeable minority. Two of the staff, the headteacher and the deputy, had attended multicultural courses; there had been visits from the Multicultural Education Support Team, and ways of developing a multicultural perspective had been considered. A structure already existed. Each term both the upper and lower school classes undertook a major topic in Social and Environmental Studies (SES). This topic generated starting points for other subjects: art, craft, music, religious education, language, mathematics. The teachers were used to working together to prepare and teach an integrated programme around a common theme. In the spring term the topic would be 'Living and growing'; for the third- and fourth-years, 9- to 11-year-olds, this would involve a study of evolution, adaptation, and change. The headteacher felt that this particularly lent itself to a consideration of different lifestyles and cultures. Our aim, then, was not to comment on the structure, content, and methodology of the project, but to try to provide a range of illustrative material drawn from observation and talk with participants during the course of the term. This would provide the starting point for a discussion by the staff on the extent to which the 'Living and growing' project had provided a framework for dealing with multicultural issues.

When we first met the headteacher in November the project was at the planning stage. The third- and fourth-years, who were taught together in three groups of about 30 children were going to study evolution and adaptation in three different climatic regions: hot and wet, hot and dry, cold and dry. The headteacher had seen an existing structure, the school's termly environmental studies topic, as an appropriate way to approach multicultural studies. There had obviously been some discussion and the two teaching teams, in conjunction with the special needs co-ordinator, were producing detailed plans, or 'forecasts', for the topic and all related curriculum areas. These would outline the concepts to be developed, the range of skills involved, the content, resources, organization, and links with the main topic. Everyone would work within this tightly organized framework. The teachers would also keep a 'precise log' in the 'continuity file'.

The headteacher felt that the teachers were good at integrating art, craft, and design into a topic in progress and at devising related assembly topics. He thought that they found it harder to incorporate other curriculum areas, particularly mathematics, science, and the reading scheme (Ginn 360), feeling that 'they had not conceptualized the absorption of maths and reading into topic work.' However, he recognized that this was in part reluctance to relinquish tried teaching skills and strategies in exchange for the unknown.

The organization of the topic seemed unproblematic, but he seemed uneasy about the multicultural input. He himself recognized that the emphasis should be on 'drawing out similarities' but feared that the topic could lead to looking at 'primitive tribes' and 'exotic groups'. He hinted that he had found 'justifying multicultural studies' difficult, religion in a Church of England school being 'the main thorny problem' among the staff. He had talked to the staff, to parents, and to governors about multiculturalism in the controlled school and a working party had been set up to discuss this. Parkside, in fact, is not in the parish of a particular church and has only a small handful of church goers; however there was a strong Christian ethos and links with the Church were in evidence.

AIMS AND OBJECTIVES

The teachers' commitment to the topic was considerable. Not only had they given up much time in preparing and planning the content, in the form of extended forecasts for each subject area, they had spent the holiday period visiting the resources centre and libraries to collect appropriate material. In each area the children were going to study animals, plants, and people. All work would finally be contained in large topic folders. The first SES lessons at the start of the project were spent making covers, each one in colours or materials reflecting the area to be studied. A great deal of attention was paid to presentation throughout the topic; classrooms were transformed into tropical forest, desert and arctic areas:

NICK	We've got cactus, well half of the room has got desert things.
CHRIS	We put things up in Mr Rogers' room.
CAROLINE	It's got some polar bears.
CHRIS	And some ice.
MARION	It's got an . . . cave sort of thing.
CHRIS	I've forgotten what it's called . . . an igloo entrance.
MARION	In Mr Rogers' room, I think it's supposed to remember the North Pole.

The topic forecasts were very detailed and seemed to aim to cover a great deal of ground. The multicultural aims expressed good intentions in a rather general way:

> We shall be looking closely at the human population – how they are governed – their rules for living. Within this aspect we hope to exploit particular multicultural opportunities – looking at different cultures, ways of life etc. and where possible including an appreciation of local/national customs and festivals . . .

This theme, which ran through the term's work, was picked up in other forecasts:

RE	To consider and understand the similarities and differences between their own way of life (culture) and that of others. To be able to emphasise and draw comparisons with and between other ways of life and their own.
MUSIC	Similarities and differences between music from different cultures.
CREATIVE	An in-depth look at the artistic expression of indigenous and immigrant cultures.

These objectives were perhaps inadequately thought out. There was no attempt to suggest how they would be able to 'look closely', nor to define what might be involved in exploring 'multicultural opportunities'. This is the rhetoric of the policy-makers and did not sit easily beside the more practical suggestions contained in the forecasts. A warning note was sounded in the main topic forecast: 'By the nature of this topic much of the content will be second- or third-hand and will therefore entail much investigative research.' This suggested that the children's experience of different cultures would only be as good as the books, films, videos, and the teachers' own knowledge and attitudes permitted it to be. As dealing with multicultural issues might involve a change of consciousness, we were particularly interested in how the children themselves recognized and understood these concepts, in their response to the term's work. The researcher talked to a small group of children on a regular basis, as well as looking at a wider range of written work in both factual and imaginative genres. A great deal of material was collected which could be used in a number of ways. For example, there were many examples of the children's growing confidence in handling factual information about the areas they were studying. By the end of each half-term's work they seemed to have acquired an impressive range of detailed information, which was the result of using well-organized research procedures and drawing on a variety of resources.

In the report prepared for the teachers, however, examples were used selectively to see whether there was any evidence to suggest that they were aware or becoming more aware of cultural differences. The study of people was likely to be the most difficult, and at half-term one of the teachers confirmed this. Finding out about plants and animals, and understanding their evolution and adaptation to different climatic conditions had been straightforward; understanding different cultures had not:

> I tried to get from them the idea that each group of people had their own special way of living that was best suited to the conditions they found themselves in, and that even though it may seem strange to us there were sensible reasons for it. I also pointed out that our way of living would be strange to them even though it was natural to us.

At the start of the project this teacher had felt that an understanding of their own way of life should underpin any consideration of cultural differences. She and her class had discussed the unwritten rules of home and school. Understanding their own responsibilities and rules for living would be the basis for looking at different religions. She hoped 'to find similarities between the rules and the reasons for some of them; also to discover that different circumstances may require different rules.' Later on in her half-term report she wrote:

> The groups studying plants and animals found their work on the whole easier than those studying people as they only had to deal with facts, whereas those studying people had to try to envisage their life-style and find out about traditions and rules for living that were not always written down in an obvious way. They had to work out a lot of what was only implied in the text and some children found this very difficult.

Perhaps one of the problems was a failure to recognize that studying the lives of people much as if they were phenomena of the same order as plants and wildlife would lead to the kind of generalization which creates stereotypes. The worksheets which had been prepared for this topic tended to encourage this. At this stage of their development most of the children were confident writers in a narrative mode but were only just beginning to write in a non-narrative, impersonal style. Using worksheets may help children to cope with factual information and to learn the conventions of objective writing, but teachers' questions will also determine the kind of text they produce (Kress 1982). Lists of facts using the present tense introduce writers to one of the ways in which we establish general and universally applicable cases. There was a lot of evidence of this in the writing that the children produced: 'Pygmies are . . . pygmies live . . . pygmies do not grow crops, pygmies have been around for at least . . .'

It could be argued that the worksheets they used limited individual interest, initiative, and expression, imposing a 'received' body of information which derived from the teachers' perceptions rather than the children's. The report to the teachers questioned whether a factual mode of writing was the most appropriate for thinking about people and the way they live. The use of the present tense and the generalizing pronoun 'they', typical of objective or expository writing, for example 'the Arctic Willow lives in the North Pole', 'the palm tree does not need long root systems', 'polar bears are half a ton when fully grown', allows the writer to state unquestionable facts. Using the same model in writing about human beings seems to produce statements which could easily become stereotypes and the basis for the sort of oversimplified points of view which give rise to all kinds of prejudice:

> They do not have houses like we have.
> The bushman's life today is not very different from the stone age people's lives.
> The people of the Sahara desert live on water and meat.
> The bushmen go around practically naked.

TIME TO REFLECT

It has been suggested that 'improving the stock of special knowledge available to the primary school teacher and the qualities of teaching deployed in the school are central to the improvement of the standards in primary education. But there are severe constraints to be overcome. For example, the time primary school teachers have for planning, reflection and appreciative judgement is severely limited (Taylor 1986). Among other constraints that Taylor points to are the persisting regularities of primary education, taken-for-granted routines. The 'Living and growing' topic typically operated to a tight schedule. This induced anxiety at all levels. There was a sense of urgency about work having to be got through. The teachers' comments were revealing:

> They took far longer than I had anticipated, searching for appropriate information from books to help them write their answers . . . research was very slow to start.
> We have only four weeks for the next group whereas the last group were with me for six weeks . . . I hope the children will get off to a much quicker start.
> We shall be doing Richmond Tests and having our author-in-residence during the four weeks, so time will be precious.

The children were also aware of this pressure:

> It was really a rush round operation on Friday.
> We only had time for the questions on the cards.
> We're just finishing off in our rough copy and then just starting in our best.

At about half-term, the headteacher tackled the staff about his feelings that they were tending to focus on exotic tribes and differences rather than similarities. He was concerned that they were concentrating on the past, looking at remote tribes like the Tuareg and the Bedouin and ignoring the way modern technological development affected everyone. The topic was not on the agenda of the meeting and the staff were a bit taken aback, especially as there had been no meetings to discuss what they had been doing so far. One of the teachers remarked afterwards that she did not see how she could make it different when these were the desert tribes and the project had to deal with second-hand sources. The headteacher had not offered any constructive advice and there seemed to be no time to discuss alternative approaches. The teachers' main concern continued to be the slow progress they were making.

Keeping the children busily engaged in highly structured tasks left little time for reflection by either pupils or teachers. The topic controlled them all, leaving no space to respond creatively to unscheduled events. There seemed to be no way of halting the well-oiled machine once it had been set in motion. One of the teachers, wanting more time, suggested that the children should remain in their original groups and concentrate on one area, rather than changing groups and tackling a second topic in the second half of the term. This idea was rejected. On two occasions, unscheduled external events, which caught the imagination of the children, were not exploited. The relentless pace and the security of the predictable programme seemed to make this impossible.

The first of these events was a trip to the Commonwealth Institute. This was enormously successful, not least because of the encounter with a Nigerian teacher who conducted a session in the education department's classroom. He talked about being an African, about the languages of Nigeria, and about his own family. He demonstrated a number of different musical instruments, taught the children to play them and then to sing a song. The session culminated in a performance in which every child participated. The children were startled, excited, interested. On their return they spoke about this incident more than any other:

ALAN	We went into this exhibition where a man was coming from Nigeria, Ali, Adi, I can't say the full name, it's so long.
ALL	Kaboo-o Kabo! (*Singing.*)
MARION	Then he choosed some people to play some instruments.
CHRISTINE	I did, I played the thumb piano.
ALAN	I played Big Daddy, the big drum that was meant to represent father.
CHRISTINE	I played the thumb piano that's meant to represent the children. It was like a wooden thing with bits of metal coming down, you had to pluck the bits of metal. You held it with your finger and you had to pluck it with your thumb.
ALAN	And the first time you plucked it, by mistake it made a very . . .
CHRISTINE	I couldn't stop laughing it was so loud.

Valerie had played a petrol can; this was also a thumb piano. She described how she put her fingers through the holes and plucked with her thumbs. Alan's drum was skin and wood; 'It was quite a decorative instrument.' He hit it with a stick which had a curved end. Marion played a shaker but she liked the 'round horns'. Alan said, 'At first it was a bit hard to understand him, but after a little while you got used to it and you began to understand.' The others agreed that at the beginning they weren't even sure whether he was speaking in English but could just about understand. Some of them were 'cracking up'. Asked why, they thought they'd probably found it 'peculiar'. They all remembered how they had been taught to say goodbye. As for what they had learned about Nigeria, they thought it was in Africa. Christine noted that 'he said that there are very big families there because men are allowed to have more than one wife.' They talked about this – and wondered whether people would get jealous. They remembered that Adi came from a family of six and was the oldest boy and that his name meant prince or crown. They thought Nigeria was the third most populous country in Africa, but after discussion among themselves thought it was the third biggest but the most highly populated.

For the first time on the project they seemed to experience aspects of a different culture which made sense to them. Yet no further reference to this event was made when they returned to school. On the playground, the children continued to sing the song they had been taught. In class they had gone over the answers on their worksheets, finishing off work so that they could move on to their new groups the following week.

Later in the term many of the children arrived at school having seen a programme on television about the Kalahari Bushmen, the second event that proved particularly meaningful to them. This news report revealed that there were only twenty-five bushmen in existence and that their future was in the balance. They had had to abandon their way of life as nomadic hunters because of animal conservation laws. South African official policy had deemed that 'civilization had overtaken them'. For these children, who had been studying the Kalahari desert and had become quite knowledgeable about the bushmen, this was shocking. In the morning they were queueing up to express real feelings of outrage to their teacher. The school secretary, fired by their enthusiasm to do something, telephoned the BBC and was given an address which the children could write to. Their teacher thought that they might do this if there was time. The relentless pace of the project meant that they did not. There was no time for unscheduled events in the programme.

THE PUPILS' PERSPECTIVE

In doing this topic, the children were on familiar ground; they had been programmed, as it were. None of them had any doubts about the kind of activity they were engaging in; rooms would be decorated, research would be undertaken, often in groups, and folders of carefully mounted work would be produced. They had done this sort of thing before and enjoyed it:

> I think all of it was good. I've enjoyed making my jungle box and I've enjoyed doing the writing as well.
> Well, the thing I found most interesting was the research work . . . the animal we found most about was the polar bear.
> My best bit was decorating the spoon. The Aborigines decorated everyday tools the spoon, it's just an idea from the Aborigines.

In a discussion about difference at the beginning of term a group of children had made it clear that they were aware of themselves as members of a multi-ethnic society. Their discussion opened up many issues which could well have been followed up during the course of the term. They had, for instance, been talking about people wearing different clothes in different countries.

RESEARCHER	Do any people in this town dress differently?
ALAN	Some do.
SALLY	Some wear saris.
RESEARCHER	Do they?
ALAN	Yes, coloured people.
RESEARCHER	What's a sari?
ALAN	It's like a piece of material wrapped round her.
SALLY	And in this town some people have different religions.
NICK	We went to visit last term, a Hindu Centre. A community centre.
RESEARCHER	Well, can you tell me about that?
ALAN	They worship quite different gods.
SALLY	There was a community centre but at the back there was a temple and pictures of all different gods.
NICK	They had a lot of pictures.
ALAN	Before we went they just had Diwali.
RESEARCHER	What's that?
ALAN	It's the time when they were getting to the Hindu Centre to celebrate. It's like us celebrating Christmas. But they don't celebrate the same as us.
SALLY	That's because they have like competition during this . . .
ALAN	They use bits of coloured stone . . . mosaic.
SALLY	And a mat, and we saw them.
ALAN	They put mats outside the doors.
NICK	And you have to take your shoes off, but if you go to church you don't.
ALAN	When we went into the Centre, the Hindu Centre, they had this bell and as you walked into the great big room you had to ring the bell.
RESEARCHER	Everybody?
ALAN	Together. If you wanted to.
SALLY	Ring it to tell their gods that you were coming in.
ALAN	We've got quite a big black population in this town.

RESEARCHER	But not very many black children in this school have you?
ALAN	No. A couple of them.
SALLY	We've got this girl. Her name's called Karen. She's in Mrs Smith's class. And we had this party here. And she wasn't allowed to come to it because her Mum and Dad didn't believe in her coming to it.
NICK	They're Jehovah's Witnesses.
RESEARCHER	Hm. Well, there's another difference.
DONNA	Yes. And we've got one in our class called Amina.
SALLY	Yes, she's doing maths with us.
DONNA	But she could come to the party though.
SALLY	It's only her colour though, she's not . . .
DONNA	She's English.
SALLY	She's not like Karen though.
DONNA	But her mum and dad come from . . .
SALLY	But she still celebrates Diwali though.
DONNA	Her mum and dad come from Kenya.
RESEARCHER	Do they?
ALAN	Yeh.
DONNA	She's a lighter colour than Karen is.
RESEARCHER	Yes.
DONNA	I've never been abroad.
SALLY	Because it was All Saints Day, and she wasn't allowed to come.
RESEARCHER	You celebrate All Saints Day here do you?
ALAN	And All-Hallows.
RESEARCHER	Yes.
ALAN	At the church.
RESEARCHER	Do you think every other school in the town celebrates All Saints and All-Hallows?
ALAN	Not all of them.
RESEARCHER	Why not?
ALAN	We're a Church of England school but not all of them are Church of England.

This long discussion, which took place in the first week of the project, seems to illustrate a potential starting-point. It is where the pupils had already got to in thinking about differences between people and about different cultures. It gives some idea of their background for thinking about multicultural issues and their confusions about difference, which they needed help to sort out. As the project developed, the children seemed to be getting a grip on the content of the topic, their conversation was more related and they exchanged information and shared ideas. However, they were often puzzled by accounts of experiences which seemed remote from their own. There was little evidence of the increased understanding or changes in attitude that their teachers were hoping for. The discussion also illustrates the hidden curriculum of the school. Amina and Karen (Kenyan Asian and Afro-Caribbean) were treated very much as honorary whites: 'It's only her colour. . .' 'She's English.' In a Church of England primary school, the knowledge that 'some people have different religions' and 'worship quite different gods', is significant. These were issues that were never confronted by the school's multicultural topic.

In fact, the pupils were often puzzled by what they were doing:

MARION	Well there's two main tribes what live in there, they are the Bedouins and the Tuaregs and we found out special rules what they live in and what they wear.
RESEARCHER	What are these special rules?
CHRISTINE	Well the Tuaregs, they're not allowed to eat pork.
VALERIE	The Indians or something aren't allowed to eat beef.
CHRISTINE	Is it their tradition?
ALAN	Religion.
MARION	Well most, right, some people, not calling them Tuaregs, but Muslims . . . they're not allowed to eat pork.
RESEARCHER	What do you mean by religion?
ALAN	Well, in quite a few countries their traditions and religions prohibit them from doing quite a few things that we would think as normal.
RESEARCHER	Do you know why?
MARION	No I just found it in this book.
CHRISTINE	Is it just because it's against their tradition to eat pork?
MARION	And in the last line it says, they give money to good customs and it puts that in this book.

Making sense of Islam on the basis of a few questions on a work card and the limited number of books available was not easy. The headteacher had spoken of his hope that the topic would be a consciousness-raising experience. By the end of term the children's grasp of information was impressive. They knew a lot about the areas they had been studying, but it seemed unlikely that there had been time for the sort of reflection which would enable them to go beyond the information and, as one of the objectives suggested, be able 'to empathise and draw comparisons with and between other ways of life than their own.'

REPORTING BACK

By the end of term a considerable amount of material, recorded talk, written work, and observation data had been collected. A report based on this was presented to the teachers as a discussion document. The taped discussions with the children were of immediate interest, as they revealed, week by week, what they had found interesting, confusing, helpful, or even boring, as well as the extent to which they were able to incorporate their new discoveries into their existing knowledge. Extracts were selected which showed their developing confidence in understanding what the topic was about, particularly those which showed them attempting to explain other people's 'rules for living'. Other material focused on teaching methods. Some methods, such as work cards and copying from books in response to teachers' questions, had often seemed to reinforce the teachers' knowledge rather than the children's. Perhaps the examples, drawn from children's work, would help teachers consider which of their approaches were most effective.

The report which was finally handed to the teachers was a chronological account of the term's work based on weekly interviews with the children and observations made while working alongside one of the teachers in the classroom. It included comments on aspects of the topic work which had seemed to occupy a good deal of the children's time: their writing, the use of prepared work sheets, the kind of books that were available and the way the children used information books, the use of video and film material, and the use of fiction in the stories which they had read and written. The following summarizes those aspects not yet discussed here.

Using books to answer questions and find out

Each climatic area had a good range of reference books, although even a ten-year-old book can seem very outdated, dangerously so where the lives of people are concerned. Changes in the earth's ecology and in world politics can radically alter what once seemed stable and unchanging. In this sense, up-to-date video programmes like *Zig Zag* can give a more honest contemporary picture and present the children with more reliable images. Some of the texts contained very glossy colour photography, which gave no impression of the hardship and poverty most of these areas endure. It is difficult, too, to see how you *can* study the lives of people much as if they are phenomena of the same order as plants and wildlife, out of the context of world politics. In many cases the children were totally unaware of the extent to which all the people they were learning about had been or were the victims of colonial oppression. In the case of the Australian Aborigine there was a book which made their political position very clear, but it was unlikely that anyone would have noticed this since the questions they were asked did not point them in this direction.

One of the books which the children were using described how the hunting and gathering way of life can be seen as the most successful adaptation that people have ever made to the environment. However, the pygmies' social organization and harmony with the environment was threatened by a rapidly changing world. But, despite the fact that this book was a resource, there was no evidence in written work of these issues being discussed. All the groups of people the children were studying were being profoundly affected by outside influences, economic, climatic, and political, but nothing was being done to ensure that the children were aware of these issues.

One of the main sources of information was the written word, and quite a lot of the children's own writing involved copying passages from books. Several children who had copied long passages from books could not read what they had written afterwards. An account of the tropical rain forest described in the vocabulary of cathedral architecture seemed to have completely confused the writer who had copied it out. She could not read what she had written; words like 'soar', 'pillar', 'buttress', and 'colossal' defeated her. Copying gives rise to phrases the children would be unlikely to use on their own, such as 'The eskimos are probably the most far-flung single tribe in the world', or, as the spelling suggests, *could* not use; 'A dangerous preditor (*sic*) to bird and beast alike . . . the Arctic Fox is nimble and athletic and produces a threat to many kinds of animals.'

Talking about videos

Where the pupils' writing was the result of watching and discussing television and film programmes, they may have had to struggle harder to present less polished information. They may have had to use a mode of writing which is less familiar to them without the help of teachers' questions or written text. What they produced often seemed to be closer to their spoken word as they attempted to explain something to a reader, rather than to record information for themselves. The writer of the Arctic Fox example above also described the Innuit:

> Innuit live almost the same as us. They have the same food as us and lorries and cars and bikes. Most people think they all live in igloos but they don't. They have all the modern things like us. There houses are the same as ours when they can not use cars they use ski-doos for skiing across the snow. Innuit have adapted to the cold by wearing thick clothes and centrally heated homes.

The following extract from a longer piece of writing seems to owe little to someone else's written text and a lot to the writer's enthusiasm for the information she is handling:

> The polar bear is very big. Its the biggest carnival in the world. Its 2 meter from top to bottom. It has very fat fur to keep out the entense cold . . . . The polar bear can kill a seal with one swipe of a paw.

Audience

The question of who all this writing is for should be addressed. There is much evidence to suggest that having a particular audience in mind is crucial to the writer. Much of the pupils' work had been lovingly copied out and mounted on coloured paper for inclusion in beautifully produced folders. When children were asked what they thought the folders were for, one said, 'Just to present your work nicely but I don't know why we make them.' Another suggested, 'You can show your children, show them how you used to work in your time, if it's changed.'

Most of the written work which went into their folders was produced in response to questions on workcards. Everyone covered similar topics. Later, they were to be asked to write a story using the information they had been gathering. They had to imagine that they had been involved in a plane crash in one of the areas they had been studying – jungle, desert, arctic – and describe how they were able to survive. The task was a difficult one, asking the children to draw together a number of facts about a particular climatic area as the framework for a fictional narrative. As one of the teachers wrote in her own appraisal of this task:

> The most demanding so far . . . in which I asked the children to imagine the area they were studying, and they had to use the facts they had learnt in SES lessons to make their story have a realistic side to it.

However, it seemed possible that this writing might provide evidence of the children's understanding of the topic and their awareness of the people they had studied.

Fictional narrative: pupils' own writing

The twenty-one pieces read showed competence in writing in the narrative mode. Clearly, everyone could cope with a basic 'story' structure. However, children as apparently confident as the writer of the first example seemed to find it hard to incorporate factual information in a fictional story:

> Where was I? It looked very much like a desert. I was very hot. I thought it was 2000C. It was only 150C I found out later. There were palm trees everywhere. There was a boy standing. I turned and looked, he said 'Ba loo'.
>
> 'Pardon', I said.
>
> 'Ca loo ma' he said. Suddenly a lot of bare people appeared round, I felt so scared. I started to cry. 'Ba loo' he said again. I thought it meant 'hello'. He pointed to a stretch of path and walked on, so I followed. We arrived at a camp of tents.

The writer is exploring the idea of feeling afraid in the presence of people who (a) do not speak your language, and (b) do not look or dress as you do. She realizes how important even one comprehensible word can be. As well as thoughtfully exploring this hypothetical situation, she tries to include factual information from various sources. There is a 'camp of tents' and they wait for missionaries to come to the rescue.

Many of the writers gave precise factual details, for instance about the geographical location of their story. It seemed to have been one way of demonstrating their knowledge of the regions they had been studying. Writing in the fictional mode, their observations or statements often seem more fluent and carefully composed than their answers to questions or to the short factual descriptions of 'animals', 'plants', or 'people' that they gave in their folders:

> Even on the hottest days Alaska can be freezing.
> Soon the sun will rise and not set for a while – summer is here.
> Icebergs are floating on the river.

Some managed to include factual information in the dialogue between their two characters:

> That's a mirage.
> What's a mirage?
> It's when you imagine something and when you go up to it it disappears.

Their knowledge of geographical detail was often impressive but their anthropological grasp was less so. When stories took place in the jungle or the desert the reference was often to 'tribes':

> Lisa pointed out a tribe about 150 metres away . . . we were OK they spoke English and told us where the nearest oasis is . . .

In another story there is a 'tribe' of little men:

> I wasn't quite sure but I thought they were pygmies, that I had been studying in my geography lesson. Not many of them wore a lot of clothes because they were very poor.

The task gave some people an opportunity to consider both how they would cope with strangers in a hostile environment and with being strangers themselves:

> They're not wearing any clothes, only a piece of cloth.
>
> Well, look at us, we're not much better.
>
> That was true, our clothes were torn and full of holes and sticking to us like mad. Then one of the men came over to us as we tried to make ourselves smaller . . . .

Another writer did not anticipate problems:

> We come to the Bedouins and made friends and my brother and I had food and water.

Several reflect or echo their reading of *Walkabout*, a novel set in the Australian bush: 'We saw a boy in a bush'; 'a boy came out of a bush'. Even in the Arctic a boy appears who says 'something we could not understand', but in all cases the boy is instrumental in finding food and getting help. In one story the protagonists meet 'bushmen', a boy and girl of their own age, who carry two large eggs with reeds sticking out of them, 'they handed us the eggs and we drank the cool water until the eggs were empty'.

Those who chose to write about the Arctic seemed to stick to animals rather than people. Sometimes these were part of the danger. One account described how polar bears 'half submerge their bodies in icy water . . . there they would swim down towards their prey and stun it, then the polar bear would strike using their paw or mouth.' Another writer is rescued by a friendly polar bear; another described 'a gang of walruses . . . all fighting each other'; yet another was cheered by the presence of some penguins. Almost all referred to the cold and to having inadequate clothing, but few of them imagined an encounter with human beings.

There were many examples of writers using language competently to create something of the atmosphere they sensed as they worked on these regions. Seeing a video may have contributed to observations like, 'The sun was shining on the ice with a blinding ray, but no heat was felt.' However, relying so heavily on secondary sources may have made the multicultural objective for this topic one of the most difficult to fulfil – understandably, other people's 'rules for living' may require starting closer to home. People whom the children perceive as 'bare' or 'peculiar', 'primitive' or 'exotic', are not the best starting-point. Many of their observations suggest that people are 'OK' when they wear clothes and speak English; men who wear 'veils' or people who are abnormally small are difficult to relate to. It seemed likely that some children might have had a stronger sense of difference than of similarities between people at the end of this topic. However, the objective to 'be able to empathise and draw comparisons with and between other ways of life and their own' had to a certain extent been met. This emerged in some of the fictional writing, illustrated above, but even more so in a discussion of the novel *Walkabout*, which was read to them.

Reading a novel

Their new knowledge about survival and adaptation in the desert seemed to help them to make sense of *Walkabout*:

CAROLINE Well it's about these two people and they were in a plane crash and they landed in the middle of the desert.
MARION The Australian desert.
ALAN The Australian desert.
CAROLINE And they're walking along and, um, they meet this Aborigine . . .
ALAN This boy.
CAROLINE Mary didn't like him at first but then when he died she did like him and then they learnt how to cope in the desert.
ALL (*Agreeing*.) Mm, yeah, in the desert.
CAROLINE And found people and eventually they . . . can't remember the end.
RESEARCHER What did they have to learn?
ALAN How to survive and find food.
RESEARCHER The boy died?
ALL The *bush* boy.
ALAN He will himself to death.
RESEARCHER How did he do that?
ALAN Well, he thought he'd got the fever and he thought he'd seen the death glare in Mary's eyes – he willed himself to death – he caught the cold that Pater had

	which he thought was the fever and he saw the death glare in Mary's eyes.
CAROLINE	He kept on shivering and going cold and they had to take her clothes off to keep him warm and she didn't like that.
CHRISTINE	And he died.
RESEARCHER	You said they had to learn how to survive, to cope, what sort of things did they have to learn?
CAROLINE	They had to learn where to get . . .
ALL	. . . food and water.

The discussion was a long one in which they speculated about the boy's death, about the way they could take doctors' and medical care for granted, about different attitudes to medicine and to death. The novel seemed to help them to empathize in the way that finding out about 'rules for living' had not. However, they were using some of their 'knowledge' in the stories and poems they had begun to write.

AN IRRELEVANCE OR A START?

It would be easy to dismiss this project as a 'superficial irrelevance' (Mullard 1984), as merely an example of a tokenistic pluralism which is likely to foster attitudes that the teachers do not intend and which only reinforce the dominant culture as a norm (Leicester 1986). The report of the term's work opened up vast areas for reflection which could not be tackled in the short term. At this point the whole issue of multicultural education came into focus. How could, or should, the school make use of this report? They had responded to the offer of a temporary researcher to help them to examine their progress. The structure and pace of the topic had not left time to identify or to challenge the kind of ethnocentricity that so often appeared in the children's writing and talking (such as 'Lisa pointed out a tribe about 150 metres away . . . we were OK they spoke English. . .'). Nor were they able to stop and reconsider alternative approaches. The teachers' very thoughtfully-prepared 'forecasts' were both a supportive structure and a strait-jacket.

Opportunities to challenge the children's assumptions and to encourage them to consider different perspectives were often missed. Perhaps this was because in planning the project the teachers had not fully considered some of the issues they might be dealing with. Presenting them with evidence of the way the children were able to reconstruct their existing knowledge and were ready to take on new perspectives could assist in future planning. The report might, at least, generate constructive discussion about ways of introducing a multicultural perspective into the curriculum.

This sort of tentative multiculturalism can be seen as a necessary prerequisite for a broader anti-racist strategy in the long term. The teachers involved were only beginning to explore these ideas themselves. In undertaking a project which was to look at alternative ways of living and belief systems, hopefully their own attitudes to cultural diversity, their own norms and value judgements might come under scrutiny. Teachers working in all-white schools have suggested that,

> before any change can take place, the staff of a school must have some overall rationale relating to anti-racist/multicultural issues in the context of a wider school policy . . . staff have to be prepared to go through a certain amount of pain if they are to remove prejudices from the curriculum as well as from their own traditionally held beliefs.
>
> (Palmer and Shan 1986: 14)

At Parkside, there were undoubtedly blind spots. One could be traced to the rhetoric of the LEA policy statement which generated the undertaking, rhetoric which saw multiculturalism in terms of teachers being able to change pupils' attitudes before looking critically at their own.

There is a limit to the change which outside agencies can bring about. 'The immunity of schools to change from outside stems from their cultural uniqueness which is rarely recognized by, or accessible to, external agents' (Oldroyd and Tiller 1987: 14). The unique social reality of Parkside, and of any school, will make it resistant to change that does not come from within. The teachers' collaborative efforts may have fallen short of their original objectives but hopefully their subsequent reflection on the outcomes of this project, aided by an independent and sympathetic assessment, would contribute to their thinking about the best ways to develop a racially unbiased curriculum in the long term.

The achievement of Parkside should not be underestimated. Recent research carried out since the publication of the Swann Report found little evidence of multicultural education being introduced in schools outside inner-city areas (Verma 1989). In a largely white area of the north-east of England a sample of teachers felt that multicultural education was not relevant to their schools. Despite the Swann Committee's recommendation that multicultural education should permeate *all* schools, and Government funding through Education Support Grants and Grant-Related In-Service training is provided to promote this, it would seem that the proposed reforms have largely foundered in predominantly white and rural areas. In this context the thoughtful way in which the teachers at Parkside attempted to work out the relevance of multiculturalism to their own culture may be seen as an important step forward.

Discussing the report of 'Living and growing', the headteacher asked his colleagues, 'Should we have done it at all?' A teacher admitted, 'The people side was far more difficult to grapple with', and another suggested, 'if we are going to try to put across the concept of adaptation and conservation, shouldn't we use something closer to home, like looking at different communities within our own community?'

10 Promoting education for all

A MODEL OF TEACHING

The broad strategy behind the work reported in this book has been to identify, describe, and analyse educational practice that appeared especially well designed to promote 'education for all'. Looking at these attempts as a whole, the more successful among them seem to involve a particular conception of teaching, one that is supported elsewhere in the literature in relation to multicultural and anti-racist education.

Person-centredness in a structured framework

The approach is marked by a distinct 'person-centredness' as opposed, for example, to 'knowledge-centredness'. The emphasis is not so much on extant bodies of knowledge and facts (though these are not unimportant) as on the development of the pupil's powers, skills, and abilities, and the appropriation of knowledge into the pupil's own scheme of relevancies. The constructivist learning theory that underpins this approach is illustrated throughout this book, but is especially evident in chapter 6, describing a school exchange, and chapter 8, on a creative mathematics project.

The teachers' concern with the development of person is not, however, an unsituated, socially decontextualized individualism. Such a narrow focus has been rightly criticized, for favouring particular groups, however unintentionally; for potentially fixing the child within his or her own racist knowledge; and for hindering the development of social education and new forms of cultural conceptualization. Their teaching steered a course between discovery-related techniques and a range of information that needed to be 'appropriated' by the pupil, and a set of committed values that needed to be learned. These included a concern for the dignity of individuals, respect for others, fairness, individual and collective responsibility, and social justice.

In this, they were not unlike the teachers discussed by Lee and Lee (1987). These authors reject the notion of liberal education as conveyed in the Plowden Report (1967) and as supported by writers such as Jeffcoate (1984). They agree with the efficacy of active learning and democratic procedures, but reject the view of the teacher as neutral chairperson. Teachers cannot be neutral with regard to racism. As Lee and Lee point out, 'the idea that children can and should learn by exploration is different when that learning is not merely a matter of individual interest but at least reflects the experience of the social group to which the child belongs' (Lee and Lee 1987: 218). At the heart of their reconciliation of a progressive primary pedagogy with anti-racist action is 'a commitment to talking as learning'. It has to be recognized that people talk on the basis of their own experience, and this differs among different groups. Thus, 'children speak not merely from the perspective of the child but from the perspective of the black child, or female child or working-class child' (ibid.). Lee and Lee compare their approach with some proponents of anti-racist education who seem to imply that teachers should instruct children into 'correct perspectives' (such as Mullard 1984). While agreeing with their aims, they feel these aims are much more likely to be met through a 'democratic process underpinned by a progressive pedagogy ... [which] values co-operation and collaboration through talk rather than simply individual exploration ...' (Lee and Lee 1987: 219). In such circumstances, young children's capacity to think and to learn has been shown to be more considerable than sometimes thought (see, for example, Blenkin 1988).

Carrington and Short see this as part of a wider programme of political education which aims

> to develop [pupils'] political (and moral) autonomy by encouraging them to take a critical stance towards ideological information; give reasons in support of a point of view; be open-minded and show respect for evidence; act with empathy and humanitarianism; explore fundamental questions relating to social justice, equality and human rights; and extend their appreciation of how power is exercised (and by whom) in our society.
>
> (Carrington and Short 1989:21)

Political education has been opposed by some on the grounds that young children are incapable of thinking about such issues. However, evidence is accumulating that this is not the case (see, for example, Epstein and Sealey 1989). Others argue that it might indoctrinate pupils with particular beliefs (Warnock 1985). But as the Swann Committee points out, it should,

> through encouraging pupils to consider how power is exercised and

> by whom at different levels in our society, how resources are allocated, how policies are determined and implemented, how decisions are taken and how conflicts are resolved, be no more likely to lead them to question and challenge the status quo, other than where this is justified, than to defend and seek to retain it.
>
> (Swann Report 1985: 334)

On this point, see also Stevens (1982), Phillips (1983), and Harber (1989). The Swann Report goes on to maintain that the ability to evaluate conflicting points of view, to argue rationally, independently, and free from prejudice, and to contribute to decision-making are essentially 'political' skills. Troyna points out that social reality is constructed through particular frames of reference, and if these are to be identified and evaluated, a broad-based approach is required, one that links racial inequality with other forms of inequality 'as girls, students, young people or as members of the working-class', and which induces 'empathy' rather than 'sympathy', and which points to the power of 'informed collective action' (Troyna 1987b: 316).

A democratic regime emphasizing co-operation, collaboration, and participation is better for this, Carrington and Short argue, than an authoritarian one featuring didacticism, hierarchy, competition and individualism. Lynch agrees, including in his tentative list of 'good practice' culled from the literature: 'democratic classrooms, collaborative methods of content presentation, high activity teaching approaches, rational methods that are attuned to pupils' judgement' (Lynch 1987: 115). This may sound like good, old-fashioned progressivism, but it is tempered with more traditional methods and attention to basics – another modification of Plowdenism. For there is a great deal of 'straight teaching' to be done; guidance, transmission of information, practice, consolidation, mass coaching. Bennett *et al.* (1984), for example, found that of the wide range of tasks sampled in their primary school pupil learning study, only 7 per cent were enrichment and restructuring tasks; 60 per cent were practice tasks, and 25 per cent incremental. Teachers cannot be hyper-active, brilliant, exciting, pedagogical pioneers all the time. But the learning, the motivation, the insights involved in some of the examples given here, such as the school exchange (chapter 6) and the mathematics project (chapter 8), show what can be done in bursts. They are initiated by flashes of enlightenment that illuminate, and are consolidated by, more formal areas of the curriculum. The typical primary school teacher, therefore, has a vast array of techniques, and rings the changes in the course of the day to secure the maximum educational output within the conditions. The style of our teachers, therefore, featured a kind of 'disciplined creativity', with the pupil and the pupils' constructions of meaning as focus.

Person-centredness applied also to the teachers themselves. These teachers were highly committed and greatly concerned to advance their own teaching skills and professionalism. They regarded themselves as individuals with their own distinctive input to make, but it was one that was sharpened by inputs from others, and that also contributed to them. Individuals thus had the freedom to innovate and debate, and to implement collective decisions in ways that accorded with their own particular local circumstances. They were reflective about their own practice, in the sense that they were concerned with 'aims and consequences as well as means', combined 'enquiry and implementation skills with attitudes of open-mindedness, responsibility and wholeheartedness', and 'monitored and evaluated their own practice continuously' (Pollard 1988: 57). They were not wedded to old routines or defensive about old practices. Rather, they were more often raising questions about their teaching, as if accepting Stenhouse's point that 'teaching is not to be regarded as a static accomplishment like riding a bicycle or keeping a ledger; it is like all arts of high ambition, a strategy in the face of an impossible task' (Stenhouse 1985: 124).

They appear to be good examples of what Hoyle has described as 'the extended professional', that is, one who is 'concerned with locating one's classroom teaching in a broader educational context, comparing one's work with that of other teachers, evaluating one's work systematically, and collaborating with other teachers' (Hoyle 1980: 43). They were prepared to 'question their attitudes, perceptions and beliefs, their teaching styles, professionalism and the very fabric of the structure which determines their value responses' (Matthews 1983, quoted in Arora 1986: 57). Such a teacher is theory-friendly, concerned about educational and teacher development, and sees 'teaching as a rational activity amenable to improvement on the basis of research and development' (ibid.). Perhaps, then, the educational gains made through the practices and projects reported here might basically be attributed not so much to what the teachers did, as to what they were – committed, critical, creative, and curious.

Collaboration and participation

The kind of person-centredness adhered to implies integration in terms of relationships. The prominent features of this are co-operation, collectivism, collaboration, and participation, and this applies to all groups and all levels. There seems to be a consensus on this in other literature on multicultural anti-racist education. James, for example, argues that multicultural education needs

> a context where children are encouraged to articulate their own ideas, to question, to listen to each other, to co-operate rather than compete – and as they grow, to take an increasing part in the practice of democracy – in debate and negotiation, and the election of representatives within school, and in informed and critical use of information and opinion in society.
>
> (James 1981: 28)

The effectiveness of pupils working in collaborative groups in the area of multicultural anti-racism is illustrated in Francis (1984) and Lee and Lee (1987). Carrington and Short also stress that 'if such policies are to have a lasting impact on pupils' attitudes and behaviour, then it will be necessary to take steps to democratize teaching and learning. In particular, the value of collaborative group work is underlined' (Carrington and Short 1989: xii).

Brandt agrees:

> This group-centred, collaborative approach to learning is, at the very base, a broadly accepted and agreed means of effective mixed ability teaching, whereby members of the group can learn from each other not only the subject matter but of the 'real life' knowledge of themselves and their counterparts as they apply to the lesson in hand. This learning approach also encourages interaction between pupils both in the classroom and outside which opens the door to a cultural education that is done through the lived experiences. Thus, given the right stimulation, pupils can be encouraged to learn respect for each other, which, when extrapolated, can be 'translated' into empathy.
>
> (Brandt 1986: 145)

This is well illustrated in this book in chapters 4, and 6 to 9. In particular, the project described in chapter 6 appears to meet the Swann principle of regarding 'cultural diversity as a valuable resource to enrich the lives of all and in which all children are able to benefit both from their own cultural heritage and also that of others' (Swann Report 1985: 326). In general, the teaching discussed in these chapters does not take the needs of ethnic minority children as separate from mainstream education but attempts to promote a 'good and relevant education for *all* pupils' (ibid.: 327) in which the needs of all, including ethnic minority children, are met. The same point applies to teachers. One of its best expressions here is in 'whole school policies', well illustrated in this book in chapters 8 and 9.

Troyna agrees that such policies 'provide the framework within which teachers might operate collaboratively in their attempts to mitigate racism in their schools', though he rightly points out that they are likely to have little impact 'unless those involved in their implementation also participate in the formulation' (Troyna 1988: 161, see also Nixon 1985, Myers 1985). At the same time, it is equally clear that the headteachers of our research schools, while establishing participatory democracies in their policy- and decision-making, provided strong leadership themselves, an element that figures large within the 'school effectiveness' literature in general (Purkey and Smith 1983, Reynolds 1985, Mortimore *et al.* 1988). Governed by the democratic parameters, however, it was leadership that was generally very much welcomed by the staff concerned. In turn, teachers had a certain freedom to experiment, and to initiate and develop their own teaching. The school exchange and the mathematics projects of chapters 6 and 8 would not have happened otherwise.

Collaboration is the favoured mode, too, in the twenty-four ESG (Education Support Grant) projects monitored by Tomlinson and Coulson. They found that

> the most appropriate and successful classroom strategies were co-operative and collaborative strategies between workers and teachers. This was important on several levels. Pupils saw teachers and project staff co-operating, discussing multicultural materials and presenting the work in a mutually acceptable rational manner, while teachers learned to adapt to new styles of teaching and learning. It became obvious that it was impossible to discuss equality, justice and fairness within an authoritarian, hierarchical framework of relationships in schools and classrooms. Allied to this was the realization that active and interactive learning strategies were crucial . . .
>
> (Tomlinson and Coulson 1988: 174)

Lynch applies the notions of co-operation, collaboration, and participation to school ethos:

> the entire school community should be included in the process of formulating a policy and delivery document, which will then be expressed in the institutional structure and values across the other areas indicated. This will help establish a 'comfortable' ambience in the school which enhances all pupils' sense of personal worth and the interaction between all cultural groups on a sensitive and just basis.
>
> (Lynch 1987: 78)

The school ethos thus formed leads to heightened effectiveness, defined in terms of 'high achievement and a sense of personal worth for all pupils, regardless of race, sex, creed or class'. The resultant feeling of justice for all pupils feeds back into and reinforces the school ethos, so that the same kind of spiralling effect between positive teaching and learning in general that Pollard (1985) noted occurs. This again suggests that what is effective multicultural anti-racist education is effective education in other respects. Nias (1989), for example, in considering the factors that aided the general teacher development in the schools of her research, draws attention to what she describes as a 'culture of collaboration' (as noted in chapter 7), where there are 'few status differentials', where teachers accepted and fostered their interdependence while valuing individuality, in an atmosphere of openness tempered by security. The general efficacy of democratic practices in educational settings is well illustrated in Harber and Meighan (1989). This research is putting flesh on the bones of the school 'ethos' and 'climate' work (Rutter *et al.* 1979, Mortimore *et al.* 1988).

One question that might be asked is whether one kind of effectiveness (for example, the heightening of pupils' social awareness) detracts from the other (cognitive achievement), but research suggests that it does not (see, for example, Yeomans 1983, King 1986). Even if there were evidence to the contrary, it might be argued that both are essential components of an education, and that ways must be found of accommodating them. They are not essentially in tension, for one can be done through the other – in fact many argue that it should; that is, that matters like social awareness can enhance and should pervade the curriculum rather than being seen as separate from it.

On the other hand, there are many unanswered questions about mixed-ability group work. In some circumstances, in some of the classrooms of our research, children seemed to spend a great deal of time 'off-task', and with no perceptible benefit to social development. Teachers showed considerable skills in orchestrating activities to preserve a semblance of 'busyness' (Sharp and Green 1975), but the management problems generated, especially when groups were on different tasks, were formidable. The answer, as noted earlier, perhaps lies in using a variety of techniques and classroom organizations, adjusting them to the situation and seeking to secure the most productive balance.

Co-operation between schools is also indicated by this study. The school exchange described in chapter 6 illustrates the added educational impetus such co-operation can impart. The multi-faith evening featured in chapter 7 shows more possibilities. In a sense, however, these are bonuses. There is a more basic need for inter-school co-operation, to do with the pupils' career progression from one school to another. The importance of this has been demonstrated in studies of transition (Measor and Woods 1984, Stillman and Maychell 1984). Our study of the experiences of ethnic minority pupils undergoing transfer, as related in chapter 5, suggests that the need is all the greater in these circumstances. Traditional problems of transition are writ large for these children, and again the language and cultural factors are prominent. Further, as these pupils adapted to their new schools, they experienced new forms of separatism, for example from boys, and lost the sense of shared values that featured strongly in their lower schools and which was so well expressed in their school assemblies. Most of the literature argues the need for curriculum continuity (for example, Gorwood 1986). Some argue that a measure of personal and social discontinuity at age 11 or 12 may, in fact, help children through the rites of passage from childhood to adolescence (Piggott 1977, Murdoch 1982). That, however, can hardly apply at age 9. In fact, this work indicates that another kind of continuity is required – that of school policy and teacher awareness *vis-à-vis* ethnic minorities.

In another part of our research not reported here (see Abbott *et al.* 1989), we saw this operationalized through the 'liaison group'; that is, a closely related group of schools consisting of a comprehensive and all its feeder middle schools, and all the schools relating to those. Meeting some two or three times a term either formally or informally, such structures are slowly coming to grips with the disintegration caused by the staged compartmentalization of formal education. Though they have many things to discuss, their policy towards multicultural anti-racism has figured large on their agenda, and knowledge and experience has been shared to mutual benefit.

Integration and collaboration applies also to parents. Arora (1986), Vassen (1986), Campbell (1986), Lynch (1987), and Carrington and Short (1989) all urge the active involvement of parents in the development and implementation of policy. This is particularly important with regard to multiculturalism and anti-racism. In this book, for example, we have seen the problems experienced by the mother of a black child during the process of being statemented (chapter 3). Balbinder's difficulties at school, and his mother's problems in understanding them, were clearly exacerbated by language and cultural factors. The complex legal process of statementing would provide a challenge to the comprehension of any parent. To Mrs Singh, it was so much worse. The chapter also illustrates how a parent's identity is closely bound up with that of her child. The separating of Balbinder from the group to which he had been accustomed was accompanied by the isolation of his mother. The chapter reinforces the messages of the Swann Report that

> if a pupil's parents are not familiar with the British education system and may not be fully fluent in English, this may call for particular sensitivity and appreciation of the situation in the school's arrangements for home/school liaison in order to enable the parents to play their full part in supporting their child's education.
>
> (Swann Report 1985: 325)

An additional point is that the involvement of parents heightens the pupils' feeling that the school is *theirs*. The importance of this is illustrated by a comment made by a student to Mac an Ghaill:

> Ye see black people don't own anything in this society. They don't belong anywhere. Ye just feel better when it's yer own place, like our church. Ye feel proud. Ye can be yerself, the pressure is off, ye can learn. The pressure is 'to be like them, to be white'.
>
> (Mac an Ghaill 1987: 6)

Given Balbinder's evident improvement in the special school, it might seem that the correct decision was made in the circumstances. However, it might be argued that a school operating more along the lines of participative democracy would have made greater attempts to integrate child and mother into the school, securing advantages not only for the pupil, but for the whole school. While as a general policy this is what the literature and our research seems to support, it still does not follow that it is the best one to implement in any given circumstance (Hammer 1989). Our case study illustrates some of the complexities in the issue and, whether the decision is one of integration or separation, the need for close teacher–parent collaboration. This includes special provision being made for parents like Mrs Singh, and help to enable her to understand the processes involved.

On the other hand, we have also seen the substantial contribution made by parents to enterprises like the school exchange discussed in chapter 6. Another aspect of the importance of parents is illustrated in respect of the all-white Church of England School of chapter 9. If this school is to advance its multicultural policy any further, it can hardly succeed without the active support of the parents. It is not the kind of policy that can be tacitly accepted. Parents have to be persuaded that it is a 'good thing' and recruited to the drive. 'Education for all' applies here too. Failure to do so can imperil an anti-racist educational strategy, as suggested by the enquiry into the events at Burnage High School (MacDonald 1988).

There are other pressures militating for closer ties with parents. Elliott, for example, who sees the Education Reform Act of 1988 as anti-educational in almost every respect, puts his hopes for educational recovery on teachers initiating a 'real dialogue with parents and employers' (Elliott 1988: 61). Hitherto, he claims, the relationship has not been active and empathetic. The professionals have defended their autonomy, not really listened to parents or promoted school–industry links in numbers and with enthusiasm. The responsibility of the professionals in any new and real dialogue, in Elliott's view, 'should be to clarify and articulate a coherent view of education, in response to the concerns expressed by [parents, employers, school governors, and elected members]. . .' (ibid. 61). In this way, the national curriculum might be reconstructed 'in a form which reflects both authentic educational values and parental concerns' (ibid. 62).

There are other ways in which such a partnership could be productive. Its potential strength in the area of equal opportunities in the new educational world following the Education Reform Act 1988 has been noted by Anderson. She argues that, with the additional powers and responsibilities given to parents and governors, 'without their co-operation equal opportunities policies may well flounder, if indeed they are not strangled at birth' (Anderson 1988: 35). Non-sexist and non-racist programmes could be undermined unless schools reach out and include parents within the discussions and debate instituting such programmes. Anderson suggests 'Workshop sessions, talks, videos, open days, special events focusing on equality', and, as reaching-out activities, 'leaflets, home-visits, phone-ins on local radio, community slots on regional television. . .' (ibid. 35–6). Epstein and Sealey (1989) describe a number of strategies teachers used in their study of 'anti-racist education in predominantly white primary schools' to persuade more parents to involve themselves more closely in the work of the school that their children attended. This included positive approaches by teachers to parents who were not regular 'parent-helpers', making sure to give them an opportunity to respond as well as to contribute; an 'open week'; and a home–school project for children of pre-school age and their parents, again run on a democratic basis. The last involved a pre-school library, which 'included a number of dual text books and stories including black children as well as the usual range of children's picture books' (Epstein and Sealey 1989: 81), which led to much discussion and a generally positive response from the parents. But not only parents should be involved. Cohen argues that effective whole-school policies, supplemented by community-led initiatives, are essential, and recommends that 'a forum should be established, with representatives from local schools, the youth service, and community organizations, to develop a more co-ordinated strategy' (Cohen 1987: 16).

TEACHER DEVELOPMENT

The teachers in the schools featuring in this book tended to be person-centred; integrationist and participatory in terms of relationships; research-, development-, and change-oriented; they worked to a constructivist theory of learning, and a holistic and processual view of knowledge; they were reflective, creative, and optimistic, committed to principles of fairness, social justice, and human rights. Not all teachers are similarly disposed. Nor are they all by any means committed to a multicultural anti-racist cause, or, where they are, able to do much about it through a combination of lack of knowledge, and the kind of constraints described in the introduction which prevent them from rectifying the lack. Some argue that the LEA policies devised in the wake of the Swann Report have not had much success (Troyna and Ball 1985, Troyna and Williams 1986). On the other hand, Tomlinson and Coulson concluded that the ESG (Education Support Grant) projects they monitored

> *Are* a support for those teachers and others in white areas who genuinely wish to change their practices and attitudes, and that the projects *are* acting as catalysts and change-agents in white areas. Short-term effects of the projects have been shown to be both positive and negative – happily the former outweighing the latter. . .
>
> (Tomlinson and Coulson 1988: 191)

The long-term effects are another matter, but will inevitably depend on the proliferation and persistence of a range of strategies and activities which keep the issue within sight, continue to refine our conceptualization of it, add to practical expertise, and prevent the submergence of the issues under the welter of demands made by the 1988 Education Reform Act. They will include close and sensitive attention to the matter at initial (IT) and in-service (INSET) teacher education (see Carrington and Short 1989, chapter 7, for a discussion of some of the possibilities; see also Burtonwood 1986). Action research by teachers seems particularly suitable and its advantages in this area have been demonstrated in a number of studies. Robertson, for example, argues that

> changes in practice may emerge from focused practical endeavours as much as cognitive activity. These practical endeavours, when identified, recorded as evidence, evaluated and systematically reflected upon should be the core of a teacher's learning processes. This kind of work, combined with inputs of information and ideas, leads teachers to reach a higher level of conceptualization of their own professional task, a higher degree of control of the educational process. Within such processes, the conceptual development of the teacher is located professionally and psychologically in the classroom and the school. This notion of teacher development will not allow the teacher to separate the rhetoric of good anti-racist and multicultural education from the practice in the classroom and the school.
>
> (Robertson 1987: 97–8)

A question that might be raised, however, is, if the focus is the teacher's own practice and classroom, how are horizons ever broadened and minds advanced? It is the same criticism noted earlier, that is directed toward some versions of child-centred education which restrict pupils to their own cognitive and cultural frameworks. But this can be an artificial distinction. To focus on one's own practice and self does not necessarily mean that any enquiry will be limited to one's own prevailing view of things. Arnot (1989), for example, in describing the development of anti-sexist approaches in some London schools, shows how part of the underlying philosophy was the need to move away from authority-based courses to school-focused projects on equal opportunities undertaken by school working parties or individual teachers. These projects in turn took girls, their biographies and their experiences, as their focus, working outward toward theory rather than the other way round. This teacher- and pupil-centredness was thought to have been the major factor behind the success of the initiative. But breadth of view was informed also by external contribution (an academic and an adviser), and collective discussion. The main 'consciousness-raiser', however, was deemed to be the focus on pupils. As Arnot explains:

> We hoped that in the long run, an increased awareness of pupils' school experiences, the range of messages they receive about relations between the sexes and the structures with which they have come to terms in their daily lives both inside and outside the school, would help teachers reflect on the impact of their teaching and of school organization.
>
> (Arnot 1989: 197)

Here is the kind of structural child-centredness discussed earlier. The same applies, of course, to ethnic minority pupils, or to any other kind of pupil. The example serves to remind us that anti-racist education is but one aspect of a general concern for equal opportunities and social justice. A location of practice here within the concept of 'education for all' would be concerned about all forms of discrimination, seek to combat them all, and gather strength from the several applications.

Some local courses for teachers have chosen to concentrate on racism awareness training (RAT). During our research, we met some headteachers who had been converted to anti-racism through attendance at such a course organized by the LEA. These courses have come under heavy criticism for, at best, bringing an individualized solution to a structural problem, for influencing surface attitudes but not on-going behaviour, for being palliatives that can lay claims to something being done while leaving things unchanged (Sivanandan 1985, Troyna 1988); at worst, it is claimed, they induce feelings of guilt, fear, and anger, and provoke confrontation (Gurnah 1984, Lloyd 1988).

As Lynch observes, however, this is an area which 'remains almost totally unevaluated' (Lynch 1987: 134). During our research, we had an opportunity to monitor the effects of one such course on some teachers. Their experiences, together with their positions of influence, seemed to offer a way round these criticisms and to promote what we might call 'effective conversion' (see Abbott *et al.* 1989 for a full account). This group of three teachers who were linked headteachers within the same liaison group had all experienced profound change after a three-day anti-racist course. The central effect of the course and ensuing reflection was to reconceptualize the problem regarding ethnic minorities as one that was located within the institution and society, and not within the pupils. Further, this realization affected the way they regarded all their pupils. For these teachers, at least, there had been no 'watering down'. Rather, the change had fed into their teaching, and they had attempted to disseminate and promote their new-found views. This applied within their own institutions, within the liaison group of schools of which they were a part, and within the LEA. Thus were links forged between the individuals and structure. These individuals were in positions of power, structurally related, and able to devise policies and plans of action and supervise their implementation and follow-up.

What factors contributed to their new awareness? First, the teachers' own 'extended professionality' which made them open to new ideas, even though they talked of being 'prejudiced' before the course. Then, the catalyst of the course itself. In their terms they were 'filleted', 'taken apart', and then 'put back together again'. It was 'punishment', but the trauma had to be gone through to engage with deep-seated prejudice. The teachers paid great compliments to the instructors, whose skill and sensitivity clearly counted for a great deal. Thirdly, the perspective transformation was aided, substantively and therapeutically, by these teachers, and the others with them on the course, operating as a team. Also, though deep, personal re-assessment was involved, the fact that a number were involved on exactly the same task aided the conception of the link between a private trouble and a public issue (Mills 1959). Fourthly, there were opportunities for continuance and development of the project, for capitalizing on the enlightenment and turning it into practice, and to bring pressure to bear on others, both within their own schools, in other schools, and in the LEA. Finally, there seemed to be a productive liaison not only within the team but between the team and others, including the LEA. This, however, is not a straightforward relationship. On occasions it was necessary for the liaison group of headteachers to meet unofficially. But to be successful it needs at least tacit official support. The secret seems to be how to keep these various inputs and interests in equilibrium – a variation of the old concept of 'partnership'. For 'bottom-up' models will not work on their own without support – from headteachers, governors, institutions, and local authorities. What seems particularly productive is a 'middle road' model, one involving a dialectic relationship between, say, local authority and teacher. This seems to be illustrated here.

This supports the point made by Allport:

> It really is not sensible to say that before we change personal attitudes we must change total structure; for in part, at least, the structure is the product of the attitudes of many single people. Change must begin somewhere. Indeed, according to the structural theory, it may start *anywhere* for every system is to some extent altered by the change in any of its parts.
>
> (Allport 1954: 506, quoted in Carrington and Short 1989)

As Celia Burgess notes,

> Because racism and sexism are so embedded in our British culture it is often difficult to work out how, as teachers, we should counteract them. We ourselves are part of the problem. Our awareness of this is the first crucial step towards looking for changes. There are those of us who are trying to put aside our professional defences and listen to other voices in education – to listen to children, to listen to voices from the black community, from the women's movement; and there are growing pressures on schools that will force us to listen. . . .
>
> (Burgess, C. 1986: 152)

Also, of course, it is possible to build such courses on anti-racist principles as with the ILEA 'Anti-Racist Strategies for Education' course for teachers. This 'strives for an understanding of the personal feelings associated with racism in the context of the dynamics of racism as a political issue. . . places interpersonal racism in the historical and political context . . . and examines the institutions and structures of society in so far as their operation helps to perpetuate racist ideology and practice'. One can construct courses, therefore, that bridge the personal and the structural.

Clearly, awareness-raising and attitude change have to be linked to action, and it has to be recognized that things might work the other way round, that is that teachers' experiences in multicultural anti-racist education and those of their colleagues, together with the promotion of opportunities for reflection, might cause them to question their own assumptions. This calls for resources being put more directly into teaching. But a measure of RAT, judiciously applied, might help draw out and direct the questioning. We would support those, therefore, who lend a degree of cautious support to such courses as one of a range of strategies that might be deployed, supported by structural linkages (Gaine 1987, Lynch 1987, Galliers 1987, Carrington and Short 1989). Another example of how this might work is provided by the City of Bradford, where RAT is a condition of the job of those who make appointments. How it actually works, however, has yet to be evaluated.

As one of the teachers remarked, in answer to a question about racism being in-built in pupils' background culture, 'It's dripped into them, isn't it? And I think we've got to drip other things into them' (Abbott *et al.* 1989: 216). This suggests permeability and persistence.

ARE AND ERA

While some comfort might be taken from the gains made in anti-sexist education from a similar strategy over recent years (though there is still a long way to go) there are concerns that the drive for multicultural anti-racist education that found official expression in the Swann Report might be slowing down. The issue, and others like it, is in danger of being swamped by the general fundamental changes involved in the implementation of the 1988 Education Reform Act. Like many such measures, the ERA offers grounds for both hope and despair. Some fear that the 'critical awareness' areas are being closed down, that the opportunities for sharing and co-operation are being reduced, that the emphasis on traditional values is to be reinforced, as is cognitive achievement (as opposed to personal, emotional, and social development). Open enrolment may lead to an increase in ethnically separated schools, and a decrease in the kind of inter-ethnic activity described in this book. Opting out will lead to another kind of divisiveness, with some schools in disadvantaged areas possibly caught in a 'spiral of decline' (Beynon 1986). Others find encouragement in the local management of schools. This will encourage the greater involvement of parents though, as Craft notes, 'in all-white areas, will the Swann Report's concern for a liberal education for *all* pupils remain a high priority?' (Craft 1989: 306). The new national curriculum is subject-specific with no expressed provision for permeation by a multicultural, or any other, perspective, though the Secretary of State has asked the National Curriculum Council to 'take account of the ethnic and cultural diversity of British society, and of the importance of the curriculum promoting equal opportunity for all pupils regardless of ethnic origin'(ibid.). The work of some of the curriculum working groups has given grounds for some optimism. The report of the working group on English, for example, recommended that all pupils be taught to write Standard English, whatever their ethnic, social, and regional origins. They should only be taught to *speak* it if motivated to do so, and should be able to choose when and where to use it if they wish. Thus, teachers must respect pupils' native language or dialect. This is not just a strategic matter, for their intrinsic value is recognized. Creole varieties of English, for example, 'are highly complex . . . governed by rules in their own right, and it is a political/ideological question as to whether they are dialects or languages in their own right' (National Curriculum Council 1988). The report recommends that schools should develop their own coherent policies, which are sensitive to local circumstances and the needs of the individual child on exactly how and when Standard English should be taught.

There are likely to be opportunities, therefore, but much would appear to depend on teachers. Some schools, however, are likely to feel more constrained. The potential contrast is illustrated by comparing the school which developed the creative mathematics project described in chapter 8 with the Church of England, all-white school of the multicultural 'Living and growing' project in chapter 9. It would be easy to criticize the latter project. In spite of their good intentions, they still seemed to be operating a traditional programme that equipped children with a number of facts which gave them no real understanding of other cultures, but simply reinforced traditional stereotypes. This was evident in the way the children reported their findings and experiences. At times, they were merely filling in workcards, and some reports were phrased in the same kind of style. On a few occasions, however, the knowledge gained was more clearly *theirs*. They had written about it with more enthusiasm, in their own idiom. This project, therefore, should be regarded as a start by a school steeped in old traditions and with many pressures on them to remain so, and should not be regarded, as 'a superficial irrelevance' (Mullard 1984). Next time round, the teachers could look to increase pupils' ownership of knowledge generated, engage a more holistic outlook which included opportunities afforded in out-of-school hours, reflect further about their own teaching and their views on multiculturalism and anti-racism.

This illustrates one of the threats of the 1988 Education Act. The teachers in the school of the mathematics project will continue to experiment. It is in their blood. They have developed a community style of teaching into which they all make an input. Within the school, as long as the present headteacher remains there, they have the power and freedom to exercise and develop their professional abilities. They do this within the context of leading opinion in the field, such as expressed in the Cockcroft Report (Cockcroft 1982), or the curriculum document *Mathematics from 5–16* (Department of Education and Science 1985). They have a good platform of results, and little to fear from national assessment. There is, though, one hazard that could slow them, and others like them, down. The mathematics project was clearly aided by a course one of the teachers had attended. The number of secondments has fallen drastically in recent years. This is unfortunate timing from another point of view. For a long while the benefits of such secondments were suspect. They operated on dubious educational principles, being external, course-based approaches which did not always match teachers' needs nor equip them with the means of implementation (Henderson 1981). More recently, however, this activity has been more teacher-based, founded on 'reflection-in-action', where knowledge is built up through practice, and theory grounded in everyday concerns (Schön 1983). Such an approach is eminently well suited to the kind of model of teaching and learning expounded here as most compatible with anti-racist education, for both pupils and teachers. An increase rather than a decrease in such provision is therefore indicated.

A bigger danger, however, is to schools like that in chapter 9. After the Act, the teachers here will be under considerable pressure to do that which they have always been best at; increase the degree of formality; and economize on the risk-taking experimentation (risk-taking because it may not feed into the 11-plus assessment in a way that is seen to do it justice in comparison with other schools who do not take such risks). There must be many schools like this second one, anxious to be fair to all children and keen to develop their abilities to the utmost, who will feel they will have to shelve their attempts to effect certain educational improvements in the deluge of reorganization under which they will be submerged (leaving them with even less time for reflection and promoting strategic teaching, i.e. teaching for bureaucratic and not primarily for educational ends); and under the pressure of clear government support (and possibly parents and governors) for traditional teaching methods, and coolness toward cross-curricula activity.

Much clearly rests with the teacher, and with the teacher's ability to develop and exercise powers of critical and creative scrutiny. We have tried to assist here, first by helping to document some of the teachers' own endeavours in this area. We have, as yet, no archive of general teacher practice (Shulman 1987), let alone one on this specific topic, though examples are beginning to appear (for example, All London Teachers Against Racism and Fascism 1984, Taylor 1987, McLean and Young 1988, Epstein and Sealey 1989).

Second, in keeping with the teaching and decision-making style discussed earlier, we have engaged in collaborative research with teachers. Collaboration was central to our research technique, and the book contains several examples of different forms. Chapter 2 is a project that was co-researched by the researcher and the class teacher concerned. Chapter 3 utilizes the researcher to gain another perspective on the issue concerned, in this case that of a parent with problems of comprehending the processes involved. Chapters 6, 7, and 9 utilize the researcher as evaluator, while chapter 8 shows the researcher participating with the teachers in the monitoring of the project.

Working with teachers in all these schools gave us a privileged view of their daily lives, their concerns and their commitment. In all the schools we visited they were pushing out the boundaries of their own understanding. Tackling the effects of racism and creating schools in which all children can feel and be seen to be equal is a never-ending challenge; multicultural input, festivals, projects, and permeation are not enough. It involves putting equal opportunities at the centre of all curriculum planning, like the head who told his staff of one of our schools at a GRIST-funded INSET meeting on developing reading:

> By failing to teach children to read we fail to make them equal . . . reading enables their further learning, opens up the world and is important in building up a positive self-image. When children can use reading to find out, they become more powerful.

Similarly, another one of our schools, a multi-ethnic lower school, has a language policy which states that:

> the use of language to develop meaning and understanding is central to all areas of the curriculum and should in its turn reflect the multicultural content of that curriculum . . . Just as the child's use of her first language while she is refining her English enables her to begin to experience a sense of power over her own learning, so that first language also gives her a sense of status in which her knowledge and an important aspect of her culture are given a relevance and standing within the school.

References

Abbott, B., Gilbert, S., and Lawson, R. (1989) 'Towards anti-racist awareness: confessions of some teacher converts', in P. Woods (ed.) *Working for Teacher Development*, Dereham: Peter Francis.

ACE Bulletins (1989) 'ACE conference: Asian children and special education', ACE, *Bulletin* 28, March–April.

Alexander, R.J. (1984) *Primary Teaching*, London: Holt, Rinehart & Winston.

All London Teachers Against Racism and Fascism (1984) *Challenging Racism*, London: ALTARF.

Allport, G.W. (1954) *The Nature of Prejudice*, Cambridge, Mass.: Addison-Wesley.

Anderson, B. (1988) 'Equal opportunities and the National Curriculum – a challenge to educators', in H. Simons (ed.) *The National Curriculum*, London: British Educational Research Association: 27–37.

Antonouris, G. (1985) 'Developing multicultural education in all primary schools: some suggestions', Trent Polytechnic, (mimeo).

Antonouris, G. and Richards, K. (1985) 'Race in education', *Trent Papers in Education*, 85/4, Trent Polytechnic.

Armstrong, M. (1980) *Closely Observed Children*, London: Writers & Readers.

Arnot, M. (1989) 'The challenge of equal opportunities: personal and professional development for secondary teachers', in P. Woods (ed.) *Working for Teacher Development*, Dereham: Peter Francis.

Arora, R.K. (1986) 'Towards a multicultural curriculum – primary', in R.K. Arora and C.G. Duncan, *Multicultural Education: towards good practice*, London: Routledge & Kegan Paul.

Arora, R.K. and Duncan, C.G. (1986) *Multicultural Education: towards good practice*, London: Routledge & Kegan Paul.

Ashton, P.T. and Webb, R.B. (1986) *Making a Difference: teachers' sense of efficacy and student achievement*, London: Longman.

Atkinson, P. and Delamont, S. (1977) 'Mock-ups and cock-ups: the stage-management of guided discovery instruction', in P. Woods and M. Hammersley (eds) *School Experience*, London: Croom Helm.

Barnes, D. (1976) *From Communication to Curriculum*, Harmondsworth: Penguin.

Barrett, G. (1986) *Starting School: an evaluation of the experience*, London: The Assistant Masters and Mistresses Association.

Bell, R.E. (1981) 'Approaches to teaching', Unit 15 of Course E200 *Contemporary Issues in Education*, Milton Keynes: Open University Press.

Bennett, N. (1987) 'The search for the effective primary school teacher', in S. Delamont (ed.) *The Primary School Teacher*, Lewes: Falmer Press.

Bennett, N., Desforges, C., Cockburn, A., and Wilkinson, B. (1984) *The Quality of Pupil Learning Experiences*, London: Lawrence Erlbaum.

Beynon, J. (1986) 'Spiral of decline: race and policy', in Z. Layton-Henry and P. Rich (eds) *Race, Government and Politics in Britain*, London: Macmillan.

Brah, A. and Minhas, R. (1985) 'Structural racism or cultural difference: schooling for Asian girls', in G. Weiner (ed.) *Just a Bunch of Girls*, Milton Keynes: Open University Press.

Brandt, G. (1986) *The Realization of Anti-Racist Teaching*, Lewes: Falmer Press.

Brown, R. and Bellugi, V. (1964) 'Three processes in the child's acquisition of syntax', *Harvard Educational Review* 34, 2: 133–51.

Bruner, J. (1960) *The Process of Education*, New York: Vintage Books.

Bruner, J. (1985) 'Vygotsky: a historical and conceptual perspective', in J.V. Wertsch (ed.) *Culture, Communication and Cognition: Vygotskian perspectives*, Cambridge: Cambridge University Press.

Bruner, J. (1986) *Actual Minds, Possible Worlds*, Harvard: Harvard University Press.

Burgess, C. (1986) 'Tackling racism and sexism in the primary classroom', in J. Gundara, J. Jones, and K. Kimberley (eds) *Racism, Diversity and Education*, London: Hodder & Stoughton.

Burgess, R.G. (1984) *In the Field: an introduction to field research*, London: Allen & Unwin.

Burgess, R.G. (ed.) (1985) *Issues in Educational Research*, Lewes: Falmer Press.

Burgess, R.G. (ed.) (1987) *Field Methods in the Study of Education*, Lewes: Falmer Press.

Burtonwood, N. (1986) 'INSET and multicultural/antiracist education: some reflections on Swann and after', *British Journal of In-service Education* 13, 1: 30–5.

Campbell, J. (1986) 'Involving parents in equal opportunities: one school's attempt', in *Primary Matters: some approaches to equal opportunities in primary schools*, London: ILEA.

Carrington, B., Millward, A., and Short, G. (1986) 'Schooling in a multiracial society: contrasting perspectives of primary and secondary teachers in training', *Educational Studies* 12, 1: 17–35.

Carrington, B. and Short, G. (1987) 'Breakthrough to political literacy: political education, antiracist teaching and the primary school', *Journal of Education Policy* 2, 1: 1–13.

Carrington, B. and Short, G. (1989) *Race, and the Primary School*, London: NFER–Nelson.

Chivers, T.S. (ed.) (1987) *Race and Culture in Education: issues arising from the Swann Committee Report*, Windsor: NFER–Nelson.

Cockcroft, W.H. (1982) *Mathematics Counts* (The Cockcroft Report), London: HMSO.

Cohen, P. (1987) *Reducing Prejudice in the Classroom and Community*, PSEC/CME Cultural Studies Project, University of London Institute of Education (mimeo).

Connell, R.W., Ashenden, D.J., Kessler, S., and Dowsett, G.W. (1982) *Making the Difference: schools, families and social division*, Sydney: Allen & Unwin.

Craft, M. (1989) 'Mixed prospects', *Education* 31 March: 306–7.

Cummins, J. (1984) *Bilingualism and Special Education: issues in assessment and pedagogy*, Clevedon: Multilingual Matters Ltd.

Davey, A.G. (1983) *Learning to be Prejudiced: growing up in multi-ethnic Britain*, London: Edward Arnold.

Davies, B. (1982) *Life in the Classroom and Playground: the accounts of primary school children*, London: Routledge & Kegan Paul.

Degenhardt, M.A.B. (1984) 'Educational research as a source of educational harm', *Culture, Education and Society* 38, 3: 232–52.

Delamont, S. and Galton, M. (1986) *Inside the Secondary Classroom*, London: Routledge & Kegan Paul.

Demaine, J. and Kadodwala, D. (1988) 'Multicultural and antiracist education: the unnecessary divide', *Curriculum* 9, 2: 99–102.

Denscombe, M. (1985) *Classroom Control: a sociological perspective*, London: Allen & Unwin.

Denscombe, M., Szule, H., Patrick, C., and Wood, A. (1986) 'Ethnicity and friendship: the contrast between sociometric research and fieldwork observation in primary school classrooms', *British Educational Research Journal* 12, 3: 221–35.

Department of Education and Science (1978) *Special Educational Needs* (The Warnock Report), London: HMSO.

Department of Education and Science (1983) *Assessments and Statements of Special Educational Needs*, Circular 1/83, London: HMSO.

Department of Education and Science (1985) *Mathematics from 5–16. Curriculum Matters 3. An HMI Series*, London: HMSO.

Desforges, C. (1985) 'Matching tasks to children', in N. Bennett and C. Desforges (eds) *Recent Advances in Classroom Research*, Edinburgh: Scottish Academic Press.

Donaldson, M. (1978) *Children's Minds*, London: Fontana.

Donaldson, M., Grieve, R., and Pratt, C. (eds) (1983) *Early Childhood Development and Education*, Oxford: Basil Blackwell.

Doyle, W. (1983) 'Academic work', *Review of Educational Research* 53, 2: 159–99.

Dulay, H., Burt, M., and Krashen, S. (1982) *Language Two*, Oxford: Oxford University Press.

Dumont, R.V. and Wax, M.L. (1971) 'Cherokee school society and the intercultural classroom', in B.R. Cosin *et al.* (eds) *School and Society*, London: Routledge & Kegan Paul.

Edwards, A.D. and Furlong, V.J. (1978) *The Language of Teaching*, London: Heinemann.
Edwards, V. (1984) 'Language issues in school', in M. Craft (ed.) *Education and Cultural Pluralism*, Lewes: Falmer Press.
Eggleston, S.J., Dunn, D.K., and Purewal, A. (1981) *In-Service Teacher Education in a Multicultural Society*, Keele: The University of Keele.
Elbaz, F. (1983) *Teacher Thinking: a study of practical knowledge*, London: Croom Helm.
Elliott, J. (1988) 'The State *v*. Education: the challenge for teachers', in H. Simons (ed.) *The National Curriculum*, London: British Educational Research Association.
Epstein, D. and Sealey, A. (1989) *Where It Really Matters: anti-racist education in predominantly white primary schools, a handbook for staff development*, Birmingham: Birmingham City Council.
Finn, G.P.T. (1987) 'Multicultural anti-racism and Scottish education', *Scottish Educational Review* 19, 1: 39–49.
Foster, P.M. (1989) *Policy and Practice in Multicultural and Anti-Racist Education: a case study of a multi-ethnic comprehensive school*, unpublished Ph.D. thesis, Milton Keynes: The Open University.
Francis, M. (1984) 'Anti-racist teaching: curricular practices', in All London Teachers Against Racism and Facism, *Challenging Racism*, London: ALTARF.
Freedman, S. (1987) 'Burntout or beached: weeding women out of women's true profession', in S. Walker and L. Barton (eds) *Changing Policies, Changing Teachers: new directions for schooling*, Milton Keynes: Open University Press.
Furlong, V.J. (1984) 'Black resistance in the liberal comprehensive', in S. Delamont (ed.) *Readings and Interaction in the Classrooms*, London: Methuen.
Gaine, C. (1987) *No Problem Here: a practical approach to education and race in white schools*, London: Hutchinson.
Galliers, D. (1987) 'A framework for anti-racist training', *British Journal of Inservice Education* 13, 2: 67–75.
Galton, M. (1987) 'An ORACLE chronicle: a decade of classroom research', in S. Delamont (ed.) *The Primary School Teacher*, Lewes: Falmer Press.
Gates, P. (1989) 'Developing consciousness and pedagogical knowledge through mutual observation', in P. Woods (ed.) *Working for Teacher Development*, Dereham: Peter Francis.
Getzels, J.W. (1977) 'Images of the classroom and visions of the learner', in J.C. Glidewell (ed.) *The Social Context of Learning and Development*, New York: Wiley.
Ghaye, A. and Pascal, C. (1988) 'Four-year-old children in reception classrooms: participant perceptions and practice', *Educational Studies* 14, 2: 187–208.
Gillborn, D.A. (1988) 'Ethnicity and educational opportunity: case studies of West Indian male-white teacher relationships', *British Journal of Sociology of Education* 9, 4: 371–85.

Gorwood, B.T. (1986) *School Transfer and Curriculum Continuity*, London: Croom Helm.

Gregory, R. (1985) *Direct Experience*, Ampthill: Teaching Media Resources Service: 24.

Grugeon, E. (1989) 'Teacher development through collaborative research' in P. Woods (ed.) *Working for Teacher Development*, Cambridge: Peter Francis.

Gurnah, A. (1984) 'The politics of racism awareness training', *Critical Social Policy* 11: 6–20.

Gurnah, A. (1987) 'Gatekeepers and caretakers: Swann, Scarman, and the social policy of containment', in B. Troyna (ed.) *Racial Inequality in Education*, London: Tavistock.

Haig, G. (1987) 'Pace-makers', *Times Educational Supplement*, 18.12.87.

Hammer, M. (1989) 'Special educational needs', Unit 26 of Course E208 *Exploring Educational Issues*, Milton Keynes: Open University Press.

Hammersley, M. (1977) 'School learning: the cultural resources required by pupils to answer a teacher's question', in P. Woods and M. Hammersley (eds) *School Experience*, London: Croom Helm.

Harber, C. (1989) 'Political education and democratic practice', in C. Harber and R. Meighan (eds) *The Democratic School: educational management and the practice of democracy*, Ticknall: Education New Publishing Cooperative Ltd.

Harber, C. and Meighan, R. (eds) (1989) *The Democratic School: educational management and the practice of democracy*, Ticknall: Education New Publishing Cooperative Ltd.

Hargreaves, A. (1988a) 'Teaching quality: a sociological analysis', *Journal of Curriculum Studies* 20, 3: 211–31.

Hargreaves, A. (1988b) 'Curriculum policy and the cultures of teaching', in I. Goodson and G. Milburn (eds) *Reconstructing Educational Research*: Althouse Press.

Hartley, D. (1985) *Understanding the Primary School: a sociological analysis*, London: Croom Helm.

Heath, S.B. (1983) *Ways with Words: language, life and work in communities and classrooms*, Cambridge: Cambridge University Press.

Henderson, E.S. (1981) 'The concept of school-focused INSET', in E.S. Henderson and G.W. Perry (eds) *Change and Development in Schools*, Maidenhead: McGraw-Hill.

Hewton, E. (1988) *School Focused Staff Development*, Lewes: Falmer Press.

Horowitz, E.L. (1936) 'Development of attitudes towards Negroes', in H. Proschansky and B. Seidenberg (eds) (1965) *Basic Studies in Social Psychology*, New York: Holt, Rinehart & Winston.

Houlton, D. (1986) *Cultural Diversity in the Primary School*, London: Batsford.

Hoyle, E. (1980) 'Professionalization and deprofessionalization in education', in E. Hoyle and J. Megarry (eds) *World Yearbook of Education 1980: professional development of teachers*, London: Kogan Page: 42–54.

Hustler, D., Cassidy, A., and Cuff, E.C. (eds) (1986) *Action Research in Classrooms and Schools*, London: Allen & Unwin.

Inglis, F. (1987) 'The condition of English in England', *English in Education* 21, 3: 10–20.
Inner London Education Authority (1988) 'Secondary transfer project, final report', *Bulletin 17*, Information Section, Research and Statistics Branch, Addington Street Annex, London, SE1 7UY.
Jackson, P.W. (1968) *Life in Classrooms*, New York: Holt, Rinehart & Winston.
James, A. (1981) 'The multicultural curriculum', in A. James and R. Jeffcoate (eds) *The School in the Multicultural Society*, London: Harper & Row.
Jeffcoate, R. (1979) *Positive Image: towards a multiracial curriculum*, London: Chameleon Books/Readers & Writers Publishing Cooperative.
Jeffcoate, R. (1984) *Ethnic Minorities and Education*, London: Harper & Row.
Jenkins, D. (1980) 'An adversary's account of SAFARI'S ethics of case-study', in C. Richards (ed.) *Power and the Curriculum*, Driffield: Nafferton Books.
King, E. (1986) 'Recent experimental strategies for prejudice in American schools and classroom', *Journal of Curriculum Studies* 18, 3: 331–8.
Knowles, W. and Masidlover, M. (1982) *Derbyshire Language Scheme*, Ripley, Derbyshire, 2nd edition (private publication).
Kress, C. (1982) *Learning to Write*, London: Routledge & Kegan Paul.
Lee, V. and J. (1987) 'Stories children tell', in A. Pollard (ed.) *Children and their Primary Schools*, Lewes: Falmer Press.
Leicester, M. (1986) 'Multicultural curriculum or anti-racist educational; denying the gulf', *Multicultural Teaching* 4, 2: 4–7.
Lever, J. (1976) 'Sex differences in the games children play', *Social Problems* 23: 478–87.
Lloyd, J. (1988) 'RAT race dilemmas', *Times Educational Supplement*, 3.6.88: 4.
Lunch, J. (1987) *Prejudice Reduction and the Schools*, London: Cassell.
Mac an Ghaill, M. (1988) *Young, Gifted and Black*, Milton Keynes: Open University Press.
MacDonald, I. (1988) *Burnage High School Inquiry*, Manchester: Manchester City Council.
McLaughlin, M. and Marsh, D. (1978) 'Staff development and school change', *Teachers College Record* 80, 1: 69–94.
McLean, B. and Young, J. (1988) *Multicultural Anti-Racist Education: a manual for primary schools*, London: Longman.
McTear, M. (1985) *Children's Conversation*, Oxford: Basil Blackwell.
Mahoney, P. (1985) *Schools for the Boys*, London: Hutchinson.
Marland, M. (1987) 'The education of and for a multi-racial and multi-lingual society: research needs post-Swann', *Educational Research* 29, 2: 116–29.
May, N. and Rudduck, J. (1983) *Sex-Stereotyping and the Early Years of Schooling*, Norwich: The Centre for Applied Research in Education.
Mead, G.H. (1934) *Mind, Self and Society*, Chicago: University of Chicago Press.
Measor, L. and Woods, P. (1984) *Changing Schools: pupil perspectives on transfer to a comprehensive*, Milton Keynes: Open University Press.
Mills, C.W. (1959) *The Sociological Imagination*, Oxford University Press: New York.

Milner, D. (1983) *Children and Race: ten years on*, London: Ward Lock Educational.

Mines, H. (1986) 'It's the Word of God, Miss', *Language Matters* 2: 14–17.

Mortimore, P., Sammons, P., Lewes, L., and Ecob, R. (1988) *School Matters: the junior years*, London: Open Books.

Mullard, C. (1984) *Anti-Racist Education: the three Os*, London: National Association for Multiracial Education.

Murdoch, A. (1982) *Forty-Two Children and the Transfer to Secondary Education*, Ph.D. thesis, University of East Anglia.

Myers, K. (1985) 'Beware of the backlash', *School Organization* 5, 1: 27–40.

Naguib, M. (1985) 'Racism as an aspect of the Swann report: a black perspective', *Multicultural Teaching* 4, 2: 8–10.

National Antiracist Movement in Education (1985) *NAME on Swann*, Walsall: National Antiracist Movement in Education.

National Curriculum Council (1988) *English For Ages 5–11* (The Cox Report), London: HMSO

Nias, J. (1988) 'The primary school staff relationships project: some findings', *Forum* 30, 3: 85–7.

Nias, J. (1989) *Teachers and their Work*, London: Methuen.

Nixon, J. (1985) 'Education for a multicultural society: reviews and reconstructions', *Curriculum* 6, 2: 29–36.

Oldroyd, D. and Tiller, T. (1987) 'Change from within: an account of school-based collaborative action research in an English secondary school', *Journal of Education for Teaching* 12, 3: 13–27.

Otty, N. (1972) *Learner–Teacher*, Harmondsworth: Penguin.

Owen-Cole, W. (1978) 'World religions in the multi-faith school', in A. James and R. Jeffcoate (eds) *The School in the Multicultural Society*, London: Harper & Row.

Palmer, C. and Shan, S. (1986) *Project for the Promotion of Racial Equality and Justice in Secondary Schools: A Report*, Birmingham: Birmingham Health Authority.

Patterson, S. (1985) 'Random Samplings from Swann', *New Community*, 12, 2: 239–48.

Phillips, G. (1983) 'Taking political autonomy seriously: a reply to Ian Gregory' *Westminster Studies in Education* 6: 13–20.

Piggott, C.A. (1977) *Transfer from Primary to Secondary Education*, unpublished MA dissertation, University of Southampton.

Plowden Report (1967) *Children and their Primary Schools*, Report of the Central Advisory Council for Education in England, London: HMSO.

Pollard, A. (1985) *The Social World of the Primary School*, London: Holt, Rinehart & Winston.

Pollard, A. (ed.) (1987) *Children and their Primary Schools*, Lewes: Falmer Press.

Pollard, A. (1988) 'Reflective teaching – the sociological contribution', in P. Woods and A. Pollard (eds) *Sociology and Teaching*, London: Croom Helm.

Pollard, A. and Tann, F. (1987) *Reflective Teaching in the Primary School*, London: Cassell.
Purkey, S. and Smith, M. (1983) 'Effective schools: a review', *The Elementary School Journal* 83, 4: 427–52.
Raban, B. and Strutt, M. (1988) 'Language is a special need', in M. Jones and A. West (eds) *Learning Me Your Language*, London: Mary Glasgow Publications.
Rattansi, A. (1988) '"Race", education and British society', in R. Dale, R. Fergusson, and A. Robinson (eds) *Frameworks for Teaching*, London: Hodder & Stoughton.
Rex, J. (1986) 'Equality of opportunity and the ethnic minority child in British schools', in S. Modgil *et al.* (eds) *Multicultural Education: the interminable debate*, Lewes: Falmer Press.
Rex, J. (1987) 'Multiculturalism, anti-racism and equality of opportunity in the Swann Report', in T.S. Chivers (ed.) *Race and Culture in Education: issues arising from the Swann Committee Report*, Windsor: NFER–Nelson.
Reynolds, D. (1985) *Studying School Effectiveness*, Lewes: Falmer Press.
Richardson, K. (1985) 'Learning theories', Units 8/9 of Course E206 *Personality, Development and Learning*, Milton Keynes: Open University Press.
Riseborough, G.F. (1981) 'Teacher careers and comprehensive schooling: an empirical study', *Sociology* 15, 3: 352–81.
Robail, D. (1985) '"You haven't changed a bit, Miss": infant–junior transition', (mimeo).
Robertson, W. (1987) 'In-service strategies for teacher education', in T.S. Chivers (ed.) *Race and Culture in Education: issues arising from the Swann Committee Report*, Windsor: NFER–Nelson.
Romaine, S. (1984) *The Language of Children and Adolescents*, Oxford: Basil Blackwell.
Rowland, S. (1984) *The Enquiring School*, Lewes: Falmer Press.
Rowland, S. (1987) 'Child in control: towards an interpretive model of teaching and learning', in S. Pollard (ed.) *Children and Their Primary Schools*, Lewes: Falmer Press.
Rubin, Z. (1980) *Children's Friendships*, London: Fontana.
Rutter, M., Maugham, B., Mortimore, P., and Ouston, J. (1979) *Fifteen Thousand Hours*, London: Open Books.
Saunders, M. (1982) *Multicultural Teaching – a guide for the classroom*, Maidenhead: McGraw-Hill.
Schön, D.A. (1983) *The Reflective Practitioner: how professionals think in action*, London: Temple Smith.
Sharp, R. and Green, A. (1975) *Education and Social Control*, London: Routledge & Kegan Paul.
Short, G. and Carrington, B. (1987) 'Towards an anti-racist initiative in the all-white primary school: a case study', in A. Pollard (ed.) *Children and their Primary Schools*, Lewes: Falmer Press.
Shulman, L. (1987) 'Knowledge and teaching: foundations of the new reform', *Harvard Educational Review* 57, 1: 1–22.

Sivanandan, A. (1985) 'RAT and the degradation of black struggle', *Race and Class* 26, 4: 1–33.

Stenhouse, L. (1985) *Research as a Basis for Teaching*, London: Heinemann.

Stevens, O. (1982) *Children Talking Politics: political learning in childhood*, Oxford: Martin Robertson.

Stillman, A. and Maychell, K. (1984) *School to School*, Windsor: NFER–Nelson.

Swann Report (1985) *Education for All. The Report of the Committee of Enquiry into the Education of Children from Ethnic Minority Groups*, Cmnd 9543, London: HMSO.

Swann, W. (1987) 'Statements of intent: an assessment of reality', in T. Booth, and W. Swann (eds) *Including Pupils with Disabilities*, Milton Keynes: Open University Press.

Taylor, B. (ed.) (1987) *Ethnicity and Prejudice in 'White Highlands' Schools*, Perspectives 35, School of Education, University of Exeter.

Taylor, P.H. (1986) *Expertise and the Primary School Teacher*, London: NFER–Nelson.

Thomas, K. (1984) 'Intercultural relations in the classroom', in M. Craft (ed.) *Education and Cultural Pluralism*, Lewes: Falmer Press.

Tizard, B., Blatchford, P., Burke, J., Farqhar, C., and Plewis, I. (1988) *Young Children at School in the Inner City*, Brighton: Lawrence Erlbaum.

Tomlinson, S. (1982) *A Sociology of Special Education*, London: Routledge & Kegan Paul.

Tomlinson, S. and Coulson, P. (1988) *Education for a Multi-Ethnic Society: a descriptive analysis of a sample of projects funded by Education Support Grants in mainly white areas*, Lancaster: University of Lancaster Press.

Tripp, D.H. (1987) 'Teachers, journals and collaborative research', in J. Smyth (ed.) *Educating Teachers: changing the nature of pedagogical knowledge*, Lewes: Falmer Press.

Troyna, B. (1984) 'Fact or artefact? The "educational underachievement" of black pupils', *British Journal of Sociology of Education* 5, 2: 153–66.

Troyna, B. (1987a) '"Swann's song": the origins, ideology and implications of Education for All', in T.S. Chivers (ed.) *Race and Culture in Education: issues arising from the Swann Committee Report*, Windsor: NFER–Nelson.

Troyna, B. (1987b) 'Beyond multiculturalism: towards the enactment of anti-racist education in policy, provision and pedagogy', *Oxford Review of Education* 13, 3: 307–20.

Troyna, B. (1988) 'The career of an anti-racist school policy: some observations on the mismanagement of change', in A.G. Green and S.J. Ball (eds) *Progress and Inequality in Comprehensive Education*, London: Routledge.

Troyna, B. and Ball, W. (1985) 'Views from the chalk-face: school responses to an LEA's policy on multicultural education', *Policy Papers in Ethnic Relations No. 1*, Centre for Research in Ethnic Relations, Coventry, University of Warwick.

Troyna, B. and Williams, J. (1986) *Racism, Education and the State: the racialization of education policy*, Beckenham: Croom Helm.

Vassen, T. (1986) 'Curriculum considerations in the primary school', in J. Gundara, J. Jones, and K. Kimberley, *Racism, Diversity and Education*, London: Hodder & Stoughton.

Verma, G. (ed.) (1989) *Education for All: a landmark in pluralism*, Lewes: Falmer Press.

Vygotsky, L.S. (1978) *Mind in Society: the development of higher psychological processes*, London: Harvard University Press.

Waller, W. (1932) *The Sociology of Teaching*, New York: Wiley.

Warnock, M. (1985) 'Teacher teach thyself', *The Listener*, 2 March: 10–12.

Weiner, G. (1985) *Just a Bunch of Girls*, Milton Keynes: Open University Press.

Wells, G. (1981) *Learning Through Interaction: the study of language development*, Cambridge: Cambridge University Press.

Whyte, J., Deem, R., Kant, L., and Cruickshank, M. (eds) (1985) *Girl Friendly Schooling*, London: Methuen.

Wiles, S. (1979) 'The multilingual classroom', in *PE232 Language and Development*, Block 5, Milton Keynes, The Open University.

Wilkinson, A. (1982) 'The implications of oracy', in B. Wade (ed.) *Language Perspectives*, London: Heinemann.

Willis, P. (1977) *Learning to Labour*, Farnborough: Saxon House.

Woodhead, M. (1989) 'School starts at five . . . or four years old', *Journal of Education Policy* 4, 1: 1–22.

Woods, P. (1980) 'The development of pupil strategies', in P. Woods (ed.) *Pupil Strategies*, London: Croom Helm.

Woods, P. (1983) *Sociology and the School*, London: Routledge & Kegan Paul.

Woods, P. (1986) *Inside Schools: ethnography in educational research*, London: Routledge & Kegan Paul.

Woods, P. (ed.) (1989) *Working for Teacher Development*, Dereham: Peter Francis.

Woods, P. and Pollard, A. (eds) (1988) *Sociology and Teaching: a new challenge for the sociology of education*, London: Croom Helm.

Wright, C. (1986) 'School processes – an ethnographic study', in J. Eggleston, D. Dunn, and M. Anjali (eds) *Education for Some: the educational and vocational experiences of 15-18 year old members of minority ethnic groups*, Stoke on Trent: Trentham Books.

Yeomans, A. (1983) 'Collaborative group work in primary and secondary schools', *Durham and Newcastle Research Review* 10: 95–105.

Author index

Subject index

For Product Safety Concerns and Information please contact our EU representative GPSR@taylorandfrancis.com Taylor & Francis Verlag GmbH, Kaufingerstraße 24, 80331 München, Germany

Printed and bound by CPI Group (UK) Ltd, Croydon, CR0 4YY

08/06/2025

01897007-0003